The Kelvedon Edition

C. H. SPURGEON'S SERMONS FOR SPECIAL OCCASIONS

Selected and Edited by
Charles T. Cook

MARSHALL, MORGAN & SCOTT

London

Marshall, Morgan & Scott, a member of the Pentos group, 1 Bath Street, LONDON ECIV 9LB.
© Marshall, Morgan & Scott 1958. This edition 1977. ISBN 0 551 05573 1. Printed in Great Britain by Hollen Street Press Ltd at Slough. 775013L20

CONTENTS

I

THE NEW YEAR'S GUEST

"I was a stranger, and ye took me in."—Matthew 25: 35.
"But as many as received him, to them gave he power to become the sons of God, even to them that believe on his name."
—John 1: 12.

I LATELY received a New Year's card, which suggested to me the topic on which I am about to speak to you. The designer of the card has, with holy insight, seen the relation of the two texts to each other, and rendered both of them eminently suggestive by placing them together. There is freshness in the thought that, by receiving Jesus as a stranger, our believing hospitality works in us a divine capacity and we thereby receive power to become the sons of God. The connection suggested between the two inspired words is really existent, and by no means strained or fanciful, as you will see by reading the context of the passage in John: "He was in the world, and the world was made by him, and the world knew him not." So he was a stranger in the world which he himself had made. "He came unto his own, and his own received him not." So he was a stranger among the people whom he had set apart for his own by many deeds of mercy. "But as many as received him,"—that is to say, gave entertainment to this blessed Stranger—"to them gave he power to become the sons of God, even to them that believe on his name."

I thought that this might prove to be a suitable and salutary passage to discourse upon at the beginning of a New Year, for this is a season of hospitality, and some among our friends will think it well to commence a New Year by saying to the Lord Jesus, "Come in, thou blessed of the Lord; wherefore standest thou without?" This divine stranger has knocked at many doors, till his head is wet with dew, and his locks with the drops of the night; and now I trust there are some who will rise up and open unto him, so that at the end of the year they may say with Job, "The stranger did not lodge in the street: but I opened my doors to the traveller." Verily, in so doing, you will not only entertain angels unawares; but you will be receiving the Lord of angels. The day in which you receive him shall be the beginning of years to you; it shall be the first of a series of years, which, whether they be few or many, shall be each one in the best sense *happy*.

I would say a few words, first, about *the Stranger taken in;* and then, about *the Stranger making strangers into sons.*

FIRST: THE STRANGER TAKEN IN: this is a simile given to us by our Lord himself: a royal metaphor presented to us from his own throne. Note that the passage begins, "I was an hungred, and ye gave me meat: I was thirsty, and ye gave me drink"; these are two good works which prove faith in Jesus and love to him, and therefore they are accepted, recorded, and rewarded; but it is a distinct and memorable growth when it comes to, "I was a Stranger, and ye took me in." House-room is a larger gift than refreshment at the door. It is good believingly to do anything for Christ, however small; but it is a much better thing to give entertainment to Jesus within our souls, admitting him into our minds and hearts. We have not come to the full of what our Lord has a right to expect of us till, having given from our stores to him, by benefiting his poor and aiding his cause, we deliberately open the doors of our entire being to him, and install him in our souls as an honoured guest. We must not be satisfied with giving him cups of cold water, or morsels of bread; but we must "constrain him, saying, Abide with us." Our hearts must be Bethanies, where, like Mary, and Martha, and Lazarus, we give our Master gladsome welcome: houses of Obed-edom, where the ark of the Lord may dwell in peace. Our prayer must be that of Abraham, "My Lord, if now I have found favour in thy sight, pass not away, I pray thee, from thy servant."

The uppermost word of our text is *stranger*, and its light casts a hue of strangeness over the whole passage. Here are three strange things. The first is, *that the Lord Jesus should be a Stranger here below.* Is it not a strange thing that "he was in the world, and the world was made by him," and yet he was a Stranger in it? Yet is it not a whit more strange than true; for when he was born there was no room for him in the inn. Inns had open doors for ordinary strangers, but not for him; for he was a greater stranger than any around him. It was Bethlehem of David, the seat of the ancient family to which he belonged; but alas! he had become "a stranger unto his brethren, and an alien unto his mother's children," and no door was open unto him. Soon there was no safe room for him in the village itself, for Herod the king sought the young child's life, and he must flee into Egypt, to be a Stranger in a strange land, and worse than a Stranger—an exile and a fugitive from the land whereof by birthright he was king. On his return, and on his public appearing, there was still no room for him among the mass of the people. He came to his own Israel, to whom prophets had revealed him, and types had set him forth; but they would have none of him. "He was despised and rejected of men." He was the man "whom men abhorred;" whom they so much detested that they cried, "Away with him! Crucify him!" Yea, the world so little knew him that they must needs hang up the Lord of glory on a cross, and put "the Holy One and the Just" to a felon's death. Jew and Gentile alike conspired to prove how truly he was a Stranger; the Jew said, "As for this fellow, we know not from whence he is;" and the Roman asked him, "Whence art thou?" Now, that Christ should be such a Stranger was indeed a sadly singular thing, and yet we need not wonder, for how should a wicked, selfish world know Jesus or receive him?

The Lord's own had been forewarned of this in ancient type, for long before the Lord appeared in the flesh he had shown himself as a stranger to the faithful. He came in angelic form to Abraham, and thus we read the story: "And he lift up his eyes and looked, and, lo, three men stood by him: and when he saw them, he ran to meet them from the tent door, and bowed himself toward the ground. And said, My Lord, if now I have found favour in thy sight, pass not away, I pray thee, from thy servant: Let a little water, I pray you, be fetched, and wash your feet, and rest yourselves under the tree: and I will fetch a morsel of bread, and comfort ye your hearts." The Lord, who stands out in the centre of the three, was a stranger, and the father of the faithful entertained him, in type of what all the faithful of every age will do. This is he of whom Jeremiah said, "O the hope of Israel, the Saviour thereof in time of trouble, why shouldest thou be as a stranger in the land, and as a wayfaring man that turneth aside to tarry for a night?" Yet with this fair warning it still remains sadly singular that, coming on an errand of mercy, our Lord should find so scant a welcome; should be so little known, so seldom recognized, so harshly entreated. Truly as Egypt made Israel to serve with rigour, so have we made this patient stranger to serve with our sins, and wearied him with our iniquities. The son of man had not where to lay his head. Luke says the barbarians showed Paul and his friends no little kindness: but men were worse than barbarians to their Saviour. Shall the servant be better treated than his Master, or the disciple than his Lord? "Behold, what manner of love the Father hath bestowed upon us, that we should be called the sons of God: therefore the world knoweth us not, because it knew him not."

Another strange thing is that *we should be able to receive the Lord Jesus as a Stranger*. He has gone into the glory, and will he ever say of us, "I was a stranger, and ye took me in"? Yes, he will say so, if we render to him that spiritual hospitality of which he here speaks. This can be done in several ways.

Brethren and sisters in Christ, for such I trust you are, we can receive Christ as a stranger when believers are few and despised in any place. We may sojourn where worldliness abounds and religion is at a discount, and it may need some courage to avow our faith in Jesus. Then have we an opportunity of winning the approving word, "I was a stranger, and ye took me in." There is a sure proof of love in receiving our Lord as a Stranger. If the Queen desired again to visit Mentone, every villa would be gladly placed at her disposal; but were she driven from her empire, and reduced to be a poor stranger, hospitality to her would be a greater test of loyalty than it is to-day. When Jesus is in low esteem in any place, and he sometimes is so, let us be all the more bold to avow our allegiance to him. I fear that many professors take their colour from their company, and are hail-fellows with the irreligious and the unbelieving. These cry "Hosanna" with the multitude of the Lord's admirers, but in heart they have no love to the Son of God. Our loyalty to Christ must never be a matter of latitude and longitude; we must love him in every land, honour him when the many disregard him, and we must speak of him when all forget him.

Again, we have the Lord's own warrant for saying that if we show brotherly kindness to a poor saint we entertain the Lord himself. If we see a sincere Christian in want, or despised, and ridiculed; and we say, "You are my brother; it matters not what garb you wear, the name of Christ is named on you, and I suffer with you. I will relieve your wants and share your reproach," then the glorious Lord himself will say to us at the last, "Inasmuch as ye have done it unto one of the least of these my brethren, ye have done it unto me." It does seem passing strange, though I thus speak, that you and I should be still able to entertain our Lord, and yet it is so. We do not wonder that the righteous with a humble truthfulness exclaim, "Lord, when saw we thee an hungred, and fed thee? or thirsty, and gave thee drink? When saw we thee a stranger, and took thee in?" Neither are we ourselves free from admiring surprise. We also cry, "Will God in very deed dwell with men upon the earth? Will he accept hospitality at our hands?" It is even so.

Again, we may entertain the stranger Christ by holding fast his faithful word when the doctrines taught by himself and his apostles are in ill repute. Nowadays the truth which God has revealed seems of less account with men than their own thoughts and dreams, and they who still believe Christ's faithful word shall have it said of them, "I was a stranger, and ye took me in." When you see revealed truth, as it were, wandering about in sheepskins and goatskins, being destitute, afflicted, tormented, and no man saith a good word for it, then is the hour come to avow it because it is Christ's truth, and to prove your fidelity by counting the reproach of Christ greater riches than all the treasures of Egypt. Oh! scorn on those who only believe what everybody else believes, just because they must be in the swim with the majority. These are but dead fish borne on the current, and they will be washed away to a shameful end. As living fish swim against the stream, so do living Christians pursue Christ's truth against the set and current of the times, defying alike the ignorance and the culture of the age. It is the believer's honour, the chivalry of a Christian, to be the steadfast friend of truth when all other men have forsaken it.

So, also, when Christ's precepts are disregarded, his day forgotten, and his worship neglected, we can come in, and take up our cross, and follow him, and so receive him as a Stranger. To be sure, some will say, "Those people are fanatical Methodists, or straitlaced Presbyterians;" but what of that? It matters nothing to us what the world thinks of us, for we are crucified to it and it to us. If our Lord has laid down a rule, it is ours to follow it, and find rest unto our souls in so doing; ay, and a special rest in doing it, when by so doing we are securing that blessed sentence, "I was a stranger, and ye took me in." Death itself for his sake would be a small matter if thereby we secured that priceless word.

Once more, that spiritual life, which is the innermost receiving of Christ; that new life, which no man knows but he that has received it; that quickening of the Spirit, which makes the Christian as much superior to ordinary men as men are above dumb, driven cattle—if we receive that blessed gift, then shall we with emphasis be entertaining our Lord as a Stranger. Profession is abundant, but the secret life is rare. The name to live is everywhere, but where is the life fully seen? To *be* rather than to talk, to *enjoy* rather than to pretend, to have Christ truly within—this is not every man's attainment, but those who have it are among the God-like ones, the true sons of God.

A third strange thing is the fact that *Jesus will deign to dwell in our hearts*. Such a one as Jesus in such a one as I am! The King of glory in a sinner's bosom! This is a miracle of grace: yet the manner of it is simple enough. A humble, repenting faith opens the door, and Jesus enters the heart at once. Love shuts to the door with the hand of penitence, and holy watchfulness keeps out intruders. Thus is the promise made good, "If any man hear my voice, and open the door, I will come in to him, and will sup with him, and he with me." Meditation, contemplation, prayer, praise, and daily obedience, keep the house in order for the Lord; and then follows the consecration of our entire nature to his use as a temple; the dedication of spirit, soul, and body, and all their powers, as holy vessels of the sanctuary; the writing of "Holiness unto the Lord" upon all that is about us, till our every-day garments become vestments, our meals sacraments, our life a ministry, and ourselves priests unto the Most High. Oh, the supreme condescension of this indwelling! He never dwelt in angel, but he resides in a contrite spirit. There is a world of meaning in the Redeemer's words, "I in them." May we know them as Paul translates them, "Christ in you, the hope of glory."

SECONDLY: THE STRANGER MAKING STRANGERS INTO SONS. "As many as received him, to them gave he power to become the sons of God, even to them that believe on his name." Yes, beloved, the moment Christ is received into our hearts by faith we are no more strangers and foreigners, but of the household of God; for the Lord *adopts us* and puts us among the children. It is a splendid act of divine grace, that he should take us who were heirs of wrath, and make us heirs of God, joint-heirs with Jesus Christ. Such honour have all the saints, even all that believe on his name.

There is more to follow: the designation of sons brings with it *a birth* into the actual condition of sons: the privilege brings with it the power, the name is backed up and warranted by the nature: for the Spirit of God enters into us when Christ comes, and causes us to be born again. To be adopted without being born again would be a lame blessing, but when we are both adopted and regenerated, then have we the fulness of son-ship, and the grace is made perfect towards us. "Except a man be born again, he cannot see the kingdom of God"; but this mysterious birth, which comes with the reception of Christ, makes us free, not only of the kingdom of God, but of the house and the heart of God.

Forget not that when the Lord Jesus enters our hearts, there springs up between us and him a living, loving, *lasting union*, and this seals our sonship: for as we become one with the Son we must be sons also. Jesus puts it, "My Father and your Father." It is the Spirit of his Son in our hearts by which we cry, "Abba, Father." "He that is joined unto the Lord is one spirit." We are unto the Father even as Jesus is, as he says "thou hast loved them as thou hast loved me." Thus you see that in receiving Jesus we receive, as the Revised Version puts it, "the right to become the sons of God."

Yet once more: the practical reception of Jesus into the life becomes a proof to ourselves and others that we are the sons of God, for *it creates in us a likeness to God* which is apparent and unquestionable. For although Jehovah, our God, be incomprehensible and infinite, and his glory is inconceivable in its splendour, yet this fact we know of him, that in his bosom lies his

Son, with whom he is always well-pleased. When we receive Jesus into our bosom, as one with us, and when our joy and delight are in him, we do in that matter become like to the Father. Having thus with the Father the same object of love and delight, we are brought into fellowship with him, and begin to walk in the light, as he is in the light.

Moreover, having received Jesus, as a Stranger, we feel a tenderness henceforth towards *all* strangers, for we see in their condition some resemblance to our own. We have love to all who like ourselves are strangers with God, and sojourners, as all our fathers were, and thus again we are made like to God, of whom it is written, "The Lord preserveth the strangers." Our God is "kind unto the unthankful and to the evil." Our Lord Jesus therefore bade us be the children of our Father which is in heaven, "For he maketh his sun to rise on the evil and on the good, and sendeth rain on the just and on the unjust." By becoming doers of good, we are known as children of the good God. "Blessed are the peacemakers: for they shall be called the children of God." A man is a son of God when he lives beyond himself by a thoughtful care for others; when his soul is not confined within the narrow circle of his own ribs, but goes abroad to bless those around him however unworthy they may be. True children of God never see a lost one without seeking to save him; never hear of misery without longing to bestow comfort. "Ye know the heart of a stranger," said the Lord to Israel; and so do we, for we were once captives ourselves, and even now our choicest Friend is still a Stranger, for whose sake we love all suffering men. When Christ is in us we search out opportunities of bringing prodigals, strangers, and outcasts to the great Father's house. Our love goes out to all mankind, and our hand is closed against none: if it be so we are made like to God, as little children are like their father. Oh! sweet result of entertaining the Son of God by faith: he dwells in us, and we gaze upon him in holy fellowship; so that "we all with open face beholding as in a glass the glory of the Lord, are changed into the same image, from glory to glory, even as by the Spirit of the Lord."

II

IMMEASURABLE LOVE

"For God so loved the world, that he gave his only begotten Son, that whosoever believeth in him should not perish, but have everlasting life."—John 3: 16.

I WAS very greatly surprised the other day, in looking over the list of texts from which I have preached, to find that I have no record of ever having spoken from this verse. This is all the more singular, because I can truly say that it might be put in the forefront of all my volumes of discourses as the sole topic of my life's ministry. It has been my one and only business to set forth the love of God to men in Christ Jesus. I heard lately of an aged minister of whom it was said, "Whatever his text, he never failed to set forth God as love, and Christ as the atonement for sin." I wish that much the same may be said of me. My heart's desire has been to sound forth as with a trumpet the good news that "God so loved the world, that he gave his only begotten Son, that whosoever believeth in him should not perish, but have everlasting life."

We are about to meet around the communion table, and I cannot preach from this text anything but a simple gospel sermon. Can you desire a better preparation for communion? We have fellowship with God and with one another upon the basis of the infinite love which is displayed in Jesus Christ our Lord. The gospel is the fair white linen cloth which covers the table on which the Communion Feast is set. The higher truths, those truths which belong to a more enlightened experience, those richer truths which tell of the fellowship of the higher life—all these are helpful to holy fellowship; but I am sure not more so than those elementary and foundation truths which were the means of our first entrance into the kingdom of God. Babes in Christ and men in Christ here feed upon one common food. Come, aged saints, be children again;

and you that have long known your Lord, take up your first spelling book, and go over your A B C again, by learning that God so loved the world, that he gave his Son to die, that man might live through him.

To-night, we have to talk about the love of God: "God so loved the world." That love of God is a very wonderful thing, especially when we see it set upon a lost, ruined, guilty world. What was there in the world that God should love it? There was nothing lovable in it. No fragrant flower grew in that arid desert. Enmity to him, hatred to his truth, disregard of his law, rebellion against his commandments; those were the thorns and briars which covered the waste land; but no desirable thing blossomed there. Yet, "God loved the world," says the text; "so" loved it, that even the writer of the book of John could not tell us how much; but so greatly, so divinely, did he love it that he gave his Son, his only Son, to redeem the world from perishing, and to gather out of it a people to his praise.

Whence came that love? Not from anything outside of God himself. God's love springs from himself. He loves because it is his nature to do so. "God is love." As I have said already, nothing upon the face of the earth could have merited his love, though there was much to merit his displeasure. This stream of love flows from its own secret source in the eternal Deity, and it owes nothing to any earth-born rain or rivulet; it springs from beneath the everlasting throne, and fills itself full from the springs of the infinite. God loved because he would love. When we enquire why the Lord loved this man or that, we have to come back to our Saviour's answer to the question, "Even so, Father, for so it seemed good in thy sight." God has such love in his nature that he must needs let it flow forth to a world perishing by its own wilful sin; and when it flowed forth it was so deep, so wide, so strong, that even inspiration could not compute its measure, and therefore the Holy Spirit gave us that great little word SO, and left us to attempt the measurement, according as we perceive more and more of love divine.

Now, there happened to be an occasion upon which the great God could display his immeasurable love. The world had sadly gone astray; the world had lost itself; the world was tried and condemned; the world was given over to perish, because of its offences; and there was need for help. The fall of Adam and

the destruction of mankind made ample room and verge enough
for love almighty. Amid the ruins of humanity there was space
for showing how much Jehovah loved the sons of men; for the
compass of his love was no less than the world, the object of it
no less than to deliver men from going down to the pit, and the
result of it no less than the finding of a ransom for them. The
far-reaching purpose of that love was both negative and positive; that, believing in Jesus, men might not perish, but have
eternal life. The desperate disease of man gave occasion for the
introduction of that divine remedy which God alone could have
devised and supplied. By the plan of mercy, and the great gift
which was needed for carrying it out, the Lord found means to
display his boundless love to guilty men. Had there been no
fall, and no perishing, God might have shown his love to us as
he does to the pure and perfect spirits that surround his throne;
but he never could have commended his love to us to such an
extent as he now does. In the gift of his only-begotten Son,
God commended his love to us, in that while we were yet sinners,
in due time Christ died for the ungodly.

I might handle my text in a thousand different ways to-night;
but for simplicity's sake, and to keep to the one point of setting
forth the love of God, I want to make you see how great that
love is by five different particulars.

The first is the GIFT: "God so loved the world, *that he gave his
only begotten Son.*" Men who love much will give much, and you
may usually measure the truth of love by its self-denials and
sacrifices. That love which spares nothing, but spends itself to
help and bless its object, is love indeed, and not the mere name
of it. Little love forgets to bring water for the feet, but great
love breaks its box of alabaster and lavishes its precious
ointment.

Consider, then, *what this gift was* that God gave. I should
have to labour for expression if I were to attempt to set forth to
the full this priceless boon; and I will not court a failure by
attempting the impossible. I will only invite you to think of
the sacred Person whom the Great Father gave in order that he
might prove his love to men. It was his only-begotten Son—his
beloved Son, in whom he was well pleased. None of us had ever
such a son to give. Ours are the sons of men; his was the Son
of God. The Father gave his other self, one with himself.

When the great God gave his Son he gave God himself, for Jesus is not in his eternal nature less than God. When God gave God for us he gave himself. What more could he give? God gave his all: he gave himself. Who can measure this love?

Judge, ye fathers, how ye love your sons: could ye give them to die for your enemy? Judge, ye that have an only son, how your hearts are entwined about your first-born, your only-begotten. There was no higher proof of Abraham's love to God than when he did not withhold from God his son, his only son, his Isaac whom he loved; and there can certainly be no greater display of love than for the Eternal Father to give his only-begotten Son to die for us. No living thing will readily lose its offspring; man has peculiar grief when his son is taken; has not God yet more?

If you desire to see the love of God in this great procedure you must consider *how he gave his Son.* He did not give his Son, as you might do, to some profession in the pursuit of which you might still enjoy his company; but he gave his Son to exile among men. He sent him down to yonder manger, united with a perfect manhood, which at the first was in an infant's form. There he slept, where horned oxen fed! The Lord God sent the heir of all things to toil in a carpenter's shop: to drive the nail, and push the plane, and use the saw. He sent him down amongst scribes and Pharisees, whose cunning eyes watched him, and whose cruel tongues scourged him with base slanders. He sent him down to hunger, and thirst, amid poverty so dire that he had not where to lay his head. He sent him down to the scourging and the crowning with thorns, to the giving of his back to the smiters and his cheeks to those that plucked off the hair. At length he gave him up to death—a felon's death, the death of the crucified. Behold that cross and see the anguish of him that dies upon it, and mark how the Father has so given him, that he hides his face from him, and seems as if he would not own him! "Lama sabachthani" ("why hast Thou forsaken Me?") tells us how fully God gave his Son to ransom the souls of the sinful. He gave him to be made a curse for us; gave him that he might die "the just for the unjust, to bring us to God."

Dear sirs, I can understand your giving up your children to go to India on her Majesty's service, or to go out to the Cameroons or the Congo upon the errands of our Lord Jesus.

I can well comprehend your yielding them up even with the fear of a pestilential climate before you, for if they die they will die honourably in a glorious cause; but could you think of parting with them to die a felon's death, upon a gibbet, execrated by those whom they sought to bless, stripped naked in body and deserted in mind? Would not that be too much? Would you not cry, "I cannot part with my son for such wretches as these. Why should he be put to a cruel death for such abominable beings, who even wash their hands in the blood of their best friend"? Remember that our Lord Jesus died what his countrymen considered to be an accursed death. To the Romans it was the death of a condemned slave, a death which had all the elements of pain, disgrace, and scorn mingled in it to the uttermost. "But God commendeth his love toward us, in that, while we were yet sinners, Christ died for us." Oh, wondrous stretch of love, that Jesus Christ should die!

Yet, I cannot leave this point till I have you notice *when God gave his Son*, for there is love in the time. "God so loved the world that he gave his Only Begotten Son." But when did he do that? In his eternal purpose he did this from before the foundation of the world. The words here used, "He gave his Only Begotten Son," cannot relate exclusively to the death of Christ, for Christ was not dead at the time of the utterance of this third chapter of John. Our Lord had just been speaking with Nicodemus, and that conversation took place at the beginning of his ministry. The fact is that Jesus was always the gift of God. The promise of Jesus was made in the garden of Eden almost as soon as Adam fell. On the spot where our ruin was accomplished, a Deliverer was bestowed whose heel should be bruised, but who should break the serpent's head beneath his foot.

Throughout the ages the great Father stood to his gift. He looked upon his Only Begotten as man's hope, the inheritance of the chosen seed, who in him would possess all things. Every sacrifice was God's renewal of his gift of grace, a reassurance that he had bestowed the gift, and would never draw back therefrom. The whole system of types under the law betokened that in the fulness of time the Lord would in very deed give up his Son, to be born of a woman, to bear the iniquities of his people, and to die the death in their behalf. I greatly admire this pertinacity of love; for many a man in a moment of generous excitement can perform a supreme act of benevolence, and yet could not bear to look at it calmly, and consider it from year to year; the slow fire of anticipation would have been unbearable. If the Lord should take away yonder dear boy from his mother, she would bear the blow with some measure of patience, heavy as it would be to her tender heart; but suppose that she were credibly informed that on such a day her boy must die, and thus had from year to year to look upon him as one dead, would it not cast a cloud over every hour of her future life? Suppose also that she knew that he would be hanged upon a tree to die, as one condemned; would it not embitter her existence? If she could withdraw from such a trial, would she not? Assuredly she would. Yet the Lord God spared not his own Son, but freely delivered him up for us all, doing it in his heart from age to age. Herein is love: love which many waters could not quench: love eternal, inconceivable, infinite!

Now, as this gift refers not only to our Lord's death, but to the ages before it, so it includes also all the ages afterwards. God "so loved the world that he gave"—and still gives—"his only begotten Son, that whosoever believeth in him should not perish, but have everlasting life." The Lord is giving Christ away to-night. Oh, that thousands of you may gladly accept the gift unspeakable! Will anyone refuse? This good gift, this perfect gift,—can you decline it? Oh, that you may have faith to lay hold on Jesus, for thus he will be yours. He is God's free gift to all free receivers; a full Christ for empty sinners. If you can but hold out your empty willing hand, the Lord will give Christ to you at this moment. Nothing is freer than a gift. Nothing is more worth having than a gift which comes fresh from the hand of God, as full of effectual power as ever it was. The fountain is eternal, but the stream from it is as fresh as when first the fountain was opened. There is no exhausting this gift.

> *Dear dying Lamb, thy precious blood*
> *Shall never lose its power*
> *Till all the ransomed church of God*
> *Be saved to sin no more.*

I call upon you from this first point to admire the love of God, because of the transcendent greatness of his gift to the world, even the gift of his only begotten Son. Now notice secondly, and, I think I may say, with equal admiration, the love of God in THE PLAN OF SALVATION. He has put it thus: "that whosoever believeth on him should not perish, but have everlasting life." The way of salvation is extremely simple to understand, and exceedingly easy to practise, when once the heart is made willing and obedient. The method of the covenant of grace differs as much from that of the covenant of works as light from darkness. It is not said that God has given his Son to all who will keep his law, for that we could not do, and therefore the gift would have been available to none of us. Nor is it said that he has given his Son to all that experience terrible despair and bitter remorse, for that is not felt by many who nevertheless are the Lord's own people. But the great God has given his own Son, that "whosoever believeth in him" should not perish. Faith, however slender, saves the soul. Trust in Christ is the certain way of eternal happiness.

Now, what is it to believe in Jesus? It is just this: it is to trust yourself with him. If your hearts are ready, though you have never believed in Jesus before, I trust you will believe in him now. O Holy Spirit, graciously make it so.

What is it to believe in Jesus?

It is, first, to give your *firm and cordial assent* to the truth, that God did send his Son, born of a woman, to stand in the room and stead of guilty men, and that God did cause to meet on him the iniquities of us all, so that he bore the punishment due to our transgressions, being made a curse for us. We must heartily believe the Scripture which saith,—"the chastisement of our peace was upon him; and with his stripes we are healed." I ask for your assent to the grand doctrine of substitution, which is the marrow of the gospel. Oh, may God the Holy Spirit lead you to give a cordial assent to it at once; for wonderful as it is, it is a fact that God was in Christ reconciling the world unto himself, not imputing their trespasses upon them. Oh that you may rejoice that this is true, and be thankful that such a blessed fact is revealed by God himself. Believe that the substitution of the Son of God is certain; cavil not at the plan, nor question its validity, or efficacy, as many do. Alas! they kick at God's great sacrifice, and count it a sorry invention. As for me, since God has ordained to save man by a substitutionary sacrifice, I joyfully agree to his method, and see no reason to do anything else but admire it and adore the Author of it. I rejoice that such a plan should have been thought of, whereby the justice of God is vindicated, and his mercy is set free to do all that he desires. Sin is punished in the person of the Christ, yet mercy is extended to the guilty. In Christ mercy is sustained by justice, and justice satisfied by an act of mercy. The worldly wise say hard things about this device of infinite wisdom; but as for me, I love the very name of the cross, and count it to be the centre of wisdom, the focus of love, the heart of righteousness.

The second thing is that you do *accept this for yourself.* In Adam's sin, you did not sin personally, for you were not then in existence; yet you fell; neither can you now complain thereof, for you have willingly endorsed and adopted Adam's sin by committing personal transgressions. You have laid your hand, as it were, upon Adam's sin, and made it your own, by committing personal and actual sin. Thus you perished by the sin of another, which you adopted and endorsed; and in like manner must you be saved by the righteousness of another, which you are to accept and appropriate. Jesus has offered an atonement, and that atonement becomes yours when you accept it by putting your trust in him. I want you now to say,

> *My faith doth lay her hand*
> *On that dear head of thine,*
> *While, like a penitent, I stand,*
> *And here confess my sin.*

Surely this is no very difficult matter. To say that Christ who hung upon the cross shall be my Christ, my surety, needs neither stretch of intellect, nor splendour of character; and yet it is the act which brings salvation to the soul.

One thing more is needful; and that is *personal trust.* First comes assent to the truth, then acceptance of that truth for yourself, and then a simple trusting of yourself wholly to Christ, as a Substitute. The essence of faith is trust, reliance, dependence. Fling away every other confidence of every sort, save confidence in Jesus. Do not allow a ghost of a shade of a shadow of a confidence in anything that you can do, or in anything that you can be; but look alone to him whom God has set forth to be the propitiation for sin. This I do at this very moment; will you not do the same? Oh, may the sweet Spirit of God lead you now to trust in Jesus!

See, then, the love of God in putting it in so plain, so easy a way. Oh, broken, crushed and despairing sinner, thou canst not work, but canst thou not believe that which is true? Thou canst not sigh; thou canst not cry; thou canst not melt thy stony heart; but canst thou not believe that Jesus died for thee, and that he can change that heart of thine and make thee a new creature? If thou canst believe this, then trust in Jesus to do so, and thou art saved; for he that believes in him is justified. "He that believeth in him *hath* everlasting life." He is a saved man. His sins are forgiven him. Let him go his way in peace, and sin no more.

I admire, first, the love of God in the great gift, and then in the great plan by which that gift becomes available to guilty men. Thirdly, the love of God shines forth with transcendent brightness in a third point, namely, in THE PERSONS FOR WHOM THIS PLAN IS AVAILABLE, and for whom this gift is given. They are described in these words—"Whosoever believeth in him." There is in the text a word which has no limit—"God so loved the world"; but then comes in the descriptive limit, which I beg you to notice with care: "He gave his Only Begotten Son *that whosoever believeth in him* should not perish." God did not so love the world that any man who does not believe in Christ shall be saved; neither did God so give his Son that any man shall be saved who refuses to believe in him. See how it is put—"God so loved the world, that he gave his only begotten Son, that whosoever believeth in him should not perish." Here is the compass of the love: while every unbeliever is excluded, every believer is included. "Whosoever believeth in him." Suppose there be a man who has been guilty of all the lusts of the flesh to an infamous degree, suppose that he is so detestable that he is only fit to be treated like a moral leper, and shut up in a separate house for fear he should contaminate those who hear or see him; yet if that man shall believe in Jesus Christ, he shall at once be made clean from his defilement, and shall not perish because of his sin. And suppose there be another man who, in the pursuit of his selfish motives, has ground down the poor, has robbed his fellow-traders, and has even gone so far as to commit actual crime of which the law has taken cognisance, yet if he believes in the Lord Jesus Christ he shall be led to make restitution, and his sins shall be forgiven him.

I once heard of a preacher addressing a company of men in chains, condemned to die for murder and other crimes. They were such a drove of beasts to all outward appearances that it seemed hopeless to preach to them; yet were I set to be chaplain to such a wretched company I should not hesitate to tell them that "God so loved the world, that he gave his Only Begotten Son, that *whosoever* believeth in him should not perish, but have everlasting life." O man, if thou wilt believe in Jesus as the Christ, however horrible thy past sins have been they shall be blotted out; thou shalt be saved from the power of thine evil habits; and thou shalt begin again like a child new-born, with a new and true life, which God shall give thee. "Whosoever believeth in him,"—that takes you in, my agèd friend, now lingering within a few tottering steps of the grave. O grey-headed sinner, if you believe in him, you shall not perish. The text also includes you, dear boy, who have scarcely entered your teens as yet: if you believe in him, you shall not perish. That takes you in, fair maiden, and gives you hope and joy while yet young. That comprehends all of us, provided we believe in the Lord Jesus Christ. Neither can all the devils in hell find out any reason why the man that believes in Christ shall be lost, for it is written, "Him that cometh to me I will in no wise cast out."

Do they say, "Lord, he has been so long in coming"? The Lord replies,—"Has he come? Then I will not cast him out for all his delays." But, Lord, he went back after making a profession. "Has he at length come? Then I will not cast him out for all his backslidings." But, Lord, he was a foul-mouthed blasphemer. "Has he come to me? Then I will not cast him out for all his blasphemies." But, says one, "I take exception to the salvation of this wicked wretch. He has behaved so abominably that in all justice he ought to be sent to hell." Just so. But if he repents of his sin and believes in the Lord Jesus Christ, whoever he may be, he shall not be sent there. He shall be changed in character, so that he shall never perish, but have eternal life.

Now, observe, that this "whosoever" makes a grand sweep; for it encircles all degrees of faith. "Whosoever believeth in him." It may be that he has no full assurance; it may be that he has no assurance at all; but if he has faith, true and childlike, by it he shall be saved. Though his faith be so little that I must needs put on my spectacles to see it, yet Christ will see it and reward it. His faith is such a tiny grain of mustard seed that I look and look again but hardly discern it, and yet it brings him eternal life, and it is itself a living thing. The Lord can see within that mustard seed a tree among whose branches the birds of the air shall make their nests.

> *My faith is feeble, I confess,*
> *I faintly trust thy word;*
> *But wilt thou pity me the less?*
> *Be that far from thee, Lord!*

O Lord Jesus, if I cannot take thee up in my arms as Simeon did, I will at least touch thy garment's hem as the poor diseased woman did to whom thy healing virtue flowed. It is written, "God so loved the world that he gave his Only Begotten Son, that whosoever believeth in him should not perish, but have everlasting life." That means me. Oh that this truth may soak into your souls. Oh you that feel yourselves guilty; and you that feel guilty because you do not feel guilty; you that are broken in heart because your heart will not break; you that feel that you cannot feel; it is to you that I would preach salvation in Christ by faith. You groan because you cannot groan; but whoever you may be, you are still within the range of this mighty word, that "whosoever believeth in Him should not perish, but have eternal life."

Thus have I commended God's love to you in those three points—the divine gift, the divine method of saving, and the divine choice of the persons to whom salvation comes. Now fourthly, another beam of divine love is to be seen in the negative blessing here stated, namely, in THE DELIVERANCE implied in the words, "that whosoever believeth in him should *not perish.*"

I understand that word to mean that whosoever believes in the Lord Jesus Christ shall not perish, though he is ready to perish. His sins would cause him to perish, but he shall never perish. At first he has a little hope in Christ, but its existence is feeble. It will soon die out, will it not? No, his faith shall not perish, for this promise covers it—"Whosoever believeth in Him should not perish." The penitent has believed in Jesus, and therefore he has begun to be a Christian; "Oh," cries an enemy, "let him alone: he will soon be back among us; he will soon be as careless as ever." Listen. "Whosoever believeth in Him should not perish," and therefore he will not return to his former state. This proves the final perseverance of the saints; for if the believer ceased to be a believer he would perish; and as he cannot perish, it is clear that he will continue a believer. If thou believest in Jesus, thou shalt never leave off believing in him; for that would be to perish. If thou believest in him, thou shalt never delight in thine old sins; for that would be to perish. If thou believest in him, thou shalt never lose spiritual life. How canst thou lose that which is everlasting? If thou wert to lose it, it would prove that it was not everlasting, and thou wouldst perish; and thus thou wouldst make this word to be of no effect. Whosoever with his heart believeth in Christ is a saved man, not for to-night only, but for all the nights that ever shall be, and for that dread night of death, and for that solemn eternity which draws so near.

What is it to perish? It is to lose all hope in Christ, all trust in God, all light in life, all peace in death, all joy, all bliss, all union with God. This shall never happen to thee if thou believest in Christ. If thou believest, thou shalt be chastened when thou dost wrong, for every child of God comes under discipline; and what son is there whom the Father chasteneth not? If thou believest, thou mayest doubt and fear as to thy state, as a man on board a ship may be tossed about; but thou hast gotten on board a ship that never can be wrecked. He that hath union with Christ hath union with perfection, omnipotence and glory. He that believeth is a member of Christ: will Christ lose his members? How should Christ be perfect if he lost even his little finger? Are Christ's members to rot off, or to be cut off? Impossible. If thou hast faith in Christ thou art a partaker of Christ's life, and thou canst not perish. If men were trying to drown me, they could not drown my foot as long as I had my head above water; and as long as our Head is above water, up yonder in the eternal sunshine, the least limb of his body can never be destroyed. He that believeth in Jesus is united to him, and he must live because Jesus lives. I do not believe that the man who is once in Christ may live in sin and delight in it, and yet be saved. That is abominable teaching, and none of mine. But I believe that the man who is in Christ will *not* live in sin, for he is saved from it; nor will he return to his old sins and abide in them, for the grace of God will continue to save him from his sins. It would be as great a miracle to undo the work of God as to do it; and to destroy the new creation would require as great a power as to make it. As only God can create, so only God can destroy; and he will never destroy the work of his own hands.

The last commendation of his love lies in *the positive*—IN THE POSSESSION. I shall have to go in a measure over the same ground again. Let me therefore be the shorter. God gives to every man that believes in Christ everlasting life. The moment thou believest there trembles into thy bosom a vital spark of heavenly flame which never shall be quenched. In that same moment when thou dost cast thyself on Christ, Christ comes to thee in the living and incorruptible word which liveth and abideth for ever. Though there should drop into thy heart but one drop of the heavenly water of life, remember this,—he hath said it who cannot lie,—"The water that I shall give him shall be in him a well of water springing up into everlasting life." When I first received everlasting life I had no idea what a treasure had come to me. I knew that I had obtained something very extraordinary, but of its superlative value I was not aware. I did but look to Christ in the little chapel, and I received eternal life. I looked to Jesus, and he looked on me: and we were one for ever. That moment my joy surpassed all bounds, just as my sorrow had aforetime driven me to an extreme of grief. I was perfectly at rest in Christ, satisfied with him, and my heart was glad; but I did not know that this grace was everlasting life till I began to read in the Scriptures, and to know more fully the value of the jewel which God had given me. The next Sunday I went to the same chapel, as it was very natural that I should. But I never went afterwards, for this reason, that during my first week the new life that was in me had been compelled to fight for its existence, and a conflict with the old nature had been vigorously carried on. This I knew to be a special token of the indwelling of grace in my soul; but in that same chapel I heard a sermon upon "O wretched man that I am! who shall deliver me from the body of this death?" And the preacher declared that Paul was not a Christian when he had that experience. Babe as I was, I knew better than to believe so absurd a statement. What but divine grace could produce such a sighing and crying after deliverance from indwelling sin? I felt that a person who could talk such nonsense knew little of the life of a true believer. I said to myself, "What! am I not alive because I feel a conflict within me? I never felt this fight when I was an unbeliever. When I was not a Christian I never groaned to be set free from sin." This conflict is one of the surest evidences of my new birth, the struggle becomes more and more intense; each victory over sin reveals another army of evil tendencies, and I am never able to sheathe my sword, nor cease from prayer and watchfulness.

I cannot advance an inch without praying my way, nor keep the inch I gain without watching and standing fast. Grace alone can preserve and perfect me. The old nature will kill the new nature if it can; and to this moment the only reason why my new nature is not dead is this—because it cannot die. If it could have died, it would have been slain long ago; but Jesus said, "I give unto my sheep eternal life"; "he that believeth on me hath everlasting life"; and therefore the believer cannot die. The only religion which will save you is one that you cannot leave, because it possesses you, and will not leave you. To have Christ living in you, and the truth ingrained in your very nature—O sirs, *this* is the thing that saves the soul, and nothing short of it. It is written in the text, "God so loved the world that he gave his only begotten Son, that whosoever believeth in him should not perish, but have everlasting life." What is this but a life that shall last through your three-score years and ten; a life that will out-shine those stars and yon sun and moon; a life that shall be co-eval with the life of the Eternal Father? As long as there is a God, the believer shall not only exist, but live.

III

SUBSTITUTION

"For he hath made him to be sin for us, who knew no sin;
that we might be made the righteousness of God in him."
—2 Cor. 5: 21.

A BOOK is the expression of the thoughts of the writer. The book of nature is an expression of the thoughts of God. We have God's terrible thoughts in the thunder and lightning; God's loving thoughts in the sunshine and the balmy breeze; God's bounteous, prudent, careful thoughts in the waving harvest and in the ripening meadow. We have God's brilliant thoughts in the wondrous scenes which are beheld from mountain-top and valley; and we have God's most sweet and pleasant thoughts of beauty in the little flowers that blossom at our feet. But you will remark that God has in nature given most prominence to those thoughts that needed to have the pre-eminence. He hath not given us broad acres overspread with *flowers*, for they were not needed in such abundance, but he hath spread the fields with corn, that thus the absolute necessities of life might be supplied. We needed most of the thoughts of his providence; and he hath quickened our industry, so that God's providential care may be read as we ride along the roads on every side. Now, God's book of grace is just like his book of nature; it is his thoughts written out. This great book, the Bible, this most precious volume is the heart of God made legible; it is the gold of God's love beaten out into leaf gold, so that therewith our thoughts might be plated, and we also might have golden, good, and holy thoughts concerning him. And you will mark that, as in nature so in grace, the most necessary is the most prominent. I see in God's word a rich abundance of flowers of glorious eloquence; often I find a prophet marshalling his words like armies for might, and like kings for majesty. But far more frequently I read simple declarations of the truth. I see, here and there, a brilliant thought of beauty, but I find whole fields of plain didactic doctrine, which is food for the soul; and I find whole chapters full of Christ which is divine manna, whereon the soul doth feed. I see starry words to make the Scriptures brilliant, sweet thoughts to make them fair, great thoughts to make them impressive, terrible thoughts to make them awful; but necessary thoughts, instructive thoughts, saving thoughts, are far more frequent, because far more necessary. Here and there a bed of flowers, but broad acres of living corn of the gospel of the grace of God. You must excuse me, then, if I very frequently dwell on the whole topic of salvation. Last Sabbath I brought you one shock of this wheat, in the fashion of Christ's promise, which saith, "He that calleth on the name of the Lord, shall be saved." And then I sought to show how men might be saved. I bring you now another shock cut down in the self same field, teaching you the great philosophy of salvation, the hidden mystery, the great secret, the wonderful discovery which is brought to light by the gospel; how God is just, and yet the justifier of the ungodly. Let us read the text again, and then at once proceed to discuss it. I shall just be as simple as ever I can; and I shall not attempt one single flight of eloquence or oratory, even if I am capable of it; but just go along the ground, so that every simple soul may be able to understand.—"For he hath made him to be sin for us, who knew no sin; that we might be made the righteousness of God in him."

Note the doctrine; the use of it; the enjoyment of it.

First, THE DOCTRINE. There are three persons mentioned here. "*He* (*that is God*) hath made *him* (*that is Christ*) who knew no sin, to be sin for *us* (*sinners*) that we might be made the righteousness of God in him." Before we can understand the plan of salvation, it is necessary for us to know something about the three persons, and, certainly, unless we understand them in some measure, salvation is to us impossible.

Here is first, GOD. Let every man know what God is. God is a very different Being from what some of you suppose. The God of heaven and of earth—the Jehovah of Abraham, of Isaac and Jacob, Creator and Preserver, the God of Holy Scripture, and the God of all grace, is not the God that some men make unto themselves, and worship. There be men in this so called Christian land, who worship a god who is no more God than Venus or Bacchus! A god made after their own hearts; a god not fashioned out of stone or wood, but fashioned from their own thoughts, out of baser stuff than ever heathen attempted to make a god of. The God of Scripture has three great attributes, and they are all three implied in the text.

The God of Scripture is a *sovereign* God; that is, he is a God who has absolute authority, and absolute power to do exactly as he pleaseth. Over the head of God there is no law, upon his arm there is no necessity; he knoweth no rule but his own free and mighty will. And though he cannot be unjust, and cannot do anything but good, yet is his nature absolutely free; for goodness is the freedom of God's nature. God is not to be controlled by the will of man, nor the desires of man, nor by fate in which the superstitious believe; he is God, doing as he willeth in the armies of heaven, and in this lower world. He is a God, too, who giveth no account of his matters; he makes his creatures just what he chooses to make them, and does with them just as he wills. And if any of them resent his acts, he saith unto them:—"Nay but, O man, who art thou that repliest against God? Shall the thing formed say to him that formed it, why hast thou made me thus? Hath not the potter power over the clay, of the same lump to make one vessel unto honour, and another unto dishonour?" God is good; but God is sovereign, absolute, knowing nothing that can control him. The monarchy of this world, is no constitutional and limited monarchy; it is not tyrannical, but it is absolutely in the hands of an all-wise God. But mark it, is in no hands but his, no cherubim, nor seraphim can assist God in the dispensation of his government.

> *He sits on no precarious throne,*
> *Nor borrows leave to be.*

This is the God of the Bible, this is the God whom we adore; no weak, pusillanimous God, who is controlled by the will of men, who cannot steer the bark of providence; but a God unalterable, infinite, unerring. This is the God we worship; a God as infinitely above his creatures, as the highest thought can fly; and higher still than that.

But, again, the God who is here mentioned, is *a God of infinite justice*. That he is a sovereign God, I prove from the words, that he *hath made* Christ to be sin. He could not have done it if he had not been sovereign. That he is a just God, I infer from my text; seeing that the way of salvation is a great plan of satisfying justice. And we now declare that the God of Holy Scripture is a God of inflexible justice; he is not the God whom some of you adore. You adore a god who winks at great sins; you believe in a god who calls your crimes peccadilloes and little faults. Some of you worship a god who does not punish sin; but who is so weakly merciful, and so mercilessly weak, that he passes by transgression and iniquity, and never enacts a punishment. You believe in a god, who, if man sins, does not demand punishment for his offence. You think that a few good works of your own will pacify him, that he is so weak a ruler, that a few good words uttered before him in prayer will win sufficient merit to reverse the sentence, if, indeed, you think he ever passes a sentence at all. Your god is no God; he is as much a false god as the god of the Greeks, or of ancient Nineveh. The God of Scripture is one who is inflexibly severe in justice, and will by no means clear the guilty. "The Lord is slow to anger, and great in power; and will not at all acquit the wicked." The God of Scripture is a ruler, who, when his subjects rebel, marks their crime, and never forgives them until he has punished it, either upon them, or upon their substitute. He is not like the god of some sectaries, who believe in a god without an atonement, with only some little show upon the cross, which was not, as they say, a real suffering of sin. Their god, the god of the Socinian, just blots out sin without exacting any punishment; he is not the God of the Scriptures. The God of the Bible is as severe as if he were unmerciful, and as just as if he were not gracious; and yet he is as gracious and as merciful as if he were not just—yea, more so.

And one more thought here concerning God, or else we cannot establish our discourse upon a sure basis. The God who is here meant, is a *God of grace:* think not that I am now contradicting myself. The God who is inflexibly severe, and never pardons sin without punishment, is yet a God of illimitable love. Although as a Ruler he will chastise, yet, as the Father-God, he loveth to bestow his blessing. "As I live, saith the Lord, I have no pleasure in the death of him that dieth; but had rather that he should turn unto me and live." God is love in its highest degree. He is love rendered more than love. Love is not God, but God is love; he is full of grace, he is the plenitude of mercy, —he delighteth in mercy. As high as the heavens are above the earth, so high are his thoughts of love above our thoughts of despair; and his ways of grace above our ways of fear. This God, in whom these three great attributes harmonize—illimitable sovereignty, inflexible justice, and unfathomable grace—these three make up the main attributes of the one God of heaven and earth whom Christians worship.

Thus, we have brought the first person before you. The second person of our text is *the Son of God*—Christ, who knew no sin. He is the Son of God, begotten of the Father before all worlds: begotten, not made; being of the same substance with the Father, co-equal, co-eternal, and co-existent. Is the Father Almighty? So is the Son Almighty. Is the Father infinite? So is the Son infinite. He is very God of very God: having dignity not inferior to the Father, but being equal to him in every respect,—God over all, blessed for evermore. Jesus Christ also, is the son of Mary, a man like unto ourselves. A man subject to all the infirmities of human nature, except the infirmities of sin; a man of suffering and of woe; of pain and trouble; of anxiety and fear; of trouble and of doubt; of temptation and of trial; of weakness and death. He is a man just as we are, bone of our bone and flesh of our flesh. Now, the person we wish to introduce to you, is this complex being, God and man. Not God humanized, not man Deified; but God, purely, essentially God; man, purely man; man, not more than man; God, not less than God,—the two standing in a sacred union together, the God-Man. Of this God in Christ, our text says that he "knew no sin." It does not say that he did not sin; that we know: but it says more than that; he did not *know* sin; he knew not what sin was. He saw it in others, but he did not know it by experience. He was a perfect stranger to it. It is not barely said, that he did not take sin into his heart; but, he did not know it. It was no acquaintance of his. He was the acquaintance of grief; but he was not the acquaintance of sin. He knew no sin of any kind,—no sin of thought, no sin of birth, no original, no actual transgression; no sin of lip, or of hand, did ever Christ commit. He was pure, perfect, spotless; like his own divinity, without spot or blemish, or any such thing. This gracious Person, is he who is spoken of in the text. He was a

B

person utterly incapable of committing anything that was wrong.

Now I have to introduce the third person. We will not go far for him. The third person is *the sinner*. And where is he? Will you turn your eyes within you, and look for him, each one of you? He is not very far from you. He has been a drunkard; he has committed drunkenness and revelling and such like, and we know that the man who committeth these things, hath no inheritance in the kingdom of God. There is another, he has taken God's name in vain; he has sometimes, in his hot passion, asked God to do most fearful things against his limbs and against his soul. Ah! there is the sinner. Where is he? I hear that man, with tearful eye, and with sobbing voice exclaim, "Sir, he is here!" Methinks I see some woman here, in the midst of us, some of us have accused her perhaps, and she standeth alone trembling, and saith not a word for herself. Oh! that the Master might say, "neither do I condemn thee; go and sin no more." I believe, I must believe, that somewhere amongst these many thousands, I hear some palpitating heart, and that heart, as it beats so hurriedly crieth, "Sin, sin, sin, wrath, wrath, wrath, how can I get deliverance?" Ah! thou art the man, a born rebel; born into the world a sinner, thou hast added to thy native guilt thine own transgressions. Thou hast broken the commandments of God, thou hast despised God's love, thou hast trampled on his grace, thou hast gone on hitherto until now, the arrow of the Lord is drinking up thy spirit; God hath made thee tremble, he hath made thee to confess thy guilt and thy transgression. Hear me, then, if your convictions are the work of God's Spirit, you are the person intended in the text, when it says, "He hath made him to be sin for us, who knew no sin, that we"—that is you—"might be made the righteousness of God in him."

I have introduced *the persons*, and now I must introduce you to *a scene* of a great exchange which is made according to the text. The third person whom we introduce is *the prisoner at the bar*. As a sinner, God has called him before him; he is about to be tried for life or death. God is gracious, and he desires to save him; God is just, and he must punish him. The sinner is to be tried; if there be a verdict of guilty brought in against him, how will the two conflicting attributes work in God's mind? He is loving, he wants to save him; he is just, he must destroy him! How shall this mystery be solved, and the riddle be solved? Prisoner at the bar, canst thou plead "Not Guilty"? He stands speechless; or, if he speaks, he cries, "I am Guilty!"

> *Shouldst thou smite my soul to hell,*
> *Thy righteous law approves it well.*

Then, you see, if he has pleaded guilty himself, there is no hope of there being any flaw in the evidence. And even if he had pleaded "not guilty," yet the evidence is most clear, for God, the Judge, has seen his sin, and recorded all his iniquities; so that there would be no hope of his escaping. The prisoner is sure to be found guilty. How can he escape? Is there a flaw in the indictment? *No!* it is drawn up by infinite wisdom, and dictated by eternal justice; and there is no hope there. Can he turn king's evidence? Ah! if we could be saved by turning king's evidence, we should all of us be saved. There is an anomaly in our law which often allows the greater criminal to escape, whilst the lesser criminal is punished. If the one is dastard and coward enough by betraying his comrade he may save himself.

If you turn to the *Newgate Calendar*—if any of you have patience enough to read so vile a piece of literature—you will see that the greatest of two murderers has escaped, whilst the other has been hanged, because he turned king's evidence. You have told of your fellows; you have said, "Lord, I thank thee, I am not as other men; I am not as that adulterer, or even as that publican. I bless thee, I am not like my neighbour, who is an extortioner, a thief, and so on." You are telling against your neighbour; you are joint sinners, and you are telling a tale against him. There is no hope for you; God's law knows of no such injustice as a man escaping by turning informer upon others. How then shall the prisoner at the bar escape? Is there any possibility? Oh! how did heaven wonder! how did the stars stand still with astonishment! and how did the angels stay their songs a moment, when for the first time, God showed how he might be just, and yet be gracious! Oh! I think I see heaven astonished, and silence in the courts of God for the space of an hour, when the Almighty said, "Sinner, I must and will punish thee on account of sin! But I love thee; the bowels of my love yearn over thee. 'How can I make thee as Admah? How shall I set thee as Zeboim?' (Hos. 11: 8.) My justice says 'smite,' but my love stays my hand, and says, 'spare, spare the sinner!' Oh! sinner, my heart hath devised it; my Son, the pure and perfect shall stand in thy stead, and be accounted guilty, and thou, the guilty, shall stand in my Son's stead and be accounted righteous!" It would make us leap upon our feet in astonishment if we did but understand this thoroughly—the wonderful mystery of the transposition of Christ and the sinner.

Do you say that such an exchange as this is unjust? Will you say that God should not have made his Son a Substitute for us, and have let us go? Let me remind you it was purely voluntary on the part of Christ. Christ was willing to stand in our stead; he had to drink the cup of our punishment, but he was quite willing to do it. And let me tell you yet one more unanswerable thing, the Substitution of Christ was not an unlawful thing, because the sovereign God made him a Substitute. We have read in history of a certain wife whose attachment to her husband was so great, that the wife has gone into the prison and exchanged clothes with him; and while the prisoner was escaping, the wife has remained in the prison-house; and so the prisoner has escaped by a kind of surreptitious substitution. In such a case there was a clear breach of law, and the prisoner escaping might have been pursued and again imprisoned. But in this case the substitution was made by the highest authority. The text says, God "hath made him to be sin for us;" and inasmuch as Christ did stand in my room, place, and stead, he did not make the exchange unlawfully. It was with the full determinate counsel of Almighty God, as well as with his own consent, that Christ stood in the sinner's place, as the sinner doth now in Christ's place. Old Martin Luther was a man for speaking a thing pretty plainly, and sometimes he spoke the truth so plainly that he made it look very much like a lie. In one of his sermons he said, "Christ was the greatest sinner that ever lived." Now, Christ never was a sinner, but yet Martin was right. He meant to say, all the sins of Christ's people were taken off them and put on Christ's head, and so Christ stood in God's sight as if he had

been the greatest sinner that ever lived. He never was a sinner;
he never knew sin; but good Martin, in his zeal to make men
understand what it was, said, "Sinner, you became Christ;
Christ, you became a sinner!" It is not quite the truth; the sinner is treated as if he were Christ, and Christ is treated as if
he were the sinner. That is what is meant by the text God
"hath made him to be sin for us, who knew no sin; that we
might be made the righteousness of God in him."

Let me just give you two illustrations of this. The first shall
be taken from the Old Testament. When, of old, men did come
before God with sin, God provided a sacrifice which should be
the representative of Christ, inasmuch as the sacrifice died
instead of the sinner. The law ran, "He that sins shall die."
When man had committed sin they brought a bullock or a
sheep before the altar; they put their hand on the bullock's
head and acknowledged their guilt; and by that deed their
guilt was typically removed from themselves to the bullock.
Then, the poor bullock, which had done no wrong, was slaugh-
tered, and cast out as a sin offering, which God had rejected.
That is what every sinner must do with Christ, if he is to be
saved. A sinner, by faith, comes and puts his hand on Christ's
head, and confessing all his sin, it is not his any longer, it is put
on Christ. Christ hangs upon the tree; he bears the cross and
endures the shame; and so the sin is all gone and cast into the
depths of the sea. Take another illustration. We read in the
New Testament, that "the Church (that is, the people of God) is
Christ's bride." We all know that, according to the law, the
wife may have many debts; but no sooner is she married than
her debts cease to be hers, and become her husband's at once.
So that if a woman be overwhelmed with debt, so that she is in
daily fear of the prison, let her but once stand up and give her
hand to a man and become his wife, and there is none in the
world can touch her; the husband is liable for all, and she says
to her creditor, "Sir, I owe you nothing; my husband did not
owe you anything; I incurred the debt; but, inasmuch as I have
become his wife, my debts are taken off from me, and become
his." It is even so with the sinner and Christ. Christ marrieth
the sinner and putteth forth his hand, and taketh the Church
to be his. She is in debt to God's justice immeasurably; she
owes to God's vengeance an intolerable weight of wrath and

punishment; Christ says, "Thou art my wife: I have chosen thee, and I will pay thy debts." And he has paid them, and got his full discharge. Now, whosoever believeth in Christ Jesus hath peace with God, because "he hath made Christ to be sin for us, though he knew no sin, that we might be made the righteousness of God in him."

And now, I shall have finished the explanation of the text, when I just bid you *remember the consequences of this great substitution*. Christ was made sin; we are made the righteousness of God. It was in the past, long further back than the memory of angels can reach—it was in the dark past, before cherubim or seraphim had flapped the unnavigated ether—when as yet worlds were not, and creation had not a name, God foresaw the sin of man, and planned his redemption. An eternal covenant was formed between the Father and the Son; wherein the Son did stipulate to suffer for his elect; and the Father on his part, did covenant to justify them through the Son. Oh, wondrous covenant, thou art the source of all the streams of atoning love. Eternity rolled on, time came, and with it soon came the fall, and then when many years had run their round the fullness of time arrived, and Jesus prepared to fulfil his solemn engagement. He came into the world, and was made a man. From that moment, when he became a man, mark the change that was wrought in him. Before, he had been entirely happy, he had never been miserable, never sad; but now, as the effects of that terrible covenant, which he had made with God, His Father begins to pour wrath upon him. What, you say, does God actually account his Son to be a sinner? Yes, he does; His Son agreed to be the Substitute, to stand in the sinner's stead. God begins with him at his birth; he puts him in a manger. If he had considered him as a perfect man, he would have provided him a throne: but considering him as a sinner, he subjects him to woe and poverty from beginning to end. And now see him grown to manhood; see him—griefs pursue him, sorrows follow him. Stop, griefs, why follow ye the perfect? why pursue ye the immaculate? Justice, why dost thou not drive these griefs away?—"the pure should be peaceful, and the immaculate should be happy." The answer comes: "This man is pure in himself, but he has made himself impure by taking his people's sin." Guilt is imputed to him, and the very imputation of guilt brings grief with all its reality.

At last, I see death coming with more than its usual horrors; I see the grim skeleton with his dart well sharpened; I see behind him, Hell. I mark the grim prince of darkness, and all the avengers uprising from their place of torment; I see them all besetting the Saviour; I notice their terrible war upon him in the garden; I note him as he lies there wallowing in his blood in fearful soul-death. I see him as in grief and sorrow he walks to Pilate's bar; I see him mocked and spit upon; I behold him tormented, maltreated, and blasphemed; I see him nailed to the cross; I behold the mocking continued, and I hear him complaining of the forsakings of God! I am astonished. Can this be just that a perfect Being should suffer thus?—Oh, God, where art thou, that thou canst thus permit the oppression of the innocent? Hast thou ceased to be King of Justice, else why dost thou not shield the perfect One? The answer comes: Be still; he is perfect in himself, but he stands in the sinner's stead; the sinner's guilt is on him, and, it is what he hath himself agreed to, that he should be punished as if he were a sinner.

And, now, take the other side of the question, and I have done with explanation. What was the effect on *us*? Do you see that sinner there dabbling his hand in lust, defiling his garments with every sin the flesh had ever indulged in? Do you hear him cursing God? Do you mark him breaking every ordinance that God hath rendered sacred? But do you see him in a little season pursuing his way to heaven? He has renounced these sins, he has been converted, and has forsaken them; he is going on the way to heaven. Justice, art thou asleep? That man has broken thy law; is he to go to heaven? Hark how the fiends come rising from the pit and cry—"That man deserves to be lost; he may not be now what he used to be, but his past sins must have vengeance." And, yet there he goes safely on his way to heaven, and I see him looking back on all the fiends that accuse him. He cries out, "Behold, who can lay anything to the charge of God's elect?" And when one would think all hell would be up in arms and accuse, the grim tyrant lieth still, and the fiends have nought to say; and I see him turning his face heavenward to the throne of God, and hear him cry "Who is he that condemneth?" as with unblushing countenance

he challengeth the Judge. Oh! justice, where art thou? This
man has been a sinner, a rebel; why not smite him to the dust
for his impertinent presumption in thus challenging the justice
of God? Nay, says Justice, he hath been a sinner, but I do
not look upon him in that light now; I have punished Christ
instead of him: that sinner is no sinner now—he is perfect.
How? perfect! Perfect, because Christ was perfect, and I look
upon him as if he were Christ, and by-and-bye, I will give
him a place among them that are sanctified, where he shall,
harp in hand, for ever praise the name of the Lord. This is the
grand result to sinners of the great exchange. "For he hath
made him to be sin for us, who knew no sin; that we might be
made the righteousness of God in him."

Now, I have to come towards the close, to my second point,
upon which I shall be brief but laborious. WHAT IS THE USE OF
THIS DOCTRINE? Turn to the Scriptures and you will see. "Now,
then, we are ambassadors for God, as though God did beseech
you by us; we pray you in Christ's stead to be reconciled to
God, for"—here is our grand argument—"He hath made him
to be sin for us, who knew no sin." I am about to pray to you;
I am about to beseech and exhort you; may the Spirit of God
help me to do it with all the earnestness which becomes me.
You and I shall face each other soon before the bar of the great
judge, and I shall be responsible in the day of account for all I
preach to you; not for my style or talent, or want of talent,
I shall only be responsible for my earnestness and zeal in this
matter. And, now, before God, I entreat you most earnestly
to be reconciled to him, you are by nature at enmity with God;
you hate him, you neglect him, your enmity shows itself in
various ways. I beseech you now be reconciled to God. I might
entreat you to be reconciled, because it would be a fearful
thing to die with God for your enemy. Who among us can
dwell with devouring fire? who can abide with the eternal
burnings? It is a fearful thing to fall into the hands of the living
God, "for our God is consuming fire." Beware, ye that forget
God, lest he tear you in pieces and there be none to deliver. I
beseech you, therefore, be reconciled to God. I might on the
other hand use another argument, and remind you that those
who are reconciled to God, are thereby proved to be the in-
heritors of the kingdom of heaven. There are crowns for God's

friends; there are harps for them that love him; there is prepared a mansion for every one that seeketh unto him. Therefore, if thou wouldst be blessed throughout eternity, be reconciled to God. But I shall not urge that; I shall urge the reason of my text. I beseech thee, be reconciled to God, because if thou repentest, it is proof that Christ has stood in thy stead. Oh, if this argument do not melt thee, there is none in heaven or earth that can. If thy heart melteth not at such an argument as this, then it is harder than the nether millstone; sure thou hast a soul of stone, and a heart of brass, if thou wilt not be reconciled to God who hath written this for thine encouragement.

I beseech thee be reconciled to God, because in this there is proof that God is loving you. Thou thinkest God to be a God of wrath. Would he have given his own Son to be punished if he had hated thee? Sinner, if God had anything but thoughts of love towards thee, I ask, would he have given up his Son to hang upon the cross? Think not my God a tyrant; think him not a wrathful God, destitute of mercy. His Son, torn from his bosom and given up to die, is the best proof of his love. Oh, sinner, I need not blame thee if thou didst hate thy enemy, but I must blame thee, call thee mad, if thou dost hate thy friend. Oh, I need not wonder if thou wouldst not be reconciled to one who would not be reconciled to thee; but, inasmuch as thou wilt not by nature be reconciled to the God who gave his own Son to die, I must marvel at the stupidity into which thine evil nature hath hurried thee. God is love; wilt thou be unreconciled to love? God is grace; wilt thou be unreconciled to grace? Oh, rebel that thou art of deepest dye if still thou art unreconciled.

He saith, "be reconciled." The child runneth away from his father when he hath sinned, because he fears his father will punish him; but when his father burns the rod, and with a smiling face says, "child, come hither," sure it must be an unloving child that would not run into such a father's arms. Sinner, thou deservest the sword; God has snapped the sword across the knee of Christ's atonement, and now he says "Come tome." You deserve infinite, eternal wrath, and the displeasure of God; God has quenched that wrath for all believers, and now he says, "Come to me and be reconciled." Do you tell me that you are not sinners? I was not preaching to you. Do you tell me that you have never rebelled against God? I warn you that though *you* cannot find your own sins out, *God* will find them out. Do you say, "I need no reconciliation, except that which I can make myself"? Be warned that if thou rejectest Christ, thou rejectest thine only hope; for all that thou canst do is less than nothing and vanity. I was not preaching to thee, when I said, "Be reconciled." I was preaching to thee, poor afflicted conscience; I was preaching to thee—thou that hast been a great sinner and transgressor, thou that feelest thy guilt; to thee, thou adulterer, trembling now under the lash of conviction; to thee, thou blasphemer, quivering now from head to foot; I preach to thee, thou thief, whose eye is now filled with the tear of penitence; thou feelest that hell must be thy portion, unless thou art saved through Christ; I preach to thee, thou that knowest thy guilt; I preach to thee and to every one such, and I beseech thee to be reconciled to God, for God is reconciled to thee. Oh, let not your heart stand out against this.

I cannot plead as I could wish. Oh! if I could, I would plead with my heart, with my eyes, and my lips, that I might lead you to the Saviour. You need not rail at me and call this an Arminian style of preaching; I care not for your opinion; this style is Scriptural. "As though God did beseech you by us, we pray you, in Christ's stead, be ye reconciled to God." Poor broken-hearted sinner, God is as much preaching to you, and bidding you be reconciled, as if he stood here himself in his own person; and though I be a mean and puny man by whom he speaketh, he speaketh now as much as if it were by the voice of angels, "Be reconciled to God." Come, friend, turn not thine eye and head away from me; but give me thine hand and lend me thine heart whilst I weep over thine hand and cry over thine heart, and beseech thee not to despise thine own mercy, not to be a suicide to thine own soul, not to damn thyself. Now that God has awakened thee to feel that thou art an enemy, I beseech thee now to be his friend. Remember, if thou art now convinced of sin, there is no punishment for thee. He was punished in thy stead. Wilt thou believe this? Wilt thou trust in it, and so be at peace with God? If thou sayest, "No!" then I would have thee know that thou hast put away thine own mercy. If thou sayest, "I need no reconciliation," thou hast thrust away the only hope thou canst ever have. Do it at thine own hazard; I wash my hands of thy blood. But, but, but, if thou knowest thyself to need a Saviour, if thou wouldst escape the hellish pit, if thou wouldst walk among them that are sanctified, I again, in the name of him that will condemn thee at the last day if thou rejectest this invitation, implore and beseech thee to be reconciled to God. I am his ambassador. When I have done this sermon, I shall go back to court. Sinner, what shall I say of thee? Shall I go back and tell my Master that thou intendest to be his enemy for ever? Shall I go back and tell him, "They heard me, but they regarded not"? They said in their hearts, "We will go away to our sins and our follies, and we will not serve your God, neither fear him!" Shall I tell him such a message as that? Must I be driven to go back to his palace with such a fearful story?

May I not go back to court to-day, and tell the Monarch on my knees, "There be some my Lord, that have been great rebels, but when they saw themselves rebels, they threw themselves at the foot of the cross, and asked for pardon. They had strangely revolted, but I heard them say, 'If he will forgive me, I will turn from my evil ways, if he will enable me!' They were gross transgressors, and they confessed it; but I heard them say, 'Jesus, thy blood and righteousness are my only trust.'" Happy ambassador! I will go back to my Master with a gladsome countenance, and tell him that peace is made between many a soul and the great God. But miserable ambassador who has to go back and say, "There is no peace made." How shall it be? The Lord decide it! May many hearts give way to Omnipotent grace now, and may enemies of grace be changed into friends, that God's elect may be gathered in, and his eternal purpose accomplished.

And now, I close up by noticing the SWEET ENJOYMENT which this doctrine brings to a believer. Mourning Christian! dry up your tears. Are you weeping on account of sin? Why weepest thou? Weep because of thy sin, but weep not through any fear of punishment. Has the evil one told thee that thou shalt be condemned? Tell him to his face that he lies. Ah! poor distressed believer; art thou mourning over thine own corruptions? Look to thy perfect Lord, and remember, thou art complete in him, thou art in God's sight as perfect as if thou hadst never sinned; nay, more than that, the Lord our righteousness hath put a divine garment upon thee, so that thou hast more than the righteousness of man—thou hast the righteousness of God. Oh! thou that art mourning by reason of in-bred sin and depravity, remember, none of thy sins can condemn thee. Thou hast learned to hate sin; but thou hast learned to know that SIN is not thine—it is put on Christ's head. Come, be of good cheer; thy standing is not in thyself—it is in Christ; thine acceptance is not in thyself, but in thy Lord; with all thy sin, thou art as much accepted to-day as in thy sanctification; thou art as much accepted of God to-day, with all thine iniquities, as thou wilt be when thou standest before his throne, rendered free from all corruption. Oh! I beseech thee, lay hold on this precious thought, perfection in Christ! For thou art perfect in Christ Jesus. With thy Saviour's garment on, thou art holy as the holy ones; thou art now justified by faith; thou hast now peace with God. Be of good cheer; do not fear to die; death has nothing terrible in it to thee; Christ hath extracted all the gall from the sting of death. Tremble not at judgment; judgment will not bring thee another acquittal, to add to the acquittal already given in thy cause.

> *Bold shalt thou stand at that great day,*
> *For who aught to thy charge can lay?*
> *Fully absolved by Christ thou art,*
> *From sin's tremendous guilt and smart.*

Ah, when thou comest to die, thou shalt challenge God; for thou shalt say, "My God, thou canst not condemn me, for thou hast condemned Christ for me, thou hast punished Christ in my stead. 'Who is he that condemneth? It is Christ that died, yea, rather, that is risen again, who also sitteth on the right hand of God and maketh intercession for us.'" Christian, be glad; let thy head lack no oil, and thy face no ointment; "go thy way; eat thy bread with joy, and drink thy wine with a merry heart, for God hath accepted thy works." Do as Solomon bids us do; live happily all the days of thy life; for thou art accepted in the Beloved—thou art pardoned through the blood, and justified through the righteousness of Christ.

IV

BONDS WHICH COULD NOT HOLD

"Whom God hath raised up, having loosed the pains of death: because it was not possible that he should be holden of it."—Acts 2: 24.

PETER is here speaking of the risen Christ, whom God had raised up, "having loosed the pains of death;" so it is clear that, whatever those pains were, our blessed Lord Jesus Christ felt them, he felt them much more than his followers do; for, in his death-agony, he was left without the sustaining help of God, and the light of his Father's countenance was hidden from him. His death was a bitter one indeed, he took the deepest draughts of wormwood and gall, for he had to "taste death for every man," whatever that mysterious expression may mean. We must never imagine that there was about Christ's death anything which took away from its bitterness; there was much that increased it, but nothing that diminished it. He was bound, as with strong cords, by the pains of death; all his powers were, for a time, fettered, he was held captive, and he did really die. After death, he was buried; but there was this remarkable fact about his dead body, it saw no corruption. In the case of ordinary corpses, corruption begins very speedily. In a climate like that of Jerusalem, it is very quick in doing its work of dissolving the mortal fabric; but, although our Lord did truly die, no taint of corruption came upon his precious body.

The reason for that was, first, because it was not necessary. Corruption is not a part of the sentence which Christ had to bear. The penalty of sin is death, and that he bore to the utmost; but there was no necessity that he should also endure the usual consequences of death; and, therefore, although he died, his flesh was not permitted to see corruption.

Again, as it was not necessary, so it would not have been seemly that our Lord Jesus Christ's body should ever be tainted by decay as all other bodies are. It was not right that One who was so pure and holy as he was, One who stood in what theologians call hypostatical union with the Godhead (it is not easy to explain exactly what is meant by that term, but it refers to our Lord's intimate and complete union with the Godhead), it would not have been comely that such a body as his should see corruption, and, therefore, it was preserved from the defilement which death usually brings in its train.

And, further, it was not even natural that the body of Christ should see corruption, for albeit that it was like our bodies in many respects, yet we must never forget that there was a vast difference even in his birth. Through the immaculate conception of our Lord, no taint of sin was in his nature; by a mysterious overshadowing which we must not attempt to understand, "that holy thing" which was born of the virgin was truly "the Son of God," "holy, harmless, undefiled, separate from sinners"; and, as there was no original taint about that sacred body, so there was never afterwards a single action, or even thought, by which its chaste and perfect purity could have been defiled. If our first parents had never sinned, it would not have been necessary for these bodies of ours to die, and to become corrupt; and in taking our place, and suffering in our stead, there did come upon Christ the necessity that he should die, but there was no natural necessity that his dead body should become corrupt, and it did not pass into a state of decay, for it was not the will of God that his soul should be left in Hades, or that his holy body should see corruption. While it is quite true that Christ is made in all things like unto his brethren, yet there is always some point of distinction to indicate that, although he is our Brother, he is "the firstborn among many brethren," "the chiefest among ten thousand"; and, if others are lovely, yet "he is altogether lovely." So, although he really died, and his body was laid in the tomb as the dead usually are, yet, inasmuch as it was preserved from corruption, it is marked out as being above and different from all the rest.

I am going now to speak upon the fact mentioned in the text, that IT WAS NOT POSSIBLE THAT THE BONDS OF DEATH SHOULD HOLD OUR LORD. God raised him up, "having loosed the pains of death: because it was not possible that he should be holden of it."

Why was it impossible that the bonds of death should hold Christ? There are several reasons; the first is, that *Christ had in himself the inherent power to die, and to live again.* I will not enlarge upon this truth, but simply give you our Lord's own words concerning it: "Therefore doth my Father love me, because I lay down my life, that I might take it again. No man taketh it from me, but I lay it down of myself. I have power to lay it down, and I have power to take it again. This commandment have I received of my Father." Now, in the realms of the dead, before that time, there had never been seen any person who had the inherent power to take up his life again. Neither had there ever been one there who had possessed the inherent power to lay down his life when he pleased, for no mere man has ever been the absolute master of his own life; so that our Lord Jesus was the first who ever entered the portals of the tomb bearing within himself the power to rise again whenever he pleased.

Next, *the dignity of his person* rendered it impossible that he should be held by the cords of death, apart from the consent of his own will; for, though Jesus Christ was truly human,—and let that blessed fact never be forgotten,—yet his humanity was in so close an alliance with the Godhead, that, though we do not say that the humanity did really become divine, yet "Jesus Christ himself" altogether is divine, and is to be worshipped and adored in the completeness of his blessed Person; and, therefore, that flesh, which he took upon himself for our sake, was uplifted, exalted, ennobled, by being taken into mysterious unity with his Deity. It could not be that a body, in which dwelt the fullness of the Godhead, could be held by the bones of death. He who slept in Joseph's tomb was the Son of God. It was he who is without beginning of days or end of years, he with whom Jehovah took counsel when he laid the foundations of the heavens and built all worlds, for "without him was not anything made that was made." It was not, therefore, possible that he should be held by the bonds of death. Marvellous condescension, not human weakness, brought him into the sepulchre; it was by his own free will that he was laid in the tomb; and, consequently, he had but to exert his royal prerogative, and he could rise again from the dead whenever he pleased.

Those two reasons might be sufficient to prove the assertion I made concerning our Lord, but I want you to notice, with delight, a third one. It was not possible that the dead Christ should be held by the bonds of death any longer than the third morning *because his redeeming work was done*. Remember—and oh! how well some of you know it, and how gladly do you welcome it!—that the reason why Jesus died was because he took the sin of his people upon himself; and being found in the sinner's place, he had to suffer the sinner's doom, which was death. But after he had endured the penalty, that is, after he had died, and remained the appointed time in the tomb, how could he be held any longer in the grave? After he had said, "It is finished," and after the predestinated hours for a full examination of his work before the throne of God had passed, why should he be detained any longer? He was the Hostage for our debt; but when the debt was paid, who could keep him in durance vile? Having borne the penalty, he was free for ever; and so, as Paul writes, "Christ being raised from the dead dieth no more; death hath no more dominion over him." In that he has satisfied all the claims of the law of God, what hand can arrest him, what power can hold him captive? He died for our sins, but he rose again for our justification, and his rising proved that all his people were accounted righteous in the sight of God. It was not possible, while there was a just God in heaven, that Christ should remain in the tomb. As his work was done, justice demanded that he should be let go;—"And now both the Surety and sinner are free."

In the next place, it was not possible that Christ should remain in the tomb because *he had his Father's promise that he should not*. I have already reminded you that David, speaking by inspiration, had said, "Thou wilt not leave my soul in Hades" (the abode of departed spirits); "neither wilt thou suffer thine Holy One to see corruption." That promise must be kept, so it was not possible that Christ should remain in the grave beyond the appointed period; indeed, this was part of the Father's purpose and plan, and an essential part of the great work of the redemption of his elect, that he who died should rise again; and what is in Jehovah's plan and purpose, none shall ever gainsay. When he openeth the door, no man is able to shut it; and while he shutteth up, no man can possibly open.

Even Nebuchadnezzar, when he came to his right mind, said concerning the Most High, "None can stay his hand, or say unto him, What doest thou?" So, when the Father had purposed and decreed that his Son, Jesus Christ, should not be held any longer by the bonds of death, it was not possible for him to be detained.

Remember, too, that there is a fifth reason for Christ's deliverance; that is to be found in *the perpetuity of his offices*. You scarcely need for me to remind you that our Lord Jesus Christ was a Priest, but not after the order of the Aaronic priests, for they died, and there was an end of them so far as their priesthood was concerned; but to Christ it was said, "Thou art a priest for ever after the order of Melchisedec." But a man cannot be a priest when he is dead; therefore, since Christ's is a Melchisedec priesthood, he "is made, not after the law of a carnal commandment, but after the power of an endless life"; and, in order that he might have that endless life, it was necessary that he should rise from the dead,—his Melchisedec priesthood required it.

Next, Jesus was King as well as Priest. You know what sort of a King he was, for it is written, "Thy throne, O God, is for ever and ever." Now Christ must reign. It is also written that "he must reign, till he hath put all enemies under his feet." But a dead king cannot reign; and, therefore, Christ must rise from the tomb. He must have death under his feet, for death is one of his enemies; but if he had not risen from the dead, he would have been under the feet of death, and that could never be. So that both his priestly and kingly offices required that he should rise from the grave.

Ay, and so did his office as our Redeemer; for, when he undertook to become our next of kin, and to redeem us, it was essential that he should continue to live, or else that ancient cry of the patriarch Job would not have remained true, "I know that my Redeemer liveth." Therefore, he must rise from the dead. I cannot stay to go further into this argument; but, if you will think over it yourself, you will see that, because Jesus Christ is "the same yesterday, and to-day, and for ever," because each of his offices is everlasting, ordained of God in perpetuity, therefore he must rise from the dead.

But it was not possible, *in the very nature of things*, for Christ to be held by the bonds of death. If he had been, think what the consequences to us would have been; for, first, we should have had no assurance of our own resurrection. The blessed hope that those who have been called away from us, and whose bodies we have committed to the earth, shall rise again, would have been without any substantial foundation. "But now is Christ risen from the dead, and become the firstfruits of them that slept." When you get the firstfruits of a harvest, you feel certain that the rest of it will be garnered in due time. So Christ has risen as the first of a great host, and we thus have an assurance, which otherwise we could not have had, but which is essential to the comfort of Christians.

Only imagine what would have been the consequences to us if that assurance had not been ours. There would have been no evidence of our justification. I might have said, "Yes, Christ took my debt, but how do I know that he paid it? Christ bore my sins, but how do I know that he put them away?" So, if he had never risen from the dead, we should have had no proof that we were justified.

Then, too, if he had never risen, and gone up to heaven in his human body, we should not have had anyone to take possession of heaven on our behalf. Now we have "a man in possession." We have a wondrous Representative before the throne, who has taken seizin and grip of the divine estates. What a joy it is to us to know that he is there to represent us before God!

Further, if Christ's body had remained in the grave, there could have been no reign of Christ, and no sitting down at the right hand of God, as there now is. He would have been in heaven in the same respect as he is here as God; but there would have been no visible appearance of the representative Man, and the once-crucified Redeemer; and the ransomed ones could not have sung, "For thou wast slain, and hast redeemed us to God by thy blood," for he would not have been there to hear the song. They might have recollected the sacrifice on Calvary; but he, as the Lamb that had been slain, wearing the marks of his priesthood and death, would not have been there.

Now I pass on to my second observation, which is that, AS CHRIST COULD NOT BE HELD BY THE BONDS OF DEATH, HE COULD NOT BE HELD BY ANY OTHER BONDS.

If he was more than a match for death, who or what shall ever be able to stand against him? Death, the slaughterer of all mankind, before whom kings and princes, as well as the meanest of their subjects, lie prostrate in the tomb—death, before whom giants bend as a rush sways to and fro in the wind—; even death is vanquished by Christ. He is the destroyer of destruction, and the death of death; then, what power can possibly stand in opposition to him? I want to cheer you, in these dark and evil days, with a strong belief in our great Master's omnipotence and invincible might. His kingdom is an everlasting kingdom. With such a Hero as he is to lead us on, victory is sure, however stern may be the conflict.

Think, for a few minutes, how many things have tried to bind the Christ of God, and to overthrow his righteous rule. At first, and even until now, *old-established error* has assailed the truth of God. What fools some people thought that those few fishermen were when they imagined that they could upset the firmly-established Judaism of the chosen people and the deeply-ingrained idolatry of other nations! The systems of the heathen were beautiful with art, adorned with poetry, intensely lascivious, and they had a tremendous power over the popular mind. If we had lived in those days, and had been unbelievers who had seen those fishermen start out to preach, we should have said to them, "Go home with you! Do you think you are ever going to overthrow the philosophies of Plato and Socrates, and all the reverence for the gods and goddesses of Greece and Rome?" Ah! but from their deep foundations that little band of men plucked up by the very roots those old idolatries, for Christ could not be held in bondage by them.

Then there came another period, in which men thought themselves exceedingly wise, and *the wisdom of this world* set itself in array against the gospel of Christ, even as it does to-day; but he who was Victor over death can never be defeated by the Academy. Think not, beloved, that the most learnèd fools can be a match for him who overcame death itself. When Christ's cause was at the lowest ebb, when he himself was dead, and all his disciples were scattered, yet even then he snatched the crown from the hands of the skeleton king, and won a complete victory over him. Think you that he, who is Wisdom Incarnate, does not know how the wise men and the scribes of to-day jest and jeer at him? Yet there is no philosopher who can bind the Christ any more than Samson could be bound by the green withs of the Philistines.

Next, there came a time when men tried to bind up the kingdom of Christ with *the bonds of ignorance*. They took away the Bible from the people, they concealed the gospel in the Latin tongue, and the nations were steeped in midnight darkness. Yet Christ could not be bound even then. He had only to call Wycliffe, and Huss, and Jerome, and Luther, and Calvin, and Melanchthon, and Zwingli, and very soon they let men know that Christ could not be held in the bonds of the Pope. The Conqueror of death was not to be vanquished by any mortal man, whoever he might be.

Since then, we have come to times in which *wealth, and rank, and fashion, and prestige*, are all against the gospel; but what matters it? Nowadays, the multitudes pour their scorn upon righteousness, and call that "cant and hypocrisy" which is really a defence of that which is right and true; and Satan is casting a fatal spell over the professing church itself, so that it is getting worldly, and is giving up its primitive simplicity. Sometimes, I am inclined to sit down and weep and grieve, as I see how sadly the battle seems to go against us today; we seem to be losing ground, instead of gaining the victory. But will I wring my hands in despair? God forbid! "The Strength of Israel will not lie," neither shall his cause fail. Let men forsake him if they will, or let them come out armed against him if they dare, his kingdom shall still stand fast, for he must reign, and, as death cannot bind him, nothing else can. The pleasure of the Lord must prosper in his hands, therefore in patience possess your souls; go on quietly witnessing for Christ; and, if you do not see the rulers of the nations converted to Christ, and the great and learned men bowing humbly before him, remember that it was never so, and is never likely to be so. Take care that you yourselves remain steadfast in faith in the Eternal, and all shall be well with you.

Now, there is a truth upon which I wish to insist with great earnestness; it is this. As CHRIST COULD NOT BE HELD BY THE BONDS OF DEATH, IT IS NOT POSSIBLE TO KEEP IN BONDAGE ANYTHING THAT BELONGS TO HIM.

You recollect that, when Pharaoh told Moses that the men

among the children of Israel might go into the wilderness to offer sacrifice, he said that they must leave their little ones behind; but Moses would not accept that condition. The next time, Pharaoh said, "Go ye, serve the Lord; only let your flocks and your herds be stayed: let your little ones also go with you." But Moses answered, "Thou must give us also sacrifices and burnt offerings, that we may sacrifice unto the Lord our God. Our cattle also shall go with us; there shall not an hoof be left behind" (Exod. 10: 24–26). All that was of Israel was to go with Israel; and that is still our Master's will and way. "Where I am," saith he, "there shall my people be also. If I am in the grave, they must be in the grave, too, buried with me; if I rise, they also shall rise, for I will not rise without them; and, if I go to heaven, I will not go without them." This is our joy, and with dear old Rowland Hill we can sing,—

> *And this do I find, we two are so joined,*
> *He'll not be in glory, and leave me behind.*

Now, where are you, *you who are struggling to get to Christ?* You are somewhere in this place, I verily believe. You have been resolving to find Christ, and you have really put your trust in him; it is a very poor little trust as yet, and no sooner have you begun to think seriously about divine things, than you are in great trouble. There are your old sins, and you wonder how you will ever get rid of the guilt of former years. Ah! if you fully trust in Christ, your old sins shall vanish away through his precious blood. They are bonds that cannot hold a soul for whom Christ hath died. "Oh, but there are also my old habits," says one, "my tendency to do what I have been doing for years. 'Can the Ethiopian change his skin, or the leopard his spots?' How then shall I, who have been accustomed to do evil, learn to do well?" Put you your trust in Christ, and those old habits shall not be able to hold you. They may, perhaps, take some time to break; but they shall all be broken, and you shall be set free. Christ could not be held by the bonds of death, neither shall you, who truly trust him, be held by the bonds of habit. Possibly you say, "My old companions get round me, and they worry me to go back to them." Let them worry as much as they like; but, if you trust in Christ,

God will give you grace to set your face like a flint against them, and you shall be a bolder and braver soldier of Christ because they oppose you. Perhaps it is better for you to be persecuted than to be allowed to live too easily. The other day, I put some primroses in my conservatory; those that were left out in the open, to endure the cold windy nights, bloomed splendidly; but those that were in the warmer atmosphere did not get on nearly so well. There are some Christians that are like the primrose, they need a little cold weather, and do not get on so well where it is too warm. The Lord sends you opposition to make you all the stronger. But the bands of the wicked cannot hold you; break loose from them, I pray you, through the power God gives you by his grace.

"Ah!" you say, "but Satan himself breaks in upon me." Very likely he does; but just resist him, steadfast in the faith. Possibly he is throwing blasphemies into your mind, injecting evil thoughts which you never had before. But, if a thousand devils were to bind you thus with cords, so that you could not move hand or foot, yet, depend upon it, you shall slip out of the cords, and come into perfect liberty, for all the devils in hell cannot hold a soul that belongs to Christ, and you do belong to him if you truly trust him.

Perhaps I am also speaking to *some child of God who has fallen into great trouble*. You are an old Christian, and yet you have got into a bad scrape. You were never in such a condition before, and you seem to be bound with the cords of trouble after trouble, as if they were tightly knotted around you so that you could not get loose. There are also the cords of depression of spirit, and they sometimes cut very painfully, and hold you bound like a poor captive. Perhaps also the devil, as well as your own depression, has tied you up. There is a diabolical temptation that has come to you; you are even afraid that you are not a child of God at all, and you begin to doubt everything. You were never before bound as you are now; you seem to be thrust into the inner prison, and your feet made fast in the stocks. If so, I believe that God has sent me to do to you as the angel did to Peter. You know that the angel went to Peter, when he was asleep in the prison, and smote him on the side. Well, I cannot get near enough to you to do that, so you must take it as done. Then what did the angel do to Peter? He raised him up, his chains fell off from his hands, and the angel said to him, "Gird thyself, and bind on thy sandals. And so he did." Then the angel said, "Cast thy garment about thee, and follow me"; and Peter did so, and he walked through the first and the second ward of the prison. At last, they came to the iron gate leading into the city, that great gate that needed half-a-dozen men to open it, and Peter was surprised to see it open of its own accord. He never saw anything like that before, and soon he found himself with the cool night air playing on his forehead, and he was a free man again. All the Herods and all the devils cannot shut up a man who trusts in God; so, you will come out of your prison again. You are like a cork in the water; men may press you below the surface, but you are bound to come to the top again. You know what Haman planned for Mordecai; he meant to hang him up on the high gallows that he had erected. He was not satisfied with that, for he intended also to kill all who belonged to the same race as Mordecai; he meant that not a Jew should be allowed to live; but, when his plans could not be carried out as he intended, his wise men and his wife said to him, "If Mordecai be of the seed of the Jews, before whom thou hast begun to fall, thou shalt not prevail against him, but shalt surely fall before him"; and so it came to pass, for there swung Haman on the gallows that he had erected for the execution of Mordecai. There may be a Haman plotting against you; leave him alone. If he is making the gallows, let him finish them; they will come in for himself in due time. If you belong to Jesus Christ, and if you belong to the seed of the believers, before whom Satan had begun to fall, he will never prevail against you, but you will overcome him, for you must reign with Christ for ever, for he himself has said so.

Finally, beloved, there is a part of Christ's redeemed possession that is under mortgage at present; it is not yet delivered from the bond that holds it. What part is that? It is *this poor body, these bones, and this flesh and blood,* for although "the spirit is life because of righteousness," the body is still "dead because of sin." And soon, that poor body of yours, unless Christ shall come first, will see corruption, and moulder, and go back to dust; but mark this, as I have already said, Christ will not leave any fragment of his people in the hands of the enemy; he will not leave any portion of his people—no, not so much as a bone of them,—under the dominion of death. The hour shall come when the trumpet shall sound, and the dead shall be raised; and, as the soul has been redeemed, so shall the body also enter into the fullness of the joy of adoption, to wit, the redemption of the body. We have buried many of the godly; there is many a *Campo Santo* ("Holy Ground") round about this great city, where sleep the pious dead; and we have wept as we have committed them to the silent clay. But they are not lost,—not one of them is lost. No baby, chosen of God to see heaven ere it saw much of the world, no man or woman in middle life, taken from the midst of the conflict, no grey-headed man, who leaned upon his staff for very age and came to the grave like a shock of corn to the garner; there shall not one of them be lost, nor an eye, nor a foot, nor a hand of any one of them; yea, and the very hairs of their head are all numbered. The Lord hath taken an inventory of all that he has bought with his precious blood, and he will have it all; not merely the souls and spirits of his people, but their bodies, too. Who is to stop him? Death knows his power, but must yield to it. The strong man armed did keep the sepulchre, but a stronger than he came in, and burst the bands of the tomb, and he came forth alive; and—

> *As the Lord our Saviour rose,*
> *So all his followers must;*

for, as it is written, "A bone of him shall not be broken"; and it is not possible that they, who are, as it were, the bones of his mystical body, should be holden by the bonds of death. O happy people, who belong to Christ! God grant that we may all be numbered amongst them, for his great name's sake!

V

SPIRITUAL RESURRECTION

"And you hath he quickened, who were dead in trespasses
and sins."—Eph. 2: 1.

IT might naturally be expected that I should have selected the
topic of the resurrection on what is usually called the Easter
Sabbath. I shall not do so. I have had pressed on my mind a
subject which is not the resurrection of Christ, but which is in
some measure connected with it—the resurrection of lost and
ruined man by the Spirit of God in this life.

The apostle is here speaking, you will observe, of the church
at Ephesus, and, indeed, of all those who were chosen in Christ
Jesus, accepted in him, and redeemed with his blood; and he
says of them, "You hath he quickened, who were dead in
trespasses and sins."

What a solemn sight is presented to us by a dead body!
When, last evening trying to realize the thought, it utterly
overcame me. The thought is overwhelming, that soon this
body of mine must be a carnival for worms; that in and out of
these places, where my eyes are glistening, foul things, the offspring of loathsomeness, shall crawl; that this body must be
stretched in still, cold, abject, passive death, must then become
a noxious, nauseous thing, cast out even by those that loved
me, who will say, "Bury my dead out of my sight." Perhaps
you can scarcely, in the moment I can afford you, appropriate
the idea to yourselves. Does it not seem a strange thing, that
you, who have walked to this place this morning, shall be carried
to your graves; that the eyes with which you now behold me
shall soon be glazed in everlasting darkness; that the tongues,
which just now moved in song, shall soon be silent lumps of
clay; and that your strong and stalwart frame, now standing in
this place, will soon be unable to move a muscle, and become a
loathsome thing, the brother of the worm and the sister of
corruption? You can scarcely get hold of the idea; death doth
such awful work with us, it is such a vandal with this mortal

57

fabric, it so rendeth to pieces this fair thing that God hath builded up, that we can scarcely bear to contemplate his works of ruin.

Now, endeavour, as well as you can, to get the idea of a dead corpse, and when you have so done, please to understand, that that is the metaphor employed in my text, to set forth the condition of your soul by nature. Just as the body is dead, incapable, unable, unfeeling, and soon about to become corrupt and putrid, so are we if we be unquickened by divine grace; dead in trespasses and sins, having within us death, which is capable of developing itself in worse and worse stages of sin and wickedness, until all of us here, left by God's grace, should become loathsome beings; loathsome through sin and wickedness, even as the corpse through natural decay. Understand, that the doctrine of the Holy Scripture is, that man by nature, since the fall, is dead; he is a corrupt and ruined thing; in a spiritual sense, utterly and entirely dead. And if any of us shall come to spiritual life, it must be by the quickening of God's Spirit, vouchsafed to us sovereignly through the good will of God the Father, not for any merits of our own, but entirely of his own abounding and infinite grace.

Now, I trust I shall not be tedious; I shall endeavour to make the subject as interesting as possible, and also endeavour to be brief. The general doctrine is, that every man that is born into the world is dead spiritually, and that spiritual life must be given by the Holy Spirit, and can be obtained from no other source. That general doctrine, I shall illustrate in rather a singular way. You remember that our Saviour raised three dead persons; I do not find that during his lifetime he caused more than three resurrections. The first was the young maiden, *the daughter of Jairus*, who, when she lay on her bed dead, rose up to life at the single utterance of Christ, "*Talitha cumi*!" The second was the case of *the widow's son*, who was on his bier, about to be carried to his tomb; and Jesus raised him up to life by saying, "Young man, I say unto thee, arise." The third, and most memorable case, was that of *Lazarus*, who was not on his bed, nor on his bier, but in his tomb, ay, and corrupt too; but, notwithstanding that, the Lord Jesus Christ, by the voice of his omnipotence, crying, "Lazarus, come forth," brought him out of the tomb.

I shall use these three facts as illustrations of *the different states of men*, though they be all thoroughly dead: secondly, as illustrations of *the different means of grace used for raising them*, though, after all, the same great agency is employed; and, in the third place, as illustrations of *the after-experience of quickened men*; for, though that to a great degree is the same, yet there are some points of difference.

I shall begin by noticing, then, first of all, THE CONDITION OF MEN BY NATURE. Men by nature are all dead. There is Jairus's daughter; she lies on her bed; she seems as if she were alive; her mother has scarce ceased to kiss her brow, her hand is still in her father's loving grasp, and he can scarcely think that she is dead; but dead she is, as thoroughly dead as she ever can be. Next comes the case of the young man brought out of his grave; he is more than dead, he has begun to be corrupt, the signs of decay are upon his face, and they are carrying him to his tomb; yet, though there are more manifestations of death about him, he is no more dead than the other. He is just as dead; they are both dead, and death really knows of no degrees. The third case goes further still in the manifestation of death; for it is the case of which Martha, using strong words, said, "Lord, by this time he stinketh; for he hath been dead four days." And yet, mark you, the daughter of Jairus was as dead as Lazarus; though the manifestation of death was not so complete in her case. All were dead alike. I have in my congregation some blessed beings, fair to look upon; fair, I mean, in their character, as well as their outward appearance; they have about them everything that is good and lovely; but, mark this, if they are unregenerate, they are dead still. That girl, dead in the room, upon her bed, had little about her that could show her death. Not yet had the loving finger closed the eyelid; there seemed to be a light still lingering in her eye; like a lily just nipped off; she was as fair as life itself. The worm had not yet begun to gnaw her cheek, the flush had not yet faded from her face; she seemed well-nigh alive. And so it is with some I have here. Ye have all that heart could wish for, except the one thing needful; ye have all things save love to the Saviour. Ye are not yet united to him by a living faith. Ah! then, I grieve to say it, ye are dead! ye are dead! As much dead as the worst of men, although your death is not so apparent. Again, I have in my presence young men who have grown to riper years than that fair damsel who died in her childhood. You have much about you that is lovely, but you have just begun to indulge in evil habits; you have not yet become the desperate sinner; you have not yet become altogether noxious in the eyes of other men; you are but beginning to sin, you are like the young man carried out on his bier; you have not yet become the confirmed drunkard; you have not yet begun to curse and blaspheme God; you are still accepted in good society; you are not yet cast out; but you are dead, thoroughly dead, just as dead as the third and worst case. But I dare say I have some characters that are illustrations of that case too. There is Lazarus in his tomb, rotten and putrid; and so there are some men not more dead than others, but their death has become more apparent, their character has become abominable, their deeds cry out against them, they are put out of decent society, the stone is rolled to the mouth of their tomb, men feel that they cannot hold acquaintance with them, for they have so utterly abandoned every sense of right, that we say, "Put them out of sight, we cannot endure them!" And yet these putrid ones may live; these last are not more dead than the maiden upon her bed, though the death has more fully revealed itself in their corruption. Jesus Christ must quicken the one as well as the other, and bring them all to know and love his name.

Now, then, I am about to enter into the minutiæ of the difference of these three cases. I will take the case of the young maiden. I have her here to-day; I have many illustrations of her present before me; at least, I trust so. Now, will you allow me to point out all the differences? Here is the young maiden; look upon her; you can bear the sight; she is dead, but oh! *beauty lingereth there*; she is fair and lovely, though the life hath departed from her. In the young man's case there is no beauty; the worm hath begun to eat him; his honour hath departed. In the third case, there is absolute rottenness. But here there is beauty still upon her cheek. Is she not amiable? Is she not lovely? Would not all love her? Is she not to be admired, even to be imitated? Is she not fairest of the fair? Ay, that she is; but God the Spirit has not yet looked upon her; she has not yet bent her knee to Jesus, and cried for mercy; she has everything, except true religion. Alas for her; alas that so fair a character should be a dead one. Alas my sister; alas that thou, the benevolent, the kind one, should yet be, after all, dead in thy trespasses and sins. As Jesus wept over that young man who had kept all the commandments, and yet one thing he lacked, so weep I over thee. Alas! thou fair one, lovely in thy character, and amiable in thy carriage, why shouldst thou lie dead? For dead thou art, unless thou hast faith in Christ. Thine excellence, thy virtue, and thy goodness, shall avail thee nought; thou art dead, and dead thou must be, unless he make thee live.

Note, too, that in the case of this maiden, whom we have introduced to you, the daughter of Jairus, *she is yet caressed*; she has only been dead a moment or two, and the mother still presses her cheek with kisses. Oh! can she be dead? Do not the tears rain on her, as if they would sow the seeds of life in that dead earth again, earth that looks fertile enough to bring forth life with but one living tear? Ay, but those salt tears are tears of barrenness. She liveth not; but she is still caressed. Not so the young man; he is put on the bier; no man will touch him any more, or else he will be utterly defiled. And as for Lazarus, he is shut up with a stone. But this young maiden is still caressed; so it is with many of you; you are loved even by the living in Sion; God's own people love you; the minister has often prayed for you; you are admitted into the assemblies of the saints, you sit with them as God's people, you hear as they hear, and you sing as they sing. Alas for you; alas for you, that you should still be dead! Oh! it grieves me to the heart, to think that some of you are all that heart could wish, except that one thing; yet lacking that which is the only thing that can deliver you. You are caressed by us, received by the living in Sion into their company and acquaintance, approved of and accepted; alas that you should yet be without life! Oh! in your case, if you are saved, you will have to join with even the worst in saying, "I have been quickened by divine grace, or else I had never lived."

And now will you look at this maiden again? Note, *she has no grave-clothes on her yet*; she is dressed in her own raiment; just as she retired to her bed a little sick, so lieth she there; not yet have the napkin and the shroud been wrapped about her; she still weareth the habiliments of sleep; she is not yet given up to death. Not so the young man yonder—he is in his grave-clothes; not so Lazarus—he is bound hand and foot. But this young maiden hath no grave-clothes upon her. So with the young person we wish to speak to-day, she has as yet no evil habits, she hath not yet reached that point; the young man yonder has begun to have evil habits; and yon grey-headed sinner is bound hand and foot by them; but as yet she appeareth just like the living, she acteth just like the Christian; her habits are fair, goodly, and comely; there seemeth to be little ill about her. Alas! alas! that thou shouldst be dead, even in thy fairest raiment. Alas! thou who hast set the chaplet of benevolence on thy brow, thou who dost gird thyself with the white robes of outward purity, if thou art not born again, thou art dead still. Thy beauty shall fade away like a moth; and in the day of judgment thou wilt be severed from the righteous, unless God shall make thee live. Oh! I could weep over those young ones who seem at present to have been delivered from forming any habits which could lead them astray, but who are yet un-quickened and unsaved. Oh! would to God, young man and young woman, you might in early years be quickened by the Spirit.

And will you notice, yet once more, that this young maiden's death was *a death confined to her chamber*. Not so with the young man; he was carried to the gate of the city, and much people saw him. Not so Lazarus; the Jews came to weep at his tomb. But this young woman's death is in her chamber. Ay, so it is with the young woman or the young man I mean to describe now. His sin is as yet a secret thing, kept to himself: as yet there has been no breaking forth of iniquity, but only the conception of it in the heart; just the embryo of lust, not as yet broken out into act. The young man has not yet drained the intoxicating cup, although he has had some whisperings of the sweetness of it; he has not yet run into the ways of wickedness, though he has had temptations thrust upon him; as yet he has kept his sin in his chamber, and most of it has been unseen. Alas! my brother, alas! my sister, that thou who in thine outward carriage art so good, should yet have sins in the chamber of thine heart, and death in the secrecy of thy being, which is as true a death as that of the grossest sinner, though not so thoroughly manifested. Would to God that thou couldst say, "And he hath quickened me, for with all my loveliness, and all my excellence, I was by nature dead in trespasses and sins." Come, let me just press this matter home. I have some in my congregation that I look upon with fear. Oh! how many there are among you, I repeat, that are all that the heart could wish, except that one thing—that you love not my Master. Oh! ye young men who come up to the house of God, and who are outwardly so good; alas for you, that you should lack the root of the matter. Oh! ye daughters of Sion, who are ever at the house of prayer, oh! that you should yet be without grace in your heart! Take heed, I beseech you, ye fairest, youngest, most upright, and most honest; when the dead are separated from the living, unless ye be regenerated, ye must go with the dead; though ye be never so fair and goodly, ye must be cast away, unless you live.

Thus, I have done with the first case; now we will go to the young man, who stands second. He is not more dead than the other, but *he is further gone.* Come, now, and stop the bier; you cannot look upon him! Why, the cheek is sunken—there is a hollowness there; not as in the case of the maiden's, whose cheek was still round and ruddy. And the eye—oh! what a blackness is there! Look on him; you can see that the gnawings of the worm will soon burst forth; corruption hath begun its work. So it is with some young men I have here. They are not what they were in their childhood, when their habits were proper and correct; but, mayhap, they have just been enticed into the house of the strange woman; they have just been tempted to go astray from the path of rectitude; their corruption is just breaking forth; they disdain now to sit at their mother's apron-strings; they think it foul scorn to keep to the rules that bind the moral! They! they are free, they say, and they will be free; they will live a jolly and a happy life; and so they run on in boisterous yet wicked merriment, and betray the marks of death about them. They have gone further than the maiden; she was still fair and comely; but here there is something that is the afterwork of death. The maiden was caressed, but the young man is untouched; he lieth on the bier, and, though men bear him on their shoulders, yet there is a shrinking from him; he is dead, and it is known that he is dead. Young man, you have got as far as that; you know that good men shrink from you. It was but yesterday that your mother's tears fell fast and thick as she warned your younger brother to avoid your sin; your very sister, when she kissed you but this morning, prayed to God that you might get good in this house of prayer; but you know that of late she has been ashamed of you; your conversation has become so profane and wicked, that even she could scarce endure it. There are houses in which you were once welcome; where you once bowed your knee with them at the family prayer, and your name was mentioned too; but now you do not choose to go there, for, when you go, you are treated with reserve. The good man of the house feels that he could not let his son go with you, for you would contaminate him; he does not sit down now side by side with you, as he used to do, and talk about the best things; he lets you sit in the room as a matter of mere courtesy; he stands far away from you, as it were; he feels that you have not a spirit congenial with his own. You are a little shunned; you are not quite avoided; you are still received amongst the people of God, yet there is a coldness that manifests that they understand that you are not a living one.

And note, too, that this young man, though carried out to his grave, was not like the maiden; she was in the garments of life, but *he was wrapped in the cerements of death*. So many of you have begun to form habits that are evil; you know that already the screw of the devil is tightening on your finger. Once it was a screw you could slip off or on; you said you were master of your pleasures—now your pleasures are master of you. Your habits are not now commendable, you know they are not; you stand convicted while I speak to you, you know your ways are evil. Ah! young man, though thou hast not yet gone so far as the open profligate and desperately profane, take heed, thou art dead! thou art dead! and unless the Spirit quicken thee, thou shalt be cast into the valley of Gehenna, to be the food of that worm which never dieth, but eateth souls throughout eternity. Ah! young man, I weep, I weep over thee; thou art not yet so far gone, that they have rolled the stone against thee; thou art not yet become obnoxious; thou art not yet the staggering drunkard, nor yet the blasphemous infidel; thou hast much that is ill about thee, but thou hast not gone all the lengths yet. Take heed; thou wilt go further still; there is no stopping in sin.

One more remark concerning this young man. The maiden's death was in her chamber; *the young man's death was in the city gates*. In the first case I described, the sin was secret. But, young man, your sin is not. You have gone so far that your habits are openly wicked; you have dared to sin in the face of God's sun. You are not as some others—seemingly good; but you go out and openly say, "I am no hypocrite; I dare to do wrong. I do not profess to be righteous; I know I am a scapegrace rascal. I have gone astray, and I am not ashamed to sin in the street." Ah! young man, young man! Thy father, perhaps, is saying now, "Would God that I had died for him—would God that I had seen him buried in his grave, ere he should have gone to such a length in wickedness! Would God that, when I first saw him, and mine eye was gladdened with my son, I had seen him the next minute smitten with disease and death! Oh, would to God that his infant spirit had been called to heaven, that he might not have lived to bring in this way my grey hairs in sorrow to the grave!" Your sport in the city gates is misery in your father's house; your open merriment before the world brings agony into a mother's heart. Oh, I beseech you, stay. Oh, Lord Jesus! touch the bier to-day! Stop some young man in his evil habits, and say unto him, "Arise!"

Now we come to the third and last case—LAZARUS DEAD AND BURIED. Ah! I cannot take you to see Lazarus in his grave. Stand, oh stand away from him. Whither shall we flee to avoid the noxious odour of that reeking corpse? Ah, whither shall we flee? There is no beauty there; we dare not look upon it. There is not even the gloss of life left. Oh, hideous spectacle! I must not attempt to describe it; words would fail me, and you would be too much shocked. Nor dare I tell the character of some men present here. I should be ashamed to tell the things which some of you have done. This cheek might mantle with a blush to tell the deeds of darkness which some of the ungodly of this world habitually practise. Ah, the last stage of death, the last stage of corruption, oh, how hideous; but the last stage of sin, hideous far more! Some writers seem to have an aptitude for puddling in this mud, and digging up this miry clay; I confess that I have none. I cannot describe to you the lusts and vices of a fullgrown sinner. I cannot tell you what are the debaucheries, the degrading lusts, the devilish, the bestial

c

sins into which wicked men will run, when spiritual death has had its perfect work in them, and sin has manifested itself in all its fearful wickedness. I may have some here. They are not Christians. They are not, like the young maiden, still fondled, not even, like the young man, still kept in the funeral procession; no, they have gone so far that decent people avoid them. Their very wife, when they go into the house, rushes upstairs to be out of the way. They are scorned. Such an one is the harlot, from whom one's head is turned in the very street. Such an one is the openly profligate, to whom we give wide quarters, lest we touch him. He is a man that is far gone. The stone is rolled before him. No one calls him respectable. He dwelleth, perhaps, in some back slum of a dirty lane; he knoweth not where to go. Even as he stands in this place, he feels that, if his next-door neighbour knew his guilt, he would give him a wide berth, and stand far away from him; for he has come to the last stage; he has no marks of life; he is utterly rotten.

And mark; as in the case of the maiden the sin was in the chamber, secret; in the next case it was in the open streets, public; but in this case it is secret again. It is in the tomb. For you will mark that men, when they are only half gone in wickedness, do it openly; but, when they are fully gone, their lust becomes so degrading that they are obliged to do it in secret. They are put into the grave, in order that all may be hidden. Their lust is one which can only be perpetrated at midnight; a deed which can only be done when shrouded by the astonished curtains of darkness. Have I any such here? I cannot tell that I have many; but still I have some. Ah! in being constantly visited by penitents I have sometimes blushed for this city of London. There are merchants whose names stand high and fair. Shall I tell it here? I know it on the best authority, and the truest, too. There are some who have houses large and tall, who on the exchange are reputable and honourable, and everyone admits them and receives them into their society; but ah! there are some of the merchants of London who practise lusts that are abominable. I have in my church and congregation—and I dare to say what men dare to do—I have in my congregation women whose ruin and destruction have been wrought by some of the most respected men in respectable society. Few would venture on so bold a statement as that; but, if you boldly do the thing, I must speak of it.

Ah! there are some that are a stench in the nostrils of the Almighty; some whose character is hideous beyond all hideousness. They have to be covered up in the tomb of secrecy; for men would scout them from society, and hiss them from existence, if they knew all. And yet—and now comes a blessed interposition—yet this last case may be saved as well as the first, and as easily too. The rotten Lazarus may come out of his tomb, as well as the slumbering maiden from her bed. The last, the most corrupt, the most desperately abominable, may yet be quickened; and he may join in exclaiming, "And I have been quickened, though I was dead in trespasses and sins."

And now I will go on to another point—THE QUICKENING. These three persons were all quickened, and they were all quickened by the same being, that is, by Jesus. But they were all quickened in a different manner. Note, first, the young maiden on her bed. When she was brought to life, it is said, "Jesus took her by the hand and said, Maiden, arise." It was a still small voice. Her heart received its pulse again, and she lived. It was the gentle touching of the hand—no open demonstration,—and the soft voice was heard: "Arise." Now, usually, when God converts young people in the first stage of sin, before they have formed evil habits, he does it in a gentle manner; not by the terrors of the law, the tempest, fire and smoke, but he makes them like Lydia, "whose heart the Lord opened" that she received the word. On such, "it droppeth like the gentle dew from heaven upon the place beneath." With hardened sinners grace cometh down in showers that rattle on them; but in young converts it often cometh gently. There is just the sweet breathing of the Spirit. They perhaps scarcely think it is a true conversion; but true it is, if they are brought to life.

Now note the next case. Christ did not do the same thing with the young man that he did with the daughter of Jairus. No; the first thing he did was, he put his hand, not on him, mark you, but *on the bier*; "and they that bare it stood still," and, after that, without touching the young man, he said in a louder voice, "Young man, I say unto thee, arise!" Note the difference: the young maiden's new life was given to her secretly.

The young man's was given more publicly. It was done in the very street of the city. The maiden's life was given gently by a touch; but in the young man's case it must be done, not by the touching of him, but by the touching of the bier. Christ takes away from the young man his means of pleasure. He commands his companions, who by bad example are bearing him on his bier to his grave, to stop, and then there is a partial reformation for awhile, and, after that, there comes the strong out-spoken voice—"Young man, I say unto thee, arise!"

But now comes the worst case; and will you please, at your leisure at home, to notice what preparations Christ made for the last case of Lazarus? When he raised the maiden, he walked up into the chamber, smiling, and said, "She is not dead, but sleepeth." When he raised the young man, he said to the mother, "Weep not." Not so when he came to the last case; there was something more terrible about that: it was, *a man in his grave corrupting*. It was on that occasion you read, "Jesus wept"; and after he had wept it is said that "he groaned in his spirit"; and then he said, "Take away the stone"; and then there came the prayer, "I know that thou hearest me always." And then, will you notice, there came, what is not expressed so fully in either of the other cases. It is written, "Jesus cried with a loud voice, Lazarus, come forth!" It is not written that he cried with the loud voice to either of the others. He spake to them; it was his word that saved all of them; but in the case of Lazarus, he cried to him in a loud voice. Now, I have, perhaps, some of the last characters here—the worst of the worst. Ah! sinner; may the Lord quicken thee! But it is a work that makes the Saviour weep. I think when he comes to call some of you from your death in sin who have gone to the utmost extremity of guilt, he comes weeping and sighing for you. There is a stone there to be rolled away—your bad and evil habits; and, when that stone is taken away, a still small voice will not do for you; it must be the loud crashing voice, like the voice of the Lord, which breaketh the cedars of Lebanon —"Lazarus, come forth!" John Bunyan was one of those rotten ones. What strong means were used in his case! Terrible dreams, fearful convulsions, awful shakings to and fro—all had to be employed to make him live. And yet some of you think, when God is terrifying you by the thunders of Sinai, that really he does not love you. It is not so: you were so dead that it needed a loud voice to arrest your ears.

This is an interesting subject; permit me to go to the third point very briefly. THE AFTER-EXPERIENCE OF THESE THREE PEOPLE WAS DIFFERENT—at least, you gather it from the commands of Christ. As soon as the maiden was alive, Christ said, "Give her meat"; as soon as the young man was alive "he delivered him to his mother"; as soon as Lazarus was alive, he said, "Loose him, and let him go." I think there is something in this. When young people are converted who have not yet acquired evil habits; when they are saved before they become obnoxious in the eyes of the world, the command is, "*Give them meat.*" Young people want instruction; they want building up in the faith; they generally lack knowledge; they have not the deep experience of the older man; they do not know so much about sin, nor even so much about salvation as the older man that has been a guilty sinner; they need to be fed. So that our business as ministers when the young lambs are brought in, is to remember the injunction, "Feed my lambs"; take care of them; give them plenty of meat. Young people, search after an instructive minister; seek after instructive books; search the Scriptures, and seek to be instructed: that is your principal business. "Give her meat."

The next case was a different one. He gave the young man up to his mother. Ah! that is just what he will do with you, young man, if he makes you live. As sure as ever you are converted, he will give you up to your mother again. You were with her when you first as a babe sat on her knee; and that is where you will have to go again. Oh, yes; grace knits together again the ties which sin has loosed. Let a young man become abandoned; he casts off the tender influence of a sister and the kind associations of a mother: but, if he is converted, one of the first things he will do will be to find the mother out, and the sister out, and he will find a charm in their society that he never knew before. Endeavour as much as possible, to be found in the company of the righteous; for, as you were carried before to your grave by bad companions, you need to be led to heaven by good ones.

And then comes the case of Lazarus. "*Loose him, and let him go.*" I do not know how it is that the young man never was loosed. I have been looking through every book I have about the manners and customs of the East, and have not been able to get a clue to the difference between the young man and Lazarus. The young man, as soon as Christ spoke to him, "sat up and began to speak"; but Lazarus, in his grave-clothes, lying in the niche of the tomb, could do no more than just shuffle himself out from the hole that was cut in the wall, and then stand leaning against it. He could not speak; he was bound about in a napkin. Why was it not so with the young man? I am inclined to think that the difference lay in the difference of their wealth. The young man was the son of a widow. Very likely he was only wrapped up in a few common things, and not so tightly bound about as Lazarus. Lazarus was of a rich family; very likely they wrapped him up with more care. Whether it was so or not, I do not know. What I want to hint at is this: when a man is far gone into sin, Christ does this for him—he breaks off his evil habits. Very likely the old sinner's experience will not be a feeding experience. It will not be the experience of walking with the saints. It will be as much as he can do to pull off his grave-clothes, to get rid of his old habits; perhaps to his death he will have to be rending off bit after bit of the cerements in which he has been wrapped. There is his drunkenness; oh, what a fight will he have with that! There is his lust; what a combat he will have with that, for many a month! There is his habit of swearing; how often will an oath come into his mouth, and he will have as hard work as he can to thrust it down again! There is his pleasure-seeking: he has given it up; but how often will his companions be after him, to get him to go with them. His life will be ever afterwards a loosing and letting go; for he will need it till he cometh up to be with God for ever and ever.

And now, I must close by asking you this question—*have you been quickened?* Oh, that he now would cry to some, "Lazarus, come forth!" and make some harlot virtuous, some drunkard sober.

VI

THE ASCENSION PRACTICALLY CONSIDERED

"And while they looked steadfastly toward heaven as he went up, behold, two men stood by them in white apparel; which also said, Ye men of Galilee, why stand ye gazing up into heaven? this same Jesus, which is taken up from you into heaven, shall so come in like manner as ye have seen him go into heaven."—Acts 1: 10, 11.

FOUR great events shine out brightly in our Saviour's story. All Christian minds delight to dwell upon his birth, his death, his resurrection, and his ascension. These make four rounds in that ladder of light, the foot of which is upon the earth, but the top whereof reacheth to heaven. We could not afford to dispense with any one of those four events, nor would it be profitable for us to forget, or to under-estimate, the value of any one of them. That the Son of God was born of a woman creates in us the intense delight of a brotherhood springing out of a common humanity. That Jesus once suffered unto the death for our sins, and thereby made a full atonement for us, is the rest and life of our spirits. The manger and the cross together are divine seals of love. That the Lord Jesus rose again from the dead is the warrant of our justification, and also a transcendently delightful assurance of the resurrection of all his people, and of their eternal life in him. Hath he not said, "Because I live, ye shall live also"? The resurrection of Christ is the morning star of our future glory. Equally delightful is the remembrance of his ascension. No song is sweeter than this— "Thou hast ascended on high; thou hast led captivity captive, thou hast received gifts for men, yea, for the rebellious also, that the Lord God might dwell among them" (Ps. 68: 18).

Each one of those four events points to another, and they all lead up to it: the fifth link in the golden chain is our Lord's second and most glorious advent. Nothing is mentioned between his ascent and his descent. True, a rich history comes between; but it lies in a valley between two stupendous mountains: we step from alp to alp as we journey in meditation from the ascension to the second advent. I say that each of the previous four events points to it. Had he not come a first time in humiliation, born under the law, he could not have come a second time in amazing glory "without a sin-offering unto salvation." Because he died once, we rejoice that he dieth no more, death hath no more dominion over him, and therefore he cometh to destroy that last enemy whom he hath already conquered. It is our joy, as we think of our Redeemer as risen, to feel that, in consequence of his rising, the trump of the archangel shall assuredly sound for the awaking of all his slumbering people, when the Lord himself shall descend from heaven with a shout. As for his ascension, he could not a second time descend if he had not first ascended; but having perfumed heaven with his presence, and prepared a place for his people, we may fitly expect that he will come again and receive us unto himself, that where he is there we may be also. I want you, therefore, as in contemplation you pass with joyful footsteps over these four grand events, as your faith leaps from his birth to his death, and from his resurrection to his ascension, to be looking forward, and even hastening, unto this crowning fact of our Lord's history; for ere long he shall so come in like manner as he was seen go up into heaven.

To-day, in our meditation, we will start from the ascension; and if I had sufficient imagination I should like to picture our Lord and the eleven walking up the side of Olivet, communing as they went, a happy company, with a solemn awe upon them, but with an intense joy in having fellowship with each other. Each disciple was glad to think that his dear Lord and Master who had been crucified was now among them, not only alive but surrounded with a mysterious safety and glory which none could disturb. The enemy was as still as a stone: not a dog moved his tongue: his bitterest foes made no sign during the days of our Lord's after-life below. The company moved onward peacefully towards Bethany—Bethany which they all knew and loved. The Saviour seemed drawn there at the time of his ascension, even as men's minds return to old and well-loved scenes when they are about to depart out of this world. His happiest moments on earth had been spent beneath the roof where lived Mary and Martha and their brother Lazarus. Perhaps it was best for the disciples that he should leave them at that place where he had been most hospitably entertained, to show that he departed in peace and not in anger. There they had seen Lazarus raised from the dead by him who was now to be taken up from them: the memory of the triumphant past would help the tried faith of the present. There they had heard the voice saying, "Loose him, and let him go," and there they might fitly see their Lord loosed from all bonds of earthly gravitation that he might go to his Father and their Father. The memories of the place might help to calm their minds and arouse their spirits to that fulness of joy which ought to attend the glorifying of their Lord.

But they have come to a standstill, having reached the brow of the hill. The Saviour stands conspicuously in the centre of the group, and, following upon most instructive discourse, he pronounces a blessing upon them. He lifts his pierced hands, and, while he is lifting them and is pronouncing words of love, he begins to rise from the earth. He has risen above them all to their astonishment! In a moment he has passed beyond the olives, which seem with their silvery sheen to be lit up by his milder radiance. While the disciples are looking, the Lord has ascended into mid-air, and speedily he has risen to the regions of the clouds. They stand spell-bound with astonishment, and suddenly a bright cloud, like a chariot of God, bears him away. That cloud conceals him from mortal gaze. Though we have known Christ after the flesh, now after the flesh know we him no more. They are riveted to the spot, very naturally so: they linger long in the place; they stand with streaming eyes, wonder-struck, still looking upward.

It is not the Lord's will that they should long remain inactive; their reverie is interrupted. They might have stood there till wonder saddened into fear. As it was, they remained long enough; for the angel's words may be accurately rendered, "Why have ye stood, gazing up into heaven?"

Their lengthened gaze needed to be interrupted, and, therefore, two shining ones, such as aforetime met the women at the sepulchre, are sent to them. These messengers of God appear in human form that they may not alarm them, and in white raiment as if to remind them that all was bright and joyous; and these white-robed ministers stood with them as if they would willingly join their company. As no one of the eleven would break silence, the men in white raiment commenced the discourse. Addressing them in the usual celestial style, they asked a question which contained its own answer, and then went on to tell their message. As they had once said to the women, "Why seek ye the living among the dead? He is not here, but is risen;" so did they now say, "Ye men of Galilee, why stand ye gazing up into heaven? this same Jesus, which is taken up from you into heaven, shall so come in like manner as ye have seen him go into heaven." The angels showed their knowledge of them by calling them "men of Galilee," and reminded them that they were yet upon earth by recalling their place of birth.

Brought back to their senses, their reverie over, the apostles at once gird up their loins for active service; they do not need twice telling, but hasten to Jerusalem. The vision of angels has singularly enough brought them back into the world of actual life again, and they obey the command, "Tarry ye at Jerusalem." They seem to say, The taking up of our Master is not a thing to weep about: he has gone to his throne and to his glory, and he said it was expedient for us that he should go away. He will now send us the promise of the Father; we scarcely know what it will be like, but let us, in obedience to his will, make the best of our way to the place where he bade us await the gift of power. Do you not see them going down the side of Olivet, taking that Sabbath-day's journey into the cruel and wicked city without a thought of fear: having no dread of the bloodthirsty crew who slew their Lord, but happy in the memory of their Lord's exaltation and in the expectation of a wonderful display of his power. They held fellowship of the most delightful kind with one another, and anon entered into the upper room, where, in protracted prayer and communion, they waited for the promise of the Father. You see I have no imagination: I have barely mentioned the incidents in the simplest language. Yet try and realise the scene, for it will be helpful so to do, since our Lord Jesus is to come in like manner as the disciples saw him go up into heaven.

My first business will be to consider *the gentle chiding* administered by the shining ones:—"Ye men of Galilee, why stand ye gazing up into heaven?" Secondly, *the cheering description* of our Lord which the white-robed messengers used,—"This same Jesus"; and then, thirdly, *the practical truth* which they taught —"This same Jesus, which is taken up from you into heaven, shall so come in like manner as ye have seen him go into heaven."

First, then, here is A GENTLE CHIDING. It is not sharply uttered by men dressed in black who use harsh speech, and upbraid the servants of God severely for what was rather a mistake than a fault. No; the language is strengthening, yet tender: the fashion of a question allows them rather to reprove themselves than to be reproved; and the tone is that of brotherly love, and affectionate concern.

Notice, that *what these saintly men were doing seems at first sight to be very right.* Methinks, if Jesus were among us now we would fix our eyes upon him, and never withdraw them. He is altogether lovely, and it would seem wicked to yield our eyesight to any inferior object so long as he was to be seen. When he ascended up into heaven it was the duty of his friends to look upon him. It can never be wrong to look up; we are often bidden to do so, and it is even a holy saying of the Psalmist, "I will direct my prayer unto thee, and will look up"; and, again, "I will lift up mine eyes unto the hills, from whence cometh my help." If it be right to look up into heaven, it must be still more right to look up while Jesus rises to the place of his glory. Surely it had been wrong if they had looked anywhere else,—it was due to the Lamb of God that they should behold him as long as eyes could follow him. He is the Sun: where should eyes be turned but to his light? He is the King; and where should courtiers within the palace gate turn their eyes but to their King as he ascends to his throne?

The truth is, there was nothing wrong in their looking up into heaven; but they went a little further than looking; they stood "gazing." A little excess in right may be faulty. It may be wise to look, but foolish to gaze. There is a very thin partition sometimes between that which is commendable and that which is censurable. There is a golden mean which it is not easy to keep. The exact path of right is often as narrow as a razor's edge, and he must be wise that doth not err either on the right hand or on the left. "Look" is ever the right word. Why, it is "Look unto me, and be saved." Look, aye, look steadfastly and intently: be your posture that of one "looking unto Jesus," always throughout life. But there is a gazing which is not commendable, when the look becomes not that of reverent worship, but of an overweening curiosity; when there mingles with the desire to know what should be known, a prying into that which it is for God's glory to conceal. It is of little use to look up into an empty heaven.

If Christ himself·be not visible in heaven, then in vain do we gaze, since there is nothing for a saintly eye to see. When the Person of Jesus was gone out of the azure vault above them and the cloud had effectually concealed him, why should they continue to gaze when God himself had drawn the curtain? If infinite wisdom had withdrawn the object upon which they desired to gaze, what would their gazing be but a sort of reflection upon the wisdom which had removed their Lord? Yet it did seem very right. Thus certain things that you and I may do may appear right, and yet we may need to be chidden out of them into something better: they may be right in themselves but not appropriate for the occasion, not seasonable, nor expedient. They may be right up to a point, and then may touch the boundary of excess. A steadfast gaze into heaven may be to a devout soul a high order of worship, but if this filled up much of our working time it might become the idlest form of folly.

Yet I cannot help adding that *it was very natural*. I do not wonder that the whole eleven stood gazing up, for if I had been there I am sure I should have done the same. How struck they must have been with the ascent of the Master out of their midst! You would be amazed if some one from among our own number now began to ascend into heaven, would you not? Our Lord did not gradually melt away from sight as a phantom, or dissolve into thin air as a mere apparition: the Saviour did not disappear in that way at all, but he rose, and they saw that it was his very self that was so rising. His own body, the materialism in which he had veiled himself, actually, distinctly and literally, rose to heaven before their eyes. I repeat, the Lord did not dissolve, and disappear like a vision of the night, but he evidently rose till the cloud intervened so that they could see him no more. I think I should have stood looking to the very place where his cloudy chariot had been. I know it would be idle to continue so to do, but our hearts often urge us on to acts which we could not justify logically. Hearts are not to be argued with.

Sometimes you stand by a grave where one is buried whom you dearly loved: you go there often to weep. You cannot help it, the place is precious to you; yet you could not prove that you do any good by your visits, perhaps you even injure yourself thereby, and deserve to be gently chidden with the question, "Why?" It may be the most natural thing in the world, and yet it may not be a wise thing. The Lord allows us to do that which is innocently natural, but he will not have us carry it too far; for then it might foster an evil nature. Hence he sends an interrupting messenger: not an angel with a sword, or even a rod; but he sends some man in white raiment,—I mean one who is both cheerful and holy, and he, by his conduct or his words, suggests to us the question, "Why stand ye here gazing?" *Cui bono?* What will be the benefit? What will it avail? Thus our understanding being called into action, and we being men of thought, we answer to ourselves, "This will not do. We must not stand gazing here for ever," and therefore we arouse ourselves to get back to the Jerusalem of practical life, where in the power of God we hope to do service for our Master.

Notice, then, that the disciples were doing that which seemed to be right, and what was evidently very natural, but that it is very easy to carry the apparently right and the absolutely natural too far. Let us take heed to ourselves, and often ask our hearts, "Why?"

For, thirdly, notice that what they *did was not after all justifiable upon strict reason.* While Christ was going up it was proper that they should adoringly look at him. He might almost have said, "If ye see me when I am taken up a double portion of my spirit shall rest upon you." They did well to look where he led the way. But, when he was gone, still to remain gazing was an act which they could not exactly explain to themselves, and could not justify to others. Put the question thus: "What purpose will be fulfilled by your continuing to gaze into the sky? He is gone; it is absolutely certain that he is gone. He is taken up, and God himself has manifestly concealed all trace of him by bidding yonder cloud sail in between him and you. Why gaze ye still? He told you 'I go unto my Father.' Why stand and gaze?" We may, under the influence of great love, act unwisely. I remember well seeing the action of a woman whose only son was emigrating to a distant colony. I stood in the station, and I noticed her many tears and her frequent embraces of her boy; but the train came up, and he entered the carriage. After the train had passed beyond the station, she was foolish enough to break away from friends who sought to detain her; she ran along the platform, leaped down upon the railroad and pursued the flying train. It was natural, but it had been better left undone. What was the use of it? We had better abstain from acts which serve no practical purpose; for in this life we have neither time nor strength to waste in fruitless action. The disciples would be wise to cease gazing, for nobody would be benefited by it, and they would not themselves be blessed. What is the use of gazing when there is nothing to see? Well, then, did the angels ask, "Why stand ye gazing up into heaven?"

Again, put another question: What precept were they obeying when they stood gazing up into heaven? If you have a command from God to do a certain thing, you need not inquire into the reason of the command, it is disobedient to begin to canvas God's will; but when there is no precept whatever, why persevere in an act which evidently does not promise to bring any blessing? Who bade them stand gazing up into heaven? If Christ had done so, then in Christ's name let them stand like statues and never turn their heads: but, as he had not bidden them, why did they do what he had not commanded, and leave undone what he had commanded? For he had strictly charged them that they should tarry at Jerusalem till they were "endued with power from on high." So what they did was not justifiable.

Here is the practical point for us: *What they did we are very apt to imitate.* "Oh," say you, "I shall never stand gazing up into heaven." I am not sure of that. Some Christians are very curious, but not obedient. Plain precepts are neglected, but difficult problems they seek to solve. I remember one who used always to be dwelling upon the vials and seals and trumpets. He was great at apocalyptic symbols; but he had seven children, and he had no family prayer. If he had left the vials and trumpets and minded his boys and girls, it would have been a deal better. I have known men marvellously great upon Daniel, and specially instructed in Ezekiel, but singularly forgetful of the twentieth of Exodus, and not very clear upon Romans the eighth. I do not speak with any blame of such folks for studying Daniel and Ezekiel, but quite the reverse; yet I wish they had been more zealous for the conversion of the sinners in their neighbourhoods, and more careful to assist the poor saints. I admit the value of the study of the feet of the image in Nebuchadnezzar's vision, and the importance of knowing the kingdoms which make up the ten toes, but I do not see the propriety of allowing such studies to overlay the common-places of practical godliness. If the time spent over obscure theological propositions were given to a mission in the dim alley near the good man's house, more benefit would come to men and more glory to God. I would have you understand all mysteries, if you could; but do not forget that our chief business here below is to cry, "Behold the Lamb!" By all manner of means read and search till you know all that the Lord has revealed concerning things to come; but, first of all, see to it that your children are brought to the Saviour's feet, and that you are workers together with God in the upbuilding of his church. The dense mass of misery and ignorance and sin which is round about us on every side demands all our powers; and, if you do not respond to the call, though I am not a man in white apparel, I shall venture to say to you, "Ye men of Christendom, why stand ye gazing up into the mysteries when so much is to be done for Jesus, and you are leaving it undone?" O ye who are curious but not obedient, I fear I speak to you in vain, but I have spoken. May the Holy Spirit also speak.

Others are contemplative but not active,—much given to the study of Scripture and to meditation thereon, but not zealous for good works. Contemplation is so scarce in these days that I could wish there were a thousand times as much of it; but, in the case to which I refer, everything runs in the one channel of thought, all time is spent in reading, in enjoyment, in rapture, in pious leisure. Religion never ought to become the subject of selfishness, and yet I fear some treat it as if its chief end was spiritual gratification. When a man's religion all lies in his saving his own self, and in enjoying holy things for his own self, there is a disease upon him. When his judgment of a sermon is based upon the one question, "Did it feed *me*?" it is a swinish judgment. There is such a thing as getting a swinish religion in which you are yourself first, yourself second, yourself third, yourself to the utmost end. Did Jesus ever think or speak in that fashion? Contemplation of Christ himself may be so carried out as to lead you away from Christ: the recluse meditates on Jesus, but he is as unlike the busy self-denying Jesus as well can be. Meditation unattended with active service in the spreading of the gospel among men, well deserves the rebuke of the angel, "Ye men of Galilee, why stand ye gazing up into heaven?"

Moreover, some are careful and anxious and deliriously impatient for some marvellous interposition. We get at times into a sad state of mind, because we do not see the kingdom of Christ advancing as we desire. I suppose it is with you as it is with me. I begin to fret, and I am deeply troubled, and I feel that there is good reason that I should be, for truth is fallen in the streets, and the days of blasphemy and rebuke are upon us. Then we pine; for the Master is away, and we cry, "When will he be back again? Oh, why are his chariots so long in coming? Why tarries he through the ages?" Our desires sour into impatience, and we commence gazing up into heaven, looking for his coming with a restlessness which does not allow us to discharge our duty as we should. Whenever anybody gets into that state, this is the word, "Ye men of Galilee, why stand ye gazing up into heaven?"

In certain cases this uneasiness has drawn to itself a wrong expectation of immediate wonders, and an intense desire for sign-seeing. Ah me, what fanaticisms come of this! In America years ago, one came forward who declared that on such a day the Lord would come, and he led a great company to believe his crazy predictions. Many took their horses and fodder for two or three days, and went out into the woods, expecting to be all the more likely to see all that was to be seen when once away from the crowded city. All over the States there were people who had made ascension-dresses in which to soar into the air in proper costume. They waited, and they waited, and

I am sure that no text could have been more appropriate for them than this, "Ye men of America, why stand ye here gazing up into heaven?" Nothing came of it; and yet there are thousands in England and America who only need a fanatical leader, and they would run into the like folly. The desire to know the times and seasons is a craze with many poor bodies whose insanity runs in that particular groove. Every occurrence is a "sign of the times": a sign, I may add, which they do not understand. An earthquake is a special favourite with them. "Now," they cry, "the Lord is coming"; as if there had not been earthquakes of the sort we have heard of lately hundreds of times since our Lord went up into heaven. When the prophetic earthquakes occur in divers places, we shall know of it without the warnings of these brethren. What a number of persons have been infatuated by the number of the beast, and have been ready to leap for joy because they have found the number 666 in some great one's name. Why, everybody's name will yield that number if you treat it judiciously, and use the numerals of Greece, Rome, Egypt, China, or Timbuctoo. I feel weary with the silly way in which some people make toys out of Scripture, and play with texts as with a pack of cards. Whenever you meet with a man who sets up to be a prophet, keep out of his way in the future; and when you hear of signs and wonders, turn you to your Lord, and in patience possess your souls. "The just shall live by his faith." There is no other way of living among wild enthusiasts. Believe in God, and ask not for miracles and marvels, or the knowledge of times and seasons. To know when the Lord will restore the kingdom is not in your power. Remember that verse: "It is not for you to know the times or the seasons." If I were introduced into a room where a large number of parcels were stored up, and I were told that there was something good for me, I should begin to look for that which had my name upon it, and when I came upon a parcel, and I saw, in pretty big letters, "*It is not for you*," I should leave it alone. Here, then, is a casket of knowledge marked, "*It is not for you* to know the times or the seasons, which the Father hath put in his own power." Cease to meddle with matters which are concealed, and be satisfied to know the things which are clearly revealed.

Secondly, I want you to notice THE CHEERING DESCRIPTION

which these bright spirits give concerning our Lord. They describe him thus,—"This same Jesus."

I appreciate the description the more because *it came from those who knew him.* "He was seen of angels"; they had watched him all his life long, and they knew him, and, when they, having just seen him rise to his Father and his God, said of him, "This same Jesus," then I know by an infallible testimony that he was the same, and that he is the same.

Jesus is gone, but he still exists. He has left us, but he is not dead; he has not dissolved into nothing like the mist of the morning. "This same Jesus" is gone up unto his Father's throne, and he is there to-day as certainly as he once stood at Pilate's bar. As surely as he did hang upon the cross, so surely does he, the self-made man, sit upon the throne of God and reign over creation. I like to think of the positive identity of the Christ in the seventh heaven with the Christ in the lowest deeps of agony. The Christ they spat upon is now the Christ whose name the cherubim and seraphim are hymning day without night. The Christ they scourged is he before whom principalities and powers delight to cast their crowns. Think of it and be glad; and do not stand gazing up into heaven after a myth or a dream. Jesus lives; mind that you live also. Do not loiter as if you had nothing at all to do, or as if the kingdom of God had come to an end because Jesus is gone from the earth, as to his bodily Presence. It is not all over; he still lives, and he has given you a work to do till he comes. Therefore, go and do it.

"This same Jesus"—I love that word, for "Jesus" means *a Saviour.* Oh, ye anxious sinners here present, the name of him who has gone up into his glory is full of invitation to you! Will you not come to "this same Jesus"? This is he who opened the eyes of the blind and brought forth the prisoners out of the prison-house. He is doing the same thing to-day. Oh that your eyes may see his light! He that touched the lepers, and that raised the dead, is the same Jesus still, able to save to the uttermost. Oh that you may look and live! You have only to come to him by faith, as she did who touched the hem of his garment; you have but to cry to him as the blind man did whose sight he restored; for he is the same Jesus, bearing about with him the same tender love for guilty men, and the same readiness to receive and cleanse all that come to him by faith.

"This same Jesus." Why, that must have meant that he who is in heaven is the same Christ who was on earth, but it must also mean that *he who is to come will be the same Jesus that went up into heaven.* There is no change in our blessed Master's nature, nor will there ever be. There is a great change in his condition:—

The Lord shall come, but not the same
As once in lowliness he came,
A humble man before his foes,
A weary man, and full of woes.

He will be "the same Jesus" in nature though not in condition: he will possess the same tenderness when he comes to judge, the same gentleness of heart when all the glories of heaven and earth shall gird his brow. Our eye shall see him in that day, and we shall recognize him not only by the nail-prints, but by the very look of his countenance, by the character that gleams from that marvellous face; and we shall say, "'Tis he! 'tis he! the self-same Christ that went up from the top of Olivet from the midst of his disciples." Go to him with your troubles, as you would have done when he was here. Look forward to his second coming without dread. Look for him with that joyous expectancy with which you would welcome Jesus of Bethany, who loved Mary, and Martha, and Lazarus.

On the back of that sweet title came this question, "Why stand ye here gazing into heaven?" They might have said, "We stay here because we do not know where to go. Our Master is gone." But it is the same Jesus, and he is coming again, so go down to Jerusalem and get to work directly. Do not worry yourselves; no grave accident has occurred; it is not a disaster that Christ has gone, but an advance in his work. Despisers tell us nowadays, "Your cause is done for! Christianity is spun out! Your divine Christ is gone; we have not seen a trace of his miracle-working hand, nor of that voice which no man could rival." Here is our answer: We are not standing gazing up into heaven, we are not paralysed because Jesus is away. He lives, the great Redeemer lives; and, though it is our delight to lift up our eyes because we expect his coming, it is equally our delight to turn our heavenly gazing into an earthward watching, and to go down into the city, and there to tell that Jesus is risen, that men are to be saved by faith in him, and that whoso-ever believeth in him shall have everlasting life. We are not defeated, far from it : his ascension is not a retreat, but an advance. His tarrying is not for want of power, but because of the abundance of his long-suffering. The victory is not questionable. All things work for it ; all the hosts of God are mustering for the final charge. "This same Jesus" is mounting his white horse to lead forth the armies of heaven, conquering and to conquer.

Our third point is this, THE GREAT PRACTICAL TRUTH. This truth is not one that is to keep us gazing into heaven, but one that is to make each of us go to his house to render earnest service. What is it?

Why, first, that *Jesus is gone into heaven*. Jesus is gone! Jesus is gone! It sounds like a knell. Jesus is taken up from you into heaven! That sounds like a marriage peal. He is gone, but he is gone up to the hills whence he can survey the battle ; up to the throne, from which he can send us succour. The reserve forces of the omnipotent stood waiting till their Captain came, and now that he is come into the centre of the universe, he can send legions of angels, or he can raise up hosts of men for the help of his cause. I see every reason for going down into the world and getting to work, for he is gone up into heaven and "all power is given unto him in heaven and in earth." Is not that a good argument, "Go ye *therefore* and teach all nations, baptising them in the name of the Father, and of the Son, and of the Holy Ghost"?

Jesus will come again. That is another reason for girding our loins, because it is clear that he has not quitted the fight, nor deserted the field of battle. Our great Captain is still heading the conflict ; he has ridden into another part of the field, but he will be back again, perhaps in the twinkling of an eye. You do not say that a commander has given up the campaign because it is expedient that he should withdraw from your part of the field. Our Lord is doing the best thing for his kingdom in going away. It was in the highest degree expedient that he should go, and that we should each one receive the Spirit. There is a blessed unity between Christ the King and the commonest soldier in the ranks. He has not taken his heart from us, nor his care from us, nor his interest from us: he is bound up heart and soul with his people and their holy warfare, and this is the evidence of it, "Behold, I come quickly; and my reward is with me, to give every man according as his work shall be" (Rev. 22: 12).

Then, moreover, we are told in the text—and this is a reason why we should get to our work—that *he is coming in like manner as he departed*. Certain of the commentators do not seem to understand English at all. "He which is taken up from you into heaven shall so come in like manner as you have seen him go into heaven"; this, they say, relates to his spiritual coming at Pentecost. Give anybody a grain of sense, and do they not see that a spiritual coming is not a coming in the same manner in which he went up into heaven? There is an analogy, but certainly not a likeness between the two things. Our Lord was taken up; they could see him rise: he will come again, and "every eye shall see him." He went up not in Spirit, but in Person: he will come down in person. "This same Jesus shall so come in like manner." He went up, not in poetic figure and spiritual symbol, but as a matter of fact. "This same Jesus" literally went up. "This same Jesus" will literally come again. He will descend in clouds even as he went up in clouds; and "he shall stand at the latter day upon the earth," even as he stood aforetime. He went up to heaven unopposed; no high priests, nor scribes, nor Pharisees, nor even one of the rabble opposed his ascension; it were ridiculous to suppose that they could; and when he comes a second time none will stand against him. His adversaries shall perish; as the fat of rams shall they melt away in his Presence. When he cometh he shall break rebellious nations with a rod of iron, for his force shall be irresistible in that day.

Do not let anybody spiritualize away all this from you. Jesus is coming as a matter of fact, therefore go down to your sphere of service as a matter of fact. Get to work and teach the ignorant, win the wayward, instruct the children, and everywhere tell out the sweet name of Jesus. As a matter of fact, give of your substance and don't talk about it. As a matter of fact, consecrate your daily life to the glory of God. As a matter of fact, live wholly for your Redeemer. Jesus is not coming in a sort of mythical, misty, hazy way, he is literally and actually coming, and he will literally and actually call upon you to give an account of your stewardship.

For this is what the men in white apparel meant, *be ready to meet your coming Lord*. What is the way to be ready to meet Jesus? If it is the same Jesus that went away from us who is coming, then let us be doing what he was doing before he went away. If it is the same Jesus that is coming we cannot possibly put ourselves into a posture of which he will better approve than by going about doing good. If you would meet him with joy, serve him with earnestness. If the Lord Jesus Christ were to come to-day I should like him to find me at my studying, praying, or preaching. Would you not like him to find you in your Sunday-school, in your class, or out there at the corner of the street preaching, or doing whatever you have the privilege of doing in his name? Would you meet your Lord in idleness? Do not think of it. I called one day on one of our members, and she was whitening the front steps. She got up all in confusion; she said, "Oh dear, sir, I did not know you were coming to-day, or I would have been ready." I replied, "Dear friend, you could not be in better trim than you are: you are doing your duty like a good housewife, and may God bless you." She had no money to spare for a servant, and she was doing her duty by keeping the home tidy: I thought she looked more beautiful with her pail beside her than if she had been dressed according to the latest fashion. I said to her, "When the Lord Jesus Christ comes suddenly, I hope he will find me doing as you were doing, namely, fulfilling the duty of the hour." I want you all to get to your pails without being ashamed of them. Serve the Lord in some way or other; serve him always; serve him intensely; serve him more and more. Go to-morrow and serve the Lord at the counter, or in the workshop, or in the field. Go and serve the Lord by helping the poor and the needy, the widow and the fatherless; serve him by teaching the children, especially by endeavouring to train your own children. Go and hold a temperance meeting, and show the drunkard that there is hope for him in Christ, or go to the midnight meeting and let the fallen woman know that Jesus can restore her. Do what Jesus has given you the power to do, and then, when he comes he will say to you, "Well done, good and faithful servant, enter thou into the joy of thy Lord." So may his grace enable us to do.

VII

GLADNESS FOR SADNESS

"Make us glad according to the days wherein thou hast afflicted us, and the years wherein we have seen evil. Let thy work appear unto thy servants, and thy glory unto their children. And let the beauty of the Lord our God be upon us: and establish thou the work of our hands upon us; yea, the work of our hands establish thou it."—Ps. 90: 15–17.

TO understand this psalm you must observe its black border. Remember the sorrows of Moses, the man of God, who saw a whole generation die in the wilderness, and was himself denied admission to the promised land. The man Moses was greatly afflicted; I might almost call him, as far as his life in the wilderness was concerned, "A man of sorrows, and acquainted with grief." He digged the desert till it became a cemetery, for he lived amid forty years of funerals. This Ninetieth Psalm is saturated with the griefs of a sentenced generation, by whom it could be truly said, "We are consumed by thine anger, and by thy wrath are we troubled" (v. 7).

How well did Moses pray, "Return, O Lord, how long? and let it repent thee concerning thy servants" (v. 13). Oh that our God would no more put his hand into the bitter box, as George Herbert calls it, but now change his dispensation and revive the spirit of his contrite ones. On our part, as we are made to sympathize with the man of God in this psalm, so let us imitate his example. Like him in multiplied bereavements, let us be like him in grace and faith.

Observe, that the first word of this painful psalm is, "Lord, thou hast been our dwelling place"; as if, touched by the rod, the sufferer remembered his Father. Will the hypocrite always call upon God? Nay, but when God dealeth roughly with him he will kick against the pricks. But the child of God when he is smitten turns to the hand that smote him and cries, "Show me wherefore thou contendest with me?" If foxes and wolves are prowling about, and the shepherd's dog appears, they fly hither and thither as far away as they can; but when the dog is sent after the sheep he fetches them back to the shepherd. Trouble drives away the carnal man from his pretended religion; but it gathers the true sheep together, and, being aroused and alarmed, they seek the Good Shepherd. The more of grief we feel the more of grace we need, and the nearer to our Comforter we come. Closer to God! is the cry of the troubled saint.

> *Nearer, my God to thee!*
> *Nearer to thee!*
> *E'en though it be a cross*
> *That raiseth me;*
> *Still all my cry shall be,*
> *Nearer, my God, to thee!*
> *Nearer to thee!*

Observe also that this psalm is "a prayer of Moses:" the comfort of a child of God in the darkness is prayer. Adversity, blessed of the Holy Spirit, calls our attention to the promise; the promise quickens our faith; faith betakes itself to prayer; God hears and answers our cry. This is the chain of a tried soul's experience. As we suffer the tribulation, as we know the promise, let us immediately exercise faith, and turn in prayer to God; for surely never did a man turn to God but the Lord also turned to him. If we are set a-praying we may depend upon it the Lord is set on blessing. Blessings are on the way from heaven; their shadow falls upon us even now. I desire at this time to stir you up to a joyful expectancy. These clouds mean rich, refreshing showers. These sharp frosts foretell heavy sheaves. The Lord by the divine Spirit make the words of our text to be our prayer this morning! May the Lord Jesus present our supplication to the Father.

The petition seems to me to be, first, for *proportionate gladness:* "Make us glad according to the days wherein thou hast afflicted us, and the years wherein we have seen evil." And, secondly, our prayer is for *peculiar gladness,* a gladness which is described in the sixteenth and seventeenth verses: "Let thy work appear unto thy servants, and thy glory unto their children. And let the beauty of the Lord our God be upon us: and establish thou the work of our hands upon us; yea, the work of our hands establish thou it.''

First, then, our prayer as a church and people should be for PROPORTIONATE GLADNESS; that our God who has filled one scale with grief would fill the other scale with grace till they balance each other. Inasmuch as he has poured out of his vial certain drops of wormwood, we pray him to measure out the like quantity of the consolation of love, whereby our hearts shall be comforted. May our covenant God, who has chastened us heavily, now revive us graciously.

We begin here by noticing that evidently the prayer desires *a gladness of the same origin as the sadness.* The psalm plainly ascribes the sadness to the Lord: '' *Thou* turnest man to destruction; and sayest, Return, ye children of men.'' '' We are consumed by *thine* anger, and by *thy* wrath are we troubled.'' God is seen in bereavements; death comes distinctly at his command; second causes are left behind. Since we have a distinct idea that the sadness comes from God, our text expresses an equally distinct desire that the gladness may come from God. We beg for divine comfort under divine chastening. The words of the prayer are eminently simple and childlike,—''Make us glad.'' They seem to say, '' Father! Thou hast made us sad; now make us glad! Thou hast saddened us grievously; now therefore, O Lord, most heartily rejoice us.'' The prayer as good as cries, ''Lord, no one but thyself can make us glad under such affliction, but thou canst bring us up from the lowest deep. The wound goes too near the heart for any human physician to heal us; but thou canst heal us even to the making of us glad!''

The prayer is full of buoyant hope; for it does not merely say, ''Comfort us; bear us up; keep our heads above water; prevent us from sinking in despair:'' no; but ''Make us glad.'' Reverse our state: lift us up from the depths to the heights. ''Make us glad!'' I hear the music of hope drowning the discord of fear; the songs of a joyous faith rising above the mournful dirges of grief.

The appeal is to the Lord alone. Moses entreats Jehovah himself to kindle the lamps of joy within the tabernacles of Israel. It is healthy sadness which the Lord sends, and it is equally safe gladness which God gives. If we make ourselves merry we may be mere mimics of mirth; if outward goods make us merry we may be no better than the rich fool in the parable; but if our God makes us glad we may take our fill of delight, and fear no ill consequences. The wine of the Kingdom cheers, but never intoxicates: the bread of God strengthens, but never surfeits. Neither pride, nor worldliness, nor carelessness comes of feasting at the table of our God. Come, then, let us together breathe this prayer: "Make us glad!" Let us paraphrase the expression thus,—"Lord, thou art the maker of all things, make us glad! By thy word thou didst make the light; make light for us! Thou wilt new-make these worn-out skies and much-polluted earth; come, then, and new-make us, and restore unto us the joy of thy salvation!" The parallel lies much in the source to which both sadness and gladness are ascribed. Lord, make both our summers and our winters, our calms and our storms; for every-thing is good which comes from thee, and it is our joy that our times are in thy hand.

But now notice that a *proportion is insisted upon:* "Make us glad according to the days wherein thou hast afflicted us, and the years wherein we have seen evil." This is an original prayer, full of thought and hope. Truly also it is a philosophical prayer; one which is in accordance with the harmonies of nature, and consonant with all the ways of God. I have been told on the Scotch lakes that the depth of the lake is almost always the same as the height of the surrounding hills; and I think I have heard that the same is true of the great ocean; so that the greatest depth is probably the same as the greatest height. Doubtless, the law of equilibrium is manifest in a thousand ways. Take an instance in the adjustment of days and nights. A long night reigns over the north of Norway; in these wintry months they do not even see the sun: but mark and admire their summer; then the day banishes the night altogether, and you may read your Bible by the light of the midnight sun. Long wintry nights find compensation in a perpetual summer day. There is a balance about the conditions of the peoples of differ-ing lands: each country has its drawbacks and its advantages. I believe it is so with the life of God's people: therein also the Lord maintains a balance. "As the sufferings of Christ abound in us, so our consolation also aboundeth by Christ" (2 Cor. 1: 5). Some the great Father permits to be little in Israel; they are none the less dear to him or that. Such are like the minnow which swims a pool proportioned to its size: no great tempest sweeps over the tiny streamlet, its ruffles and its calms suit its little inhabitants. Another of God's children is made for wide service; he may be compared to leviathan, for whom ocean is prepared; with billows, tempests, hurricanes, in due proportion. The great Architect draws everything to scale: while some lives are wisely arranged upon a small scale, others are fashioned for wider spheres and made to do business on the great waters; these have greater tribulations, but they have also greater consolations. God knoweth how to manage for us all, and we have each one a place in his thoughts. Wisdom allots each one his talent and his work, his strength and his trial. What would a sparrow do with an eagle's wing? Given the eagle's wing and the eagle's eye, there must be a soaring up above the Alps, a companionship with winds and lightnings. To the tiny humming-bird God appoints no flight into the upper air, but allots it flowers and sunshine nearer the ground. He knows the way of his people, and his love is over all.

The good Lord measures out the dark and the light in due proportions, and the result is life sad enough to be safe, and glad enough to be desirable. I do not believe that our mortal life is fitly set forth by the Thane's parable, when he said to the Saxon king, "Hast thou marked, O king, when thou art sitting in thy hall, and the fires are lit, and the lamps are burning, how the sparrow comes flying out of the thick darkness, passes through the window, glides into the bright and cheerful light, and then flits out again into the darkness? Such is our life, an interval of light amidst a long darkness." It is not so. If a believer flits out of the light he glides into the light again; if we traverse a stretch of darkness we may expect an equal breadth of brightness. If to-day we sail a stormy main we may hope to-morrow that the sea will be as glass. We have our changes, but the preponderance of life is not to misery. Rainy days are many, and yet in the long run they are outnumbered by the seasons of fair weather. God makes us glad "according to the days wherein he has afflicted us, and the years wherein we have seen evil." It may not be said of God's children that we are a wretched company. Though truly, if in this life only we had hope we should be of all men most miserable; yet since that hope is sure we are of all men the most happy! We shall not say when life is ended here below that it was an evil thing to have lived. We have the promise of the life that now is as well as of that which is to come. "Happy art thou, O Israel," is for the present as well as for the future. God has blessed us, and we are blessed; and it is not for us to speak as if the blessing were in vain.

Now, if it be so, that our gladness and our sadness are balanced, let us accept them by turns with gratitude. Let us notice, further, that *sorrow is the herald of joy*. Grief is God's usher of the black rod, sent to intimate that in the majesty of his grace the Lord is drawing near to us. There will be first to us, even as there was to Israel, the sound of Egypt's chariot-wheels and the cry of her horsemen, and a descent into the depths of the sea: and then shall come the far-resounding, never-forgotten shout of victory. The rage of Pharaoh, and the darkness of the night, and the march through the Red Sea must prepare the way for Miriam's timbrel and the loud refrain, "Sing unto the Lord, for he hath triumphed gloriously; the horse and his rider hath he thrown into the sea" (Exod. 15: 1). Israel must make bricks without straw before Moses shall come. If I had been a little child among the Israelites I think I should have known, when father set the bitter herbs upon the table, that the lamb was roasting somewhere, and would be set out too. "With bitter herbs shall ye eat it," (Exod. 12: 8) and so, if there be bitter herbs, the dainty dish is near. Job did not know, and he could not guess it; but in the light of Job's book we ought to know that the preparation for making a man twice as rich as he was before is to take away all that he has. Often-times, in building a bigger house, it is the way of wisdom to clear away the old building altogether. Keeping up the old structure is often an expensive economy; it is better to demolish it. Even so do I believe that the adversities of the saints are to their lasting profit, by removing that which would hinder greater prosperity. Troubles come clothed in black; but to the eye of faith they carry silver trumpets, and they proclaim the approach of great mercies. God is hastening in the richness of his favour to bless his children: sorrow is the outrider of joy.

A step further, and we have it thus, *sorrow often prepares for joy*. It might not be safe that you should enjoy worldly prosperity at the outset of life. Your adversities in business are meant to teach you the worthlessness of earthly things, so that when you have them you may not be tempted to make idols of them. I am persuaded that many men have been ruined by rising suddenly to fame and power: had they at first been abused and trodden down like mire in the streets, their spirits might have been hardened to endure that sharpest of all tests, namely, human honour; for "as the fining pot for silver, and the furnace for gold; so is a man to his praise" (Prov. 27: 21). You are not ready yet to bear the weight of an elevated super-structure: you must be dug out first, and a deep foundation must be laid to bear a lofty building. In the spiritual life God does not run us up with glittering virtues all of a sudden; but deep prostration of spirit and thorough humiliation prepare the under-courses; and then, afterwards, stone upon stone, as with rows of jewels, we are built up to be a palace for the indwelling of God. Sorrow furnishes the house for joy. The preparation for an eternal heaven is temporary affliction. Jesus has gone to prepare heaven for us; but he has left his cross behind him that the Holy Spirit may by its means prepare us for heaven. You could not enjoy the rest of Paradise if you had not first known the labours of pilgrimage; you could not understand the bound-less felicity of heaven if your hearts had not been enlarged by the endurance of tribulation. Let not this be forgotten, then, that our troubles build a house and spread a table for our joys.

Did you ever read of a Roman triumph? Have you ever stood upon the Via Sacra which led up to the Capitol? There, when the glad day was come, the people crowded all along the road: every house-roof was loaded, the very chimney-tops bore each a man, while along the sacred way the conqueror rode, drawn by white horses, amid the blast of trumpets, and the thundering acclamations of myriads. What glory! What re-nown! Rome's millions did their best to crown their hero. But there had been to him full many a battle before that hour of pride. Victory needs conflict as its preface. The conqueror's scars are his truest decorations, his wounds his best certificates of valour. Because he had been smothered with the dust and defiled with the blood of battle, therefore the hero stood erect, and all men paid him reverence. It must be so in the present condition of things; no man can wear the garland till he has first contended for it.

Sure we must fight if we would reign;
Increase our courage, Lord.

The way to the crown is by the cross: the palm branch cometh
not to the idle hand.

The path of sorrow, and that path alone,
Leads to the place where sorrow is unknown.

Once again, let me say to you, there is such a connection
between sorrow and joy that *no saint ever has a sorrow but what
it has a joy wrapped up in it.* It is a rough oyster, but a pearl lies
within those shells if you will but look for it. Do not think I
mock at grief by saying that it is the husk of joy: far from it, I
would console grief by asserting solemnly that within the black
envelope of affliction there is a precious love-token from God:
be sure of that. We find the treasure of communion with Christ
in the earthen vessel of sorrow. We ask to have fellowship with
Jesus in his sufferings; and we cannot do so except we suffer.
It is a joy to remember in our woe that by these things we are
made like unto our Lord, and conformed unto his image. If there
were only this comfort it might suffice to sweeten every suffering.

Beside this, there is generally with sorrow a manifestation
of the Lord amid our weakness. I have known many forms of
happiness; but I think, upon the whole, I do consider the purest
and sweetest to be that of fainting in weakness upon the breast
of Jesus and dying into his life. "Oh to be nothing, nothing,
only to lie at his feet!" To be as a lily broken off at the stalk,
and therefore taken up into his hand, This is unutterable
happiness. The Lord's love to his poor and afflicted ones is
most choice and tender. "He carrieth the lambs in his bosom."
Favoured feebleness to be thus laid in the heaven of Jesus'
bosom! I love to cower down under the divine wings like a
chick under the hen, finding myself by losing myself in God. I
have found it precious to feel that no more strength is left to
suffer with, and therefore I must die away into the divine will.
Certain is it that in every tribulation there are consolations,
even as every night has its own stars. Said I not truly that
every sorrow contains a joy?

Once more, *the day will come when all the sorrows of God's
sending will be looked upon as joys.* Hear ye this! By some

strange alchemy, known only to "the King eternal, immortal, invisible," our sorrows shall be turned into joys. Ye see this in your own homes,—I quote it because it is the Lord's own metaphor,—a woman when she is in travail hath sorrow because her hour is come; but soon she remembereth no more her travail, for joy that a man is born into the world. Our troubles and travails are sharp, but they will all be forgotten in the joy that will come of them. Before we enter heaven we shall thank God for most of our sorrow; and when we are once in glory we shall thank him for it all. Perhaps in heaven, among all the things which have happened to us that will excite our wonder and delight, our furnace experience, and the hammer and the file, will take the lead. Sorrow will contribute rich stanzas to our everlasting psalm. Wherefore comfort one another with these words, and breathe the prayer each one to-day, "Make us glad according to the days wherein thou hast afflicted us, and the years wherein we have seen evil." In each case may divine love weigh out the ingredients of a sanctified life according to the art of the apothecary, each one in due proportion.

Bear with me while I come to the second part of my subject, which I desire to make eminently practical. The gladness desired is also described: it is PECULIAR GLADNESS. The Psalmist wishes for a fourfold gladness: the first is *gladness at the sight of God's work.*

Notice; "THY work." There is always something cheering in God's work. Have you never felt it so? I think you must have done so. When Mungo Park was cheered by that little bit of moss which he picked up in the wilderness, he was but comforted as many of us have been. The flowers of the garden, the wild beauties of the wood, the chance tufts by the roadside, are all God's work, and, therefore, breathe consolation to God's servants. Nature is kindly; her stars speak light to our hearts; her winds chase away our gloom; and her waves flash with health for us. Nature is a fond foster-mother to the Lord's children, because she is like ourselves, the work of the Lord. When we are in deep tribulation it is a sweet quietus to survey the handiwork of our Father in Heaven. His work in providence, also, is often a consolation to us. Let us but see what God has done for his people and for ourselves in years past, and we are cheered. Trouble itself, when we see it to be God's work, has lost its terror. A certain Persian nobleman found himself surrounded by soldiers, who sought to take him prisoner; he drew his sword and fought right valiantly, and might have escaped had not one of the company said, "The king has sent us to convey you to himself." He sheathed his sword at once. Yes, we can contend against what we call a misfortune; but when we learn that the Lord hath done it, our contest is ended, for we joy and rejoice in what the Lord doeth; or, if we cannot get the length of rejoicing in it, we acquiesce in his will. This is our song:—

> *I would not contend with thy will,*
> *Whatever that will may decree;*
> *But oh, may each trial I feel*
> *Unite me more fondly to thee.*

The great comfort which this church wants now is to see God's work in the midst of her revived and glorified. If the Lord will but come among us and save men, and if he will build up and edify his people and give them help to accomplish their holy service—this will be our richest possible comfort: "Let thy work appear unto thy servants." Lord, our brethren fade away, they go into the shadow land, we see them no more; but, oh, if we can see thy hand at work among us we shall not be discouraged! May the Lord make you to see his work on your own hearts; may he make you to see his work in the congregation, in the Sunday School, and everywhere throughout the world, bringing men to himself; and you will find therein a sovereign balm for all your wounds.

The next consolation is also a very rich one—*gladness at the revelation of God to our children;*—"and thy glory unto their children." If our God will but make his glory to be seen by our children, what more can we ask? "I have no greater joy than this, my children walk in the truth." No better comfort can be found for bereaved mothers than to see their sons and daughters converted. There is a sorrow for those who have departed; but I could almost say, "Weep not for the dead, neither bewail them,"—for there is a sharper grief by far, and that is our anxiety for those who survive, and yet are dead unto God. Did you ever see a chain-gang of convicts marching to their labour? I could wish never to see the sad scene again. Suppose that among those convicts there was a boy of yours! Ah me! it were better for you that he had never been born. But think of those who are prisoners in the chains of sin. Is there a boy or girl of yours in such bonds? Oh, then, I am sure you will pray the Lord to rescue you from so sharp a trial, and to set your sons and daughters free from the fetters of iniquity. Pray ye each one fervently, "O Lord, let thy glory as their emancipator appear to my children, and then do what thou wilt."

Did you ever visit a condemned cell? To peep through the gate and to see a man sitting there condemned to die is enough to make one faint. Suppose it were your boy! Suppose it were your husband! Suppose it were your brother! But listen: "He that believeth not is condemned already." Pardon us, dear unconverted relatives, if we say that yours is a terrible plight, to be even now sitting in the condemned cell, doomed to be taken out to execution before long unless infinite mercy shall grant a free pardon. What dreadful sights must meet the eye upon a battle-field. If I see a man bleeding by a common cut my heart is in my mouth, and I cannot bear the sight: but what must it be to see men dismembered, disembowelled, writhing to and fro in the last agonies of death! What horror to walk among mounds of dead bodies, and stumble at each step over a human corpse! Yet, what is natural death compared with spiritual death? What terror to dwell in the same house with relatives who are dead while they live,—dead unto God. The thought is full of anguish. If God will quicken our spiritually dead; if he will give life to those who are " free among the slain, as they that go down into the pit," what a consolation we shall find therein!

Did you see that alarming fire the other day? Did you hear of the hotel in flames, wherein there were many guests, and they were in the upper story, and the flames had grasped the whole edifice, so that numbers perished? It must be dreadful to see persons at the upper windows of a burning house, and to be powerless to rescue them. But if your child were there, your boy, your girl, or if your husband or your wife were there, or even if anyone you knew were there, your grief would have a double sting about it, and you would cry, "Lord, do what thou wilt with me, but do save those precious lives." Remember, then, that your ungodly friends are in a like condition, and what

D

greater mercy can God bestow upon you than for him to make his glory to be seen by your children in their eternal salvation?

Therefore I turn your thoughts to that prayer. May you breathe it now, and may the Lord, for Christ's sake, answer it right speedily,—"Let thy glory appear unto our children."

The third consolation which Moses here describes is *gladness at beauty bestowed*—"Let the beauty of the Lord our God be upon us." Sorrow mars the countenance and clothes the body with sackcloth; but if the Lord will come to us and adorn us with his beauty, then the stains of mourning will speedily disappear. What a beauty is this which the Lord giveth— "the beauty of the Lord our God!" This comeliness is the beauty of his grace; for our covenant God is the God of all grace. If the Lord makes us to know that we are his our faces shine. If he fills us with his life and love, then brightness flashes from the eyes, and there is a grace about every movement.

This "beauty" means holiness; for holiness is the beauty of God. If the Holy Spirit works in you the beauty of holiness, you will rise superior to your afflictions. If this church shall be made the holier by its bereavements, we shall gain much by our losses.

This beauty of the Lord must surely mean his Presence with us. As the sun beautifies all things, so does God's Presence. When we know that Jesus is with us, when we feel that he is our Helper, when we bask in his love, when he abides with us in power, this is the beauty of the saints. If we have Christ in us, Christ with us, we can bear any amount of trouble.

> *I can do all things, or can bear*
> *All suffering if my Lord be there.*

This beauty gives to the believer an attractiveness in the eyes of men: they perceive that we have been with Jesus, and they behold our faces shining like the faces of angels. It is a great thing when a Christian is so happy, so holy, and so heavenly that he attracts others to Christ, and people seek his company because they perceive that he has been in the company of the blessed Lord. God give you this, and, if you have it, you may forget your sorrows: they are transfigured into joy.

The last comfort that Moses speaks of is *gladness at our own work being established*—"Establish thou the work of our hands upon us; yes, the work of our hands establish thou it." Do you notice the wonderful blending in the fifteenth and seventeenth verses: there it is, "Let *thy* work appear unto thy servant;" here it is "Let *our* work be established." Alas, I have heard divines rightly say that salvation is God's work, and then they have harshly added that, in our preaching of the gospel, we make it out to be our own work. Thus they speak hard things against us, and their speech is not after the Lord's mind. Others, again, make out this work to be so much man's work that God is forgotten. Neither of these is correct: we must blend the two: to build up the church and win souls for Jesus is first of all God's work, and then our work. Why should a Christian work to win souls? Answer: because God works in him to win souls. Remember the verses,—"Work out your own salvation with fear and trembling." Why? "For it is God that worketh in you to will and to do of his good pleasure" (Phil. 2: 12, 13). God works to set us working: our work is the result of his work.

Our work is often a very effectual means of comfort to us. On the battle-field of Gettysburg there had been a terrible fight, and among the wounded lay a certain chaplain of the name of Eastman who had been seriously injured in the back by his horse falling upon him. The dark and dreary night came on, and as he lay there in intense pain, unable to rise, he heard a voice at a little distance cry, "O God!" His interest was excited, and he rolled himself over and over through pools of blood, and among the slain, till he reached the side of the dying man, and there lay, talking of Jesus and his free salvation. The man expired in hope, and just then two soldiers came and told Eastman that a captain was dying a little further down the field, and they must carry him there: so he was borne in anguish upon the work of mercy, and while the night wore on he spoke of Jesus to many dying men. Could he have had a surer relief from his pain? I think not. Why, it seems to me that to lie there on his back with nothing to do but moan and groan would have been horrible: but in all his pain and anguish to be carried about to proclaim mercy to dying men made the anguish of an injured back endurable! So is it when you miss a friend, or have lost property, or are heavy in spirit, you shall find your surest comfort in serving God with all your might.

The text prays for our work *that it may succeed*: "Establish thou the work of our hands." Oh, if God will but prosper us in our work for him how happy we shall be! One day this week I had a great lift up out of deep distress when I was informed that a captain was here last Sunday morning, and was so impressed that he found the Saviour, and made the fact known at one of the noonday prayer-meetings, asking for himself that he might be kept faithful to his God. This is good. We do not always see our seed grow so quickly as that.

Then we pray that our *work may be lasting,*—that is the chief point. I look forward to the future of this church with prayerful, hopeful anxiety! I am not old, not very old at any rate; but I am not all that I was in my earlier days, and mistrust whispers that soon things will decline. Though dear ones, who seemed to be pillars, are taken away, the Lord will find other pillars; and though just now there are breaches in Zion's wall here and there, yet the wall shall again be repaired, and not a broken place shall remain. If we may see this accomplished we shall be abundantly comforted. "Establish thou the work of our hands upon us; yea, the work of our hands establish thou it." We belong to an established church; established, not by men, but by the Lord. This church will flourish when you and I have passed into our rest. Meanwhile, I beg you to take a deep interest in it, and do all you can for its prosperity. Make it more and more the model of what a church of Christ should be. I long that the truth which I have preached may be established in the earth.

God will establish his work upon us from day to day, and this shall be our comfort. Keep everything in the best possible working order. Plead with the Holy Spirit to clothe us with his power. Maintain all forms of holy labour vigorously, and sustain every fund by your spontaneous liberality. Never need pressing, but let each one enquire, "What can I do to keep the church well supplied to God's glory?" I believe this is the way to church comfort. God will comfort Zion, he will comfort all her waste places; but we must each one take pleasure in her stones, and favour the dust thereof. Close up your ranks. Leave no empty spaces. Let every man stand closer to his fellow: and then *"Forward!"* Forward to a fuller consecration and a braver faith in God.

VIII

"THOUGH HE WERE DEAD"

"Martha saith unto him, I know that he shall rise again in the resurrection at the last day. Jesus said unto her, I am the resurrection, and the life: he that believeth in me, though he were dead, yet shall he live: and whosoever liveth and believeth in me shall never die. Believest thou this?"—John 11: 24–26.

MARTHA is a very accurate type of a class of anxious believers. They do believe truly, but not with such confidence as to lay aside their care. They do not distrust the Lord, or question the truth of what he says, yet they puzzle their brain about "How shall this thing be?" and so they miss the major part of the present comfort which the word of the Lord would minister to their hearts if they received it more simply. *How?* and *why?* belong unto the Lord. It is his business to arrange matters so as to fulfil his own promises. If we would sit at our Lord's feet with Mary, and consider what he has promised, we should choose a better part than if we ran about with Martha, crying, "How can these things be?"

Martha, you see, in this case, when the Lord Jesus Christ told her that her brother would rise again, replied, "I know that he shall rise again in the resurrection at the last day." She was a type, I say, of certain anxious believers, for she *set a practical bound to the Saviour's words.* "Of course there will be a resurrection, and then my brother will rise with the rest." She concluded that the Saviour could not mean anything beyond that. The first meaning and the commonest meaning that suggests itself to her must be what Jesus means. Is not that the way with many of us? We had a statesman once, and a good man too, who loved reform; but, whenever he had accomplished a little progress, he considered that all was done. We called him at last "Finality John," for he was always coming to an ultimatum, and taking for his motto "Rest, and be thankful." Into that style Christian people too frequently drop with regard to the promises of God. We limit the Holy One of Israel as to the meaning of his words. Of course they mean so much, but we cannot allow that they intend more. It were well if the spirit of progress would enter into our faith, so that we felt within our souls that we had never beheld the innermost glory of the Lord's words of grace. We often wonder that the disciples put such poor meanings upon our Lord's words, but I fear we are almost as far off as they were from fully comprehending all his gracious teachings. Are we not still as little children, making little out of great words? Have we grasped as yet a tithe of our Lord's full meaning, in many of his sayings of love? When he is talking of bright and sparkling gems of benediction, we are thinking of common pebble-stones in the brook of mercy; when he speaketh of stars and heavenly crowns, we think of sparks and childish coronals of fading flowers. Oh that we could but have our intellect cleared; better still, could have our understanding expanded, or, best of all, our faith increased, so as to reach to the height of our Lord's great arguments of love!

Martha also had another fault in which she was very like ourselves: she *laid the words of Jesus on the shelf*, as things so trite and sure that they were of small practical importance. "Thy brother shall rise again." Now, if she had possessed faith enough, she might truthfully have said, "Lord, I thank thee for that word! I expect within a short space to see him sitting at the table with thee. I put the best meaning possible upon thy words, for I know that thou art always better than I can think thee to be; and therefore I expect to see my beloved Lazarus walk home from the sepulchre before the sun sets again." But no, she lays the truth aside as a matter past all dispute, and says, "I know that my brother shall rise again in the resurrection at the last day." A great many precious truths are laid up by us like the old hulks in the Medway, never to see service any more, or like aged pensioners at Chelsea, as relics of the past. We say "Yes, quite true, we fully believe that doctrine." Somehow it is almost as bad to lay up a doctrine in lavender as it is to throw it out of the window. When you so believe a truth as to put it to bed and smother it with the bolster of neglect, it is much the same as if you did not believe it at all. An official belief is very much akin to infidelity.

Some persons never question a doctrine: that is not their line of temptation; they accept the gospel as true, but then they never expect to see its promises practically carried out; it is a proper thing to believe, but by no means a prominent, practical factor in actual life. It is true but it is mysterious, misty, mythical, far removed from the realm of practical common sense. We do with the promises often as a poor old couple did with a precious document, which might have cheered their old age had they used it according to its real value.

A gentleman stepping into a poor woman's house saw framed and glazed upon the wall a French note for a thousand francs. He said to the old folks, "How came you by this?" They informed him that a poor French soldier had been taken in by them and nursed until he died, and he had given them that little picture when he was dying as a memorial of him. They thought it such a pretty souvenir that they had framed it, and there it was adorning the cottage wall. They were greatly surprised when they were told that it was worth a sum which would be quite a little fortune for them if they would but turn it into money. Are we not equally unpractical with far more precious things? Have you not certain of the words of your great Lord framed and glazed in your hearts, and do you not say to yourselves, "They are so sweet and precious"? and yet you have never turned them into actual blessing, never used them in the hour of need. You have done as Martha did when she took the words, "Thy brother shall rise again," and put round about them this handsome frame, "in the resurrection at the last day." Oh that we had grace to turn God's bullion of gospel into current coin, and use them as our present spending money.

Moreover, Martha made another blunder, and that was *setting the promise in the remote distance.* This is a common folly, this distancing the promises of the Most High. "In the resurrection at the last day"; no doubt she thought it a very long way off, and therefore she did not get much comfort out of it. Telescopes are meant to bring objects near to the eye, but I have known people use the mental telescope in the wrong way: they always put the big end of it to their eye, and then the glass sends the object further away. Her brother was to be raised that very day: she might so have understood the Saviour, but instead of it she looked at his words through the wrong end of the glass, and said, "I know that he will rise again in the resurrection a the last day." Do not refuse the present blessing. Death and heaven, or the advent and the glory, are at your doors. A little while and he that will come shall come, and will not tarry. Think not that the Lord is slack concerning his promise. Do not say in your heart, "My Lord delayeth his coming"; or dream that his words of love are only for the dim future. In the ages to come marvels shall be revealed, but even the present hour is bejewelled with loving-kindness. To-day the Lord has rest, and peace, and joy to give to you. Lose not these treasures by unbelief.

Martha also appears to me to have *made the promise unreal and impersonal*. "Thy brother shall rise again": to have realized that would have been a great comfort to her, but she mixes Lazarus up with all the rest of the dead. "Yes, he will rise in the resurrection at the last day; when thousands of millions shall be rising from their graves, no doubt Lazarus will rise with the rest." That is the way with us; we take the promise and say, "This is true to all the children of God." If so it is true to us; but we miss *that* point. What a blessing God has bestowed upon the covenanted people! Yes, and you are one of them: but you shake your head, as if the word was not for you. It is a fine feast, and yet you are hungry; it is a full and flowing stream, but you remain thirsty. Why is this? Somehow the generality of your apprehension misses the sweetness which comes of personal appropriation. There is such a thing as speaking of the promises in a magnificent style, and yet being in deep spiritual poverty; as if a man should boast of the wealth of old England and the vast amount of treasure in the Bank, while he does not possess a penny wherewith to bless himself. In your case you know it is your own fault that you are poor and miserable, for if you would but exercise an appropriating faith you might possess a boundless heritage. If you are a child of God all things are yours, and you may help yourself. If you are hungry at this banquet it is for want of faith: if you are thirsty by the brink of this river it is because you do not stoop down and drink. Behold, God is your portion: the Father is your shepherd, the Son of God is your food, and the Spirit of God is your comforter. Rejoice and be glad, and grasp with the firm hand of a personal faith that royal boon which Jesus sets before you in his promises.

I beg you to observe how the Lord Jesus Christ in great wisdom dealt with Martha. In the first place, he did not grow angry with her. There is not a trace of petulance in his speech. He did not say to her, "Martha, I am ashamed of you that you should have such low thoughts of me." She thought that she was honouring Jesus when she said,—"I know, that even now, whatsoever thou wilt ask of God, God will give it thee." Her idea of Jesus was that he was a great prophet who would ask of God and obtain answers to his prayers; she has not grasped the truth of his own personal power to give and sustain life. But the Saviour did not say, "Martha, these are low and grovelling ideas of your Lord and Saviour." He did not chide her, though she lacked wisdom, wisdom which she ought to have possessed. I do not think God's people learn much by being scolded; it is not the habit of the great Lord to scold his disciples, and therefore they do not take it well when his servants take upon themselves to rate them. If ever you meet with one of the Lord's own who falls far short of the true ideal of the gospel, do not bluster and upbraid. Who taught you what you know? He that has taught you did it of his infinite love and grace and pity, and he was very tender with you, for you were doltish enough; therefore be tender with others, and give them line upon line, even as your Lord was gentle towards you. It ill becomes a servant to lose patience where his Master shows so much.

The Lord Jesus, with gentle spirit, proceeded to teach her more of the things concerning himself. More of Jesus! That is the sovereign cure for our faults. He revealed himself to her, that in him she might behold reasons for a clearer hope and a more substantial faith. How sweetly fell those words upon her ear: "I am the resurrection and the life"! Not "I can get resurrection by my prayers," but "I am, myself, the resurrection." God's people need to know more of what Jesus is, more of the fulness which it has pleased the Father to place in him. Some of them know quite enough of what they are themselves, and they will break their hearts if they go on reading much longer in that black-letter book: they need, I say, to rest their eyes upon the Person of their Lord, and to spy out all the riches of grace which lie hidden in him; then they will pluck up courage, and look forward with surer expectancy. When our Lord said, "I am the resurrection and the life," he indicated to

Martha that resurrection and life were not gifts which he must seek, nor even boons which he must create; but that he himself was the resurrection and the life: these things were wherever he was. He was the Author, and Giver, and Maintainer of Life, and that Life was himself. He would have her to know that he was himself precisely what she wanted for her brother. She did know a little of the Lord's power, for she said, "If thou hadst been here, my brother had not died," which being very kindly interpreted might mean, "Lord, thou art the life." "Ah, but," saith Jesus, "you must also learn that I am the resurrection! You already admit that if I had been here Lazarus would not have died; I would have you further learn that I being here your brother shall live though he has died; and that when I am with my people none of them shall die for ever, for I am to them the resurrection and the life." Poor Martha was looking up into the sky for life, or gazing down into the deeps for resurrection, when the Resurrection and the Life stood before her, smiling upon her, and cheering her heavy heart. She had thought of what Jesus might have done if he had been there before; now let her know what he *is* at the present moment.

Thus I have introduced the text to you, and I pray God the Holy Spirit to bless these prefatory observations; for if we learn only these first lessons we shall not have been here in vain. Let us construe promises in their largest sense, let us regard them as real, and set them down as facts. Let us look to the Promiser, even to Jesus the Lord, and not so much to the difficulties which surround the accomplishment of the promise. In beginning the divine life let us look to Jesus, and in afterwards running the heavenly race let us still be looking unto Jesus, till we see in him our all in all. When both eyes look on Jesus we are in the light; but, when we have one eye for him, and one eye for self, all is darkness. Oh, to see him with all our soul's eyes!

Now, I am going to speak as I am helped of the Spirit; and I shall proceed thus—first, by asking you to *view the text as a stream of comfort to Martha and other bereaved persons*; and, secondly, to *view it as a great deep of comfort to all believers*.

First, I long for you to VIEW THE TEXT AS A STREAM OF COMFORT TO MARTHA AND OTHER BEREAVED PERSONS.

Observe, in the beginning, that *the presence of Jesus Christ means life and resurrection*. It meant that to Lazarus. If Jesus comes to Lazarus, Lazarus must live. Had Martha taken the Saviour's words literally, as she should have done, as I have already told you, she would have had immediate comfort from them; and the Saviour intended her to understand them in that sense. He virtually says, "I am to Lazarus the Power that can make him live again; and I am the Power that can keep him in life. Yea, I am the Resurrection and the Life." A statement so understood would have been very comfortable to her. Nothing could have been more so. It would there and then have abolished death so far as her brother was concerned. Somebody says, "But I do not see that this is any comfort *to us*, for if Jesus be here, yet it is only a spiritual Presence, and we cannot expect to see our dear mother, or child, or husband raised from the dead thereby." I answer that our Lord Jesus is able at this moment to give us back our departed ones, for he is still the Resurrection and the Life. But let me ask you whether you really wish that Jesus would raise your departed ones from the dead. You say at first, "Of course I do wish it"; but I would ask you to reconsider that decision; for I believe that upon further thought you will say, "No, I could not wish it." Do you really desire to see your glorified husband sent back again to this world of care and pain? Would you have your father or mother deprived of the glories which they are now enjoying in order that they might help you in the struggles of this mortal life? Would you discrown the saints? You are not so cruel. That dear child, would you have it back from among the angels, and from the inner glory, to come here and suffer again? You would not have it so. And, to my mind, it is a comfort to you, or should be, that it is not within your power to have it so; because you might be tempted in some selfish moment to accept the doubtful boon. Lazarus could return, and fit into his place again, but scarcely one in ten thousand could do so.

There would be serious drawbacks in the return of those whom we have loved best. Do you cry, "Give back my father! Give me back my friend"? You know not what you ask. It might be a cause of regret to you as long as they lingered here, for you would each morning think to yourself, "Beloved one, I have brought you out of heaven by my wish. I have robbed you of infinite felicity to gratify myself." For my own part, I had rather that the Lord Jesus should keep the keys of death than that he should lend them to me. It would be too dreadful a privilege to be empowered to rob heaven of the perfected merely to give pleasure to imperfect ones below. Jesus would raise them now if he knew it to be right; I do not wish to take the government from his shoulder. It is more comfortable to me to think that Jesus Christ could give them back to me, and would if it were for his glory and my good. My dear ones that lie asleep could be awakened in an instant if the Master thought it best; but it would not be best, and therefore even I would hold his skirt, and say, "Tread softly, Master! Do not arouse them! I shall go to them, but they shall not return to me. It is not my wish they should return: it is better that they should be with thee where thou art, to behold thy glory." It does not seem to me, then, that you are one whit behind Martha; and you ought to be comforted while Jesus says to you, "I am even now the Resurrection and the Life."

Furthermore, here is comfort which we may each one safely take, namely, that *when Jesus comes the dead shall live*. The Revised Version has it, "He that believeth on me, though he die, yet shall he live." We do not know when our Lord will descend from heaven, but we do know the message of the angel, "This same Jesus, which is taken up from you into heaven, shall so come in like manner as ye have seen him go into heaven" (Acts 1: 11). The Lord will come; we may not question the certainty of his appearing. When he cometh, all his redeemed shall live with him. The trump of the archangel shall startle the happy sleepers, and they shall wake to put on their beauteous array; the body transformed and made like unto Christ's glorious body shall be once more wrapt about them as the vesture of their perfected and emancipated spirits. Then our brother shall rise again, and all our dear ones who have fallen asleep in Jesus the Lord will bring with him. This is the glorious hope of the church, wherein we see the death of death, and the destruction of the grave. Wherefore comfort one another with these words.

Then we are also told that *when Jesus comes, living believers shall not die*. After the coming of Christ there shall be no more death for his people. What does Paul say? "Behold, I show you a mystery. We shall not all *die*, but we shall all be changed." Did I see a little schoolgirl put up her finger? Did I hear her say, "Please, sir, you made a mistake." So I did; I made it on purpose. Paul did not say, "We shall not all *die*," for the Lord had already said, "Whosoever liveth and believeth in me shall never *die*"; so Paul would not say that any of us should die, but he used his Master's own term, and said, "We shall not all sleep, but we shall all be changed." When the Lord comes there will be no more death; we who are alive and remain (as some of us may be—we cannot tell) will undergo a sudden transformation—for flesh and blood, as they are, cannot inherit the kingdom of God—and by that transformation our bodies shall be made meet to be "partakers of the inheritance of the saints in light" (Col. 1: 12). There shall be no more death then. Here, then, we have two sacred handkerchiefs with which to wipe the eyes of mourners: when Christ cometh the dead shall live; when Christ cometh those that live shall never die. Like Enoch, or Elias, we shall pass into the glory state without wading through the black stream, while those who have already forded it shall prove to have been no losers thereby. All this is in connection with Jesus. Resurrection with Jesus is resurrection indeed. Life in Jesus is life indeed. It endears to us resurrection, glory, eternal life, and ultimate perfection, when we see them all coming to us in Jesus. He is the golden pot which hath this manna, the rod which beareth these almonds, the life whereby we live.

But further, I have not made you drink deep enough of this stream yet. I think our Saviour meant that *even now his dead are alive*. "He that believeth on me, though he die, yet shall he live." Those that believe in Jesus Christ appear to die, but yet they live. They are not in the grave; they are for ever with the Lord. They are not unconscious; they are with their Lord in Paradise. Death cannot kill a believer; it can only usher him into a freer form of life. Because Jesus lives, his people live. God is not the God of the dead, but of the living: those who have departed have not perished. We laid the precious body in the cemetery, and we set up stones at the head and foot; but we might engrave on them the Lord's words, "She is not dead, but sleepeth." True, an unbelieving generation may laugh us to scorn, but we scorn their laughing.

Again, *even now his living do not die*. There is an essential difference between the decease of the godly and the death of the ungodly. Death comes to the ungodly man as a penal infliction, but to the righteous as a summons to his Father's palace: to the sinner it is an execution, to the saint an undressing. Death to the wicked is the King of terrors: death to the saint is the end of terrors, the commencement of glory. To die in the Lord is a covenant blessing. Death is ours; it is set down in the list of our possessions among the all things, and it follows life in the list as if it were an equal favour. No longer is it death to die. The name remains, but the thing itself is changed. Wherefore, then, are we in bondage through fear of death? Why do we dread the process which gives us liberty? I am told that persons who in the cruel ages had lain in prison for years suffered much more in the moment of the knocking off of their fetters than they had endured for months in wearing the hard iron; and yet I suppose that no man languishing in a dungeon would have been unwilling to stretch out his arm or leg, that the heavy chains might be beaten off by the smith. We should all be content to endure that little inconvenience to obtain lasting liberty. Now, such is death—the knocking off of the fetters; yet the iron may never seem to be so truly iron as when that last liberating blow of grace is about to fall. Let us not mind the harsh grating of the key as it turns in the lock; if we understand it aright it will be as music to our ears. Imagine that your last hour is come! The key turns with pain for a moment; but, lo, the bolt is shot! The iron gate is open! The spirit is free! Glory be unto the Lord for ever and ever!

I leave the text now as a stream of comfort for the bereaved, for I wish you to VIEW IT AS A GREAT DEEP OF COMFORT FOR ALL BELIEVERS. I cannot fathom it, any more than I could measure the abyss, but I can invite you to survey it by the help of the Holy Ghost.

Methinks, first, this text plainly teaches that *the Lord Jesus Christ is the life of his people.* We are dead by nature, and you can never produce life out of death: the essential elements are wanting. Should a spark be lingering among the ashes, you may yet fan it to a flame; but from human nature the last spark of heavenly life is gone, and it is vain to seek for life among the dead. The life of every Christian is Christ. He is the beginning of life, being the Resurrection: when he comes to us we live.

Regeneration is the result of contact with Christ: we are begotten again unto living hope by his resurrection from the dead. The life of the Christian in its commencement is in Christ alone; not a fragment of it is from himself, and the continuance of that life is equally the same; Jesus is not only the resurrection to begin with, but the life to go on with. "I have life in myself," saith one. I answer: not otherwise than as you are one with Christ; your spiritual life in every breath it draws is in Christ. If you are regarded for a moment as separated from Christ, you are cast forth as a branch and are withered. A member severed from the head is dead flesh and no more. In union to Christ is your life. Oh that our hearers would understand this! I see a poor sinner look into himself, and look again, and then cry, "I cannot see any life within!" Of course you cannot; you have no life of your own. "Alas," cried a Christian, "I cannot find anything within to feed my soul with!" Do you expect to feed upon yourself? Must not Israel look up for the manna? Did one of all the tribes find it in his own bosom? To look to self is to turn to a broken cistern which can hold no water. I tell you you must learn that Jesus is the Resurrection and the Life. Hearken to that great "I"—that infinite EGO! This must cover over and swallow up your little *ego*. "I live; yet not I, but Christ liveth in me" (Gal. 2: 20). What are you? Less than nothing, and vanity; but over all springs up that divine, all-sufficient personality, "I am the resurrection and the life." Take the two first words together, and they seem to me to have a wondrous majesty about them—"I AM!" Here is Self-Existence. Life in himself! Even as the Mediator, the Lord Jesus tells us that it is given him to have life in himself, even as the Father hath life in himself (John 5: 26). "*I am*" fills the yawning mouth of the sepulchre. He that liveth and was dead and is alive for evermore, the Alpha and the Omega, the beginning and the end, declares, "*I am* the resurrection and the life." If, then, I want to live unto God, I must have Christ; and if I desire to continue to live unto God I must continue to have Christ; and if I aspire to have that life developed to the utmost fulness of which it is capable, I must find it all in Christ. He has come not only that we may have life, but that we may have it more abundantly. Anything that is beyond the circle of Christ is death. If I conjure up an experience over which I foolishly dote, which puffs me up as so perfect that I need not come to Christ now as a poor empty-handed sinner, I have entered into the realm of death, I have introduced into my soul a damning leaven. Away with it! Everything of life is put into this golden casket of Christ Jesus: all else is death. We have not a breath of life anywhere but in Jesus, who ever liveth to give life. He saith, "Because I live, ye shall live also," and this is true. We live not for any other reason—not because of anything in us or connected with us, but only because of Jesus. "For ye are dead, and your life is hid with Christ in God" (Col. 3: 3).

Now, further, in this great deep to which we would conduct you, *faith is the only channel by which we can draw from Jesus our life.* "I am the resurrection, and the life: *he that believeth in me*": that is it. He does not say, "He that loves me," though love is a bright grace, and very sweet to God: he does not say, "He that serves me," though every one that believes in Christ will endeavour to serve him; but it is not put so: he does not even say, "He that imitates me," though every one that believes in Christ must and will imitate him; but it is put, "He that believeth in me." Why is that? Why does the Lord so continually make faith to be the only link between himself and the soul? I take it, because faith is a grace which arrogates nothing to itself, and has no operation apart from Jesus, to whom it unites us. You want to conduct the electric fluid, and, in order to do this, you find a metal which will not create any action of its own; if it did so, it would disturb the current which you wish to send along it. If it set up an action of its own, how would you know the difference between what came of the metal and what came of the battery? Now, faith is an empty-handed receiver and communicator; it is nothing apart from that upon which it relies, and therefore it is suitable to be a conductor for grace. When an auditorium has to be erected for a speaker in which he may be plainly heard, the essential thing is to get rid of all echo. When you have no echo, then you have a perfect building: faith makes no noise of its own, it allows the Word to speak. Faith cries, "*Non nobis Domine!* Not unto us! Not unto us." Christ puts his crown on faith's head, exclaiming, "Thy faith hath saved thee;" but faith hastens to ascribe all the glory of salvation to Jesus only. So you see why the Lord selects faith rather than any other grace, because it is a self-forgetting thing. It is best adapted to be the tubing through which the water of life runs, because it will not communicate a flavour of its own, but will just convey the stream purely and simply from Christ to the soul. "He that believeth in me."

Now notice, *to the reception of Christ by faith there is no limit.* "He that believeth in me, though he were dead, yet shall he live: and whosoever"—I am deeply in love with that word "whosoever." It is a splendid word. A person who kept many animals had some great dogs and some little ones, and in his eagerness to let them enter his house freely he had two holes cut in the door, one for the big dogs and another for the little dogs. You may well laugh, for the little dogs could surely have come in wherever there was room for the larger ones. This "whosoever" is the great opening, suitable for sinners of every size. "Whosoever liveth and believeth in me shall never die." Has any man a right to believe in Christ? The gospel gives every creature the right to believe in Christ, for we are bidden to preach it to every creature, with this command, "Hear, and your soul shall live." Every man has a right to believe in Christ, because he will be damned if he does not, and he must have a right to do that which will bring him into condemnation if he does it not. It is written, "He that believeth and is baptized shall be saved; but he that believeth not shall be damned," and that makes it clear that I, whoever I may be, as I have a right to endeavour to escape from damnation, have a right to avail myself of the blessed command, "Believe in the Lord Jesus Christ, and live." Oh that word "whosoever," that hole in the door for the big dog! Do not forget it! Come along with you, and put your trust in Christ. If you can only get linked with Christ you are a living man; if but a finger touches his garment's hem you are made whole. Only the touch of faith, and the virtue flows from him to you, and he is to you the Resurrection and the Life.

I desire you to notice that *there is no limit to this power.* Before I was ill this time, and even since, I have had to deal with such a swarm of despairing sinners, that if I have not pulled them up they have pulled me down. I have been trying to speak very large words for Christ when I have met with these disconsolate ones. I hear one say, "How far can Christ be life to a sinner? I feel myself to be utterly wrong, I am altogether wrong; there is nothing right about me: though I have eyes I cannot see, though I have ears I do not hear; if I have a hand I cannot use it; if I have a foot I cannot run with it—I seem altogether wrong." Yes, but if you believe in Christ, though you were still more wrong—that is to say, though you were dead, which is the wrongest state in which a man's body can be, —though you were dead yet shall you live. You look at the spiritual thermometer, and you say, "How low will the grace of God go? will it descend to summer heat? will it touch the freezing point? will it go to zero?" Yes, it will go below the lowest conceivable point,—lower than any instrument can indicate: it will go below the zero of death. If you believe in Jesus, though you are not only wrong, but dead, yet shall you live.

But, says another, "I feel so weak. I cannot understand, I cannot lay hold of things; I cannot pray. I cannot do anything. All I can do is feebly to trust in Jesus." All right! Though you had gone further than that, and were so weak as to be dead, yet should you live. Though the weakness had turned to a dire paralysis, that left you altogether without strength, yet it is written, "He that believeth in me, though he were dead, yet shall he live." "Oh, sir," says one, "I am so unfeeling." Mark you, these generally are the most feeling people in the world. "I am sorry every day because I cannot be sorry for my sin"— that is the way they talk; it is very absurd, but still very real to them. "Oh," cried one, "the earth shook, the sun was darkened, the rocks rent, the very dead came out of their graves at the death of Christ.

Of feeling all things show some sign
But this unfeeling heart of mine."

Yet if thou believest, unfeeling as thou art, thou livest; for if thou wert gone further than numbness to deadness, yet if thou believest in him thou shalt live.

But the poor creature fetches a sigh, and cries, "Sir, it is not only that I have no feeling, but I am become objectionable and obnoxious to everybody. I am a weariness to myself and to others. I am sure when I come to tell you my troubles you must wish me at Jericho, or somewhere else far away." Now, I admit that such a thought *has* occurred to us sometimes when we have been very busy, and some poor soul has grown prosy with rehearsing his seven-times-repeated miseries; but if you were to get more wearisome still, if you were to become so bad that people would as soon see a corpse as see you, yet remember Jesus says, "He that believeth in me, though he were dead, yet shall he live." Ay, if you went so far as to go in and out among men like an unquiet ghost, so that everybody got out of your way, it would not put you beyond the promise, "He that believeth in me, though he were dead, yet shall he live."

"Oh, sir, I have no hope; my case is quite hopeless!" Very well; but if you had got beyond that, so that you were dead, and could not even know you had no hope, yet if you believed in him you should live. "Oh, but I have tried everything, and there is nothing more for me to attempt. I have read books, I have spoken to Christians, and I am nothing bettered." No doubt it is quite so; but if you had even passed beyond that stage, so that you could not try anything more, yet if you did believe in Jesus you should live. Oh, the blessed power of faith! Nay, rather say the matchless power of him who is the Resurrection and the Life; for though the poor believer were dead, yet shall he live! Glory be to the Lord who works so wonderfully.

To conclude, if you once do believe in Christ, and come to live, there is this sweet reflection for you, "*Whosoever liveth and believeth in me shall never die.*" Here is a very literal translation—"And every one who lives and believes on me, in no wise shall die for ever." This is from "The Englishman's Greek New Testament," and nothing can be better.

The believer may pass through the natural change called death, as far as his body is concerned; but as for his soul it cannot die, for it is written, "I give unto my sheep eternal life; and they shall never perish, neither shall any man pluck them out of my hand." "He that believeth in me hath everlasting life." "The water that I shall give him shall be in him a well of water springing up into everlasting life." "He that believeth and is baptized shall be saved." These are not "ifs" and "buts," and faint hopes; but they are dead certainties, nay, living certainties, out of the mouth of the living Lord himself. You get the life of God in your soul, and you shall never die.

"Do you mean that I may do as I like, and live in sin?" No, I mean nothing of the sort; what right have you to impute such teaching as that to me? I mean that you shall not love sin and live in it, for that is death; but you shall live unto God. Your likes shall be so radically changed that you shall abhor evil all your days, and long to be holy as God is holy; and you shall be kept from transgression, and shall not go back to wallow in sin. If in some evil hour you backslide, yet shall you be restored; and the main current of your life shall be from the hour of your regeneration towards God, and holiness, and heaven. The angels that rejoiced over you when you repented made no mistake; they shall go on to rejoice till they welcome you amidst the everlasting songs and Hallelujahs of the blessed at the right hand of God. Believest thou this? Come, poor soul, believest thou this? Who are you? That does not matter, you can get into the "whosoever." That ark will hold all God's Noahs. What have you done? One said to me the other day, "I should like to tell you some of my sins!" I answered quickly, "*You* would like; *I* would not; I have enough of my own without being infected with yours." What is any man that he should have the filth of another man's drains poured into his ear? No, no: confess to God, but not to man unless you have wronged him, and confession of the wrong is due to him.

"Ah," saith one, "you don't know what I am." No, and I don't want to know what you are; but if you are so far gone that there seems to be not even a ghost of a shade of a shadow of a hope anywhere about you, yet if you believe in Jesus you shall live. Trust the Lord Jesus Christ, for he is worthy to be trusted. Throw yourself upon him, and he will carry you in his bosom. Cast your whole weight upon his atonement; it will bear the strain. Hang on him as the vessel hangs on the nail, and seek no other support. Depend upon Christ with all your might just as you now are, and as the Lord liveth you shall live, and as Christ reigneth you shall reign over sin, and as Christ cometh to glory you shall partake of that glory for ever and ever.

IX

THE HOLY SPIRIT GLORIFYING CHRIST

"He shall glorify me: for he shall receive of mine, and shall shew it unto you."—John 16: 14.

THE needs of spiritual men are very great, but they cannot be greater than the power of the Divine Trinity is able to meet. We have one God,—Father, Son, and Holy Ghost,—One in Three, and Three in One; and that blessed Trinity in Unity gives himself to sinners that they may be saved. In the first place, every good thing that a sinner wants is in the Father. The prodigal son was wise when he said, "I will arise and go to my father." Every good and perfect gift comes from God the Father, the first Person in the blessed Trinity, because every good gift and every perfect gift can only be found in him. But the needy soul says, "How shall I get to the Father? He is infinitely above me. How shall I reach up to him?" In order that you might obtain the blessings of grace, God was in Christ Jesus, the second ever-blessed Person of the Sacred Trinity. Let me read you part of the verse that follows my text: "All things that the Father hath are mine." So, you see, everything is in the Father first; and the Father puts all things into Christ. "It pleased the Father that in him should all fulness dwell" (Col. 1: 19). Now you can get to Christ because he is man as well as God. He is "over all, God blessed for ever;" but he came into this world, was born of the Virgin Mary, lived a life of poverty, "suffered under Pontius Pilate, was crucified, dead, and buried." He is the conduit-pipe, conveying to us all blessings from the Father. In the Gospel of John we read, "Of his fulness have all we received, and grace for grace." Thus you see the Father, with every good thing in himself, putting all fulness into the Mediator, the Man Christ Jesus who is also the Son of God.

Now I hear a poor soul say, "But I cannot even get to Christ; I am blind and lame. If I could get to him, he would open my eyes; but I am so lame that I cannot run or even walk to him. If I could get to him, he would give me strength; but I lie as one dead. I cannot see Christ, or tell where to find him." Here comes in the work of the Holy Spirit, the third Person of the blessed Unity. It is his office to take of the things of Christ, and show them unto saints and sinners, too. We cannot see them, but we shall see them fast enough when he shows them to us. Our sin puts a veil between us and Christ. The Holy Spirit comes and takes the veil away from our heart, and then we see Christ. It is the Holy Spirit's office to come between us and Christ, to lead us to Christ, even as the Son of God comes between us and the Father, to lead us to the Father; so that we have the whole Trinity uniting to save a sinner, the Triune God bowing down out of heaven for the salvation of rebellious men. Every time we dismiss you from this house of prayer, we pronounce upon you the blessing of the Sacred Trinity: "May the grace of our Lord Jesus Christ, and the love of God, and the communion of the Holy Ghost be with you!" And you want all that to make a sinner into a saint, and to keep a saint from going back to be a sinner again. The whole blessed Godhead, Father, Son, and Holy Spirit, must work upon every soul that is to be saved.

See how divinely they work together, how the Father glorifies the Son, how the Holy Spirit glorifies Jesus, how both the Holy Spirit and the Lord Jesus glorify the Father! These Three are One, sweetly uniting in the salvation of the chosen seed.

Now our work is to speak of the Holy Spirit. Oh, what a blessed Person he is; not merely a sacred influence, but a Divine Person, "very God of very God." He is the Spirit of holiness to be reverenced, to be spoken of with delight, yet with trembling; for, remember, there is a sin against the Holy Ghost. A word spoken against the Son of man may be forgiven, but blasphemy against the Holy Ghost (whatever that may be, I know not), is put down as a sin beyond the line of divine forgiveness. Therefore reverence, honour, and worship God the Holy Spirit, in whom lies the only hope that any of us can ever have of seeing Jesus, and so of seeing God the Father.

First, I shall try to speak of *what the Holy Spirit does:* "He shall receive of mine, and shall shew it unto you;" secondly, I shall seek to set forth *what the Holy Spirit aims at:* "He shall glorify me: for he shall receive of mine, and shall shew it unto you;" and, thirdly, I shall explain how *in both these things he acts as the Comforter*, for we read, in the seventh verse, that our Saviour says, "If I go not away, the Comforter will not come unto you;" and it is of the Comforter that he says, "He shall glorify me; for he shall receive of mine, and shall shew it unto you."

First, we are to consider WHAT THE HOLY SPIRIT DOES. Jesus says, "He shall receive of mine, and shall shew it unto you."

The Holy Ghost, then, *deals with the things of Christ.* How I wish that all Christ's ministers would imitate the Holy Spirit in this respect! When you are dealing with the things of Christ, you are on Holy Ghost ground; you are following the track of the Holy Spirit. Does the Holy Ghost deal with science? What is science? Another name for the ignorance of men. Does the Holy Ghost deal with politics? What are politics? Another name for every man getting as much as he can out of the nation. Does the Holy Ghost deal with these things? Nay, "He shall receive of mine." The Holy Ghost will leave you if you go gadding about after these insignificant trifles! He will leave you, if you aim at magnifying yourself, and your wisdom, and your plans; for the Holy Spirit is taken up with the things of Christ. "He shall receive of mine, and shall shew it unto you." I like what Mr. Wesley said to his preachers. "Leave other things alone," said he; "you are called to win souls." So I believe it is with all true preachers. We may let other things alone. The Holy Ghost, who is our Teacher, will own and bless us if we keep to his line of things. O preacher of the gospel, what canst thou receive like the things of Christ? And what canst thou talk of so precious to the souls of men as the things of Christ? Therefore, follow thou the Holy Ghost in dealing with the things of Christ.

Next, the Holy Spirit *deals with feeble men.* "He shall receive of mine, and shall shew it unto you." "Unto you." He is not above dealing with simple minds. He comes to those who have no training, no education, and he takes the things of Christ, and shows them to such minds. The greatest mind of man that was ever created was a poor puny thing compared with the infinite mind of God. We may boast about the great capacity of the human intellect; but what a narrow and contracted thing it is at its utmost width! So, for the Holy Spirit to come and teach the little mind of man, is a great condescension. But we see the great condescension of the Holy Ghost even more when we read, "Not many wise men after the flesh, not many mighty, not many noble, are called;" (1 Cor. 1: 26), and when we hear the Saviour say, "I thank thee, O Father, Lord of heaven and earth, because thou hast hid these things from the wise and prudent, and hast revealed them unto babes" (Matt. 11: 25). The Holy Ghost takes of the things of Christ, and shows them to those who are babes compared with the wise men of this world. The Lord Jesus might have selected princes to be his apostles; he might have gathered together twelve of the greatest kings of the earth, or at least twelve senators from Rome; but he did not so. He took fishermen, and men belonging to that class, to be the pioneers of his kingdom; and God the Holy Ghost takes of the things of Christ, high and sublime as they are, and shows them unto men like these apostles were, men ready to follow where the Lord led them, and to learn what the Lord taught them.

If you think of the condescension of the Holy Spirit in taking of the things of Christ, and showing them unto us, you will not talk any more about coming down to the level of children when you talk to them. I remember a young man, who was a great fool, but did not know it, and therefore was all the greater fool, once, speaking to children, said, "My dear children, it takes a great deal to bring a great mind down to your capacities." You cannot show me a word of Christ of that kind. Where does the Holy Ghost ever talk about its being a great come-down for him to teach children, or to teach us? Nay; but he glorifies Christ by taking of his things, and showing them unto us, even such poor ignorant scholars as we are.

If I understand what is meant here, I think that it means, first, that the Holy Ghost *helps us to understand the words of Christ.* If we will study the teaching of the Saviour, it must be with the Holy Spirit as the light to guide us; he will show us what Christ meant by the words he uttered. We shall not lose ourselves in the Saviour's verbiage; but we shall get at the inner meaning of Christ's mind, and be instructed therein; for the Lord Jesus says, "He shall receive of mine, and shall shew it unto you." A sermon of Christ, even a single word of Christ, set in the light of the Holy Spirit, shines like a diamond; nay, like a fixed star, with light that is never dim. Happy men and happy women who read the words of Christ in the light shed upon them by the Holy Ghost! But I do not think that this is all that the text means.

It means this: "Not only shall he reveal my words, but my *things;*" for Christ says, "All things that the Father hath are mine: therefore said I, that he shall take of mine, and shall shew it unto you."

The Holy Ghost takes the *nature* of Christ, and shows it unto us. It is easy to say, "I believe him to be God and man;" but the point is, to apprehend that he is God, and therefore able to save, and even to work impossibilities; and to believe that he is man, and therefore feels for you, sympathizes with you, and therefore is a brother born to help you in your adversities. May the Holy Ghost make you see the God-Man now. May he show you the humanity and the Deity of Christ, as they are most blessedly united in his adorable Person; and you will be greatly comforted thereby.

The Holy Ghost shows to us the *offices* of Christ. He is Prophet, Priest, King. Especially to you, sinner, Christ is a Saviour. Now, if you know that he takes up the work of saving sinners, and that it is his business to save men, why, then, surely you will have confidence in him, and not be afraid to come to him! If I wanted my shoes mended, I should not take my hat off when I went into a cobbler's shop, and say, "Please excuse me. May I beg you to be so good as to mend my shoes?" No, it is his trade: it is his business. He is glad to see me. "What do you want, sir?" says he; and he is glad of work. And when Christ puts over his door, "Saviour," I, wanting to be saved, go to him, for I believe that he knows his calling, and that he can carry it out, and that he will be glad to see me, and that I shall not be more glad to be saved than he will be to save me. I want you to catch that idea. If the Holy Spirit will show you that, it will bring you very near to joy and peace.

May the Holy Ghost also show you Christ's *engagements!* He has come into the world engaged to save sinners. He pledged himself to the Father to bring many sons unto glory, and he must do it. He has bound himself to his Father, as the Surety of the covenant, that he will bring sinners into reconciliation with

God. May the Holy Ghost show that fact to you; and right gladly you will leap into the Saviour's arms!

It is very sweet when the Holy Spirit shows us the *love* of Christ,—how intensely he loves men, how he loved them of old, for his delights were with the sons of men, not because he had redeemed them, but he redeemed them because he loved them, and delighted in them. Christ has had an eternal love to his people.

> *His heart is made of tenderness,*
> *His bowels melt with love.*

It is his heaven to bring men to heaven. It is his glory to bring sons to glory. He is never so happy as when he is receiving sinners. But if the Holy Ghost will show you the depth and the height, the length and the breadth, of the love of Christ to sinners, it will go a long way towards bringing all who are in this house to accept the Saviour.

But when the Holy Ghost shows you the *mercy* of Christ; how willingly he forgives; how he passes by iniquity, transgression, and sin; how he casts your sins into the sea, throws them behind God's back, puts them away for ever; ah! when you see this, then will your hearts be won to him.

Specially I would desire the Holy Ghost to show you the *blood* of Christ. A Spirit-taught view of the blood of Christ is the most wonderful sight that ever a weeping eye beheld. There is your sin, your wicked, horrible, damnable sin; but Christ comes into the world, and takes the sin, and suffers in your room and place and stead; and the blood of such an One as he, perfect Man and infinite God—such blood as was poured out on Calvary's tree,—must take away sin. Oh, for a sight of it! If any of you are now despairing, and the Holy Ghost will take of the blood of Christ, and show it unto you, despair will have no place in you any longer. It must be gone, for "the blood of Jesus Christ his Son cleanseth us from all sin," (1 John 1: 7), and he that believeth in him is forgiven all his iniquities.

And if the Holy Ghost will also take of the *prayers* of Christ, and show them unto you, what a sight you will have! Christ on earth, praying till he gets into a bloody sweat; Christ in heaven, praying with all his glorious vestments on, accepted by the Father, glorified at the Father's right hand, and making intercession for transgressors, praying for you, praying for all who come to God by him, and able, therefore, to save them to the uttermost; this is the sight you will have. A knowledge of the intercession of Christ for guilty men is enough to make despair flee away once for all. I can only tell you these things; but if the Holy Ghost will take of them, and show them unto you, oh, you will have joy and peace through believing!

One thing I must add, however, and then I will leave this point, upon which we could dilate for six months, I think; that is, that *whatever the Holy Ghost shows you, you may have.* Do you see that? He takes of the things of Christ, and shows them to us; but why? Not as a boy at school does to one of his companions when he is teasing him. I remember often seeing it done. He pulls out of his pocket a beautiful apple, and shows it to his schoolmate. "There," says he, "do you see that apple?" Is he going to say, "Now I am going to give you a piece of it"? No, not he. He only shows him the apple just to tantalize him. Now, it would be blasphemy to imagine that the Holy Ghost would show you the things of Christ, and then say, "You cannot have them." No, whatever he shows you, you may have. Whatever you see in Christ, you may have. Whatever the Holy Ghost makes you to see in the person and work of the Lord Jesus, you may have it. And he shows it to you on purpose that you may have it, for he is no Tantalus to mock us with the sight of a blessing beyond our reach; he waits to bless us. Lay that thought up in your heart; it may help you some day, if not now. You remember what God said to Jacob, "The land whereon thou liest, to thee will I give it"? If you find any promise in this Book, and you dare to lie down upon it, it is yours. If you can just lie down and rest on it, it is yours; for it was not put there for you to rest on it without its being fulfilled to you. Only stretch yourself on any covenant blessing, and it is yours for ever. God help us so to do!

But now, secondly, let us consider WHAT THE HOLY SPIRIT AIMS AT. Well, he aims at this, Jesus says, "He shall glorify me." When he shows us the things of Christ, his object is to glorify Christ. The Holy Spirit's object is to make Christ appear to be great and glorious to you and to me. The Lord Jesus Christ is infinitely glorious; and even the Holy Ghost cannot make him glorious except to our apprehension; but his desire is that we may see and know more of Christ, that we may honour him more, and glorify him more.

Well, how does the Holy Spirit go about this work? In this simple way, by *showing us the things of Christ*. Is not this a blessedly simple fact, that when even the Holy Ghost intends to glorify Christ, all that he does is to show us Christ? Well, but does he not put fine words together, and weave a spell of eloquence? No; he simply shows us Christ. Now, if you wanted to praise Jesus Christ, what would you have to do? Why, you would only have to speak of him as he is,—holy, blessed, glorious! You would show him, as it were, in order to praise him, for there is no glorifying Christ except by making him to be seen. Then he has the glory that rightly belongs to him. No words are wanted, no descriptions are needed. "He shall glorify me: for he shall receive of mine, and shall shew it unto you."

And is it not strange that Christ should be glorified by his *being shown to you? To you*. Perhaps you are saying, "I am a nobody." Yes, but Christ is glorified by being shown to you. "Oh, but I am very poor, very illiterate, and besides, very wicked!" Yes, but Christ is glorified by being shown to you. Now, a great king or a great queen would not be rendered much more illustrious by being shown to a little Sunday School girl, or exhibited to a crossing-sweeper boy. At least, they would not think so; but Christ does not act as an earthly monarch might. He reckons it to be his glory for the poorest pair of eyes that ever wept to look by faith upon him. He reckons it to be his greatest honour for the poorest man, the poorest woman, or the poorest child that ever lived, to see him in the light in which the Holy Ghost sets him. Is not this a blessed truth? I put it very simply and briefly. The Holy Ghost, you see, glorifies Christ by showing him to sinners. Therefore, if you want to glorify Christ, do the same. Do not go and write a ponderous tome, and put fine words together. Tell sinners, in simple language, what Christ is. "I cannot praise him," says one. You do not want to praise him. Say what he is. If a man says to me, "Show me the sun," do I say, "Well, you must wait till I strike a match and light a candle, and then I will show you the sun"? That would be ridiculous, would it not? And for our candles to be held up to show Christ, is absurd. Tell what he is. Tell what he is to you. Tell what he did for you. Tell what he did for sinners. That is all. "He shall glorify me: for he shall receive of mine, and shall shew it unto you."

I will not say more on this point, except that, if any of us are to glorify Christ, we must talk much of him. We must tell what the Holy Spirit has told to us; and we must pray the Holy Spirit to bless to the minds of men the truth we speak, by enabling them to see Christ as the Spirit reveals him.

But now, thirdly, in both of these things—showing unto us the things of Christ, and glorifying Christ—, THE HOLY SPIRIT IS A COMFORTER. Gracious Spirit, be a Comforter now to some poor struggling ones, by showing them the things of Christ, and by glorifying him in their salvation!

First, in showing to men the things of Christ, the Holy Spirit is a Comforter. *There is no comfort like a sight of Christ.* Sinner, your only comfort must lie in your Saviour, in his precious blood, and in his resurrection from the dead. Look that way, man! If you look inside, you will never find any comfort there. Look where the Holy Ghost looks. "He shall receive of mine, and shall shew it unto you." When a thing is shown to you, it is meant for you to look at it. If you want real comfort, I will tell you where to look, namely, to the person and work of the Lord Jesus Christ. "Oh!" say you, "but I am a wretched sinner." I know you are. You are a great deal worse than you think you are. "Oh, but I think myself the worst that ever lived." Yes, you are worse than that! You do not know half your depravity. You are worse than you ever dreamed that you were. But that is not where to look for comfort. "I am brutish," says one; "I am proud; I am self-righteous; I am envious; I have everything in me that is bad, sir, and if I have a little bit that is good sometimes, it is gone before I can see it. I am just lost, ruined, and undone." That is quite true; but I never told you to look there. Your comfort lies in this, "He shall receive of mine,"—that is, of Christ's,—"and shall shew it unto you." Your hope of transformation, of gaining a new character altogether, of eternal life, lies in Christ, who quickeneth the dead, and maketh all things new. Look away from self, and look to Christ, for he alone can save you.

A sight of Christ is the destruction of despair. "Oh, but the devil tells me that I shall be cast into hell! There is no hope for me." What matters it what the devil tells you? He was a liar from the beginning. Let him say what he likes; but if you will look away to Christ, there will be an end of the devil's power over you. If the Holy Ghost shows you what Christ came to do on the cross, and what he is doing on his throne in heaven, there will be an end to these troublous thoughts from Satan, and you will be comforted.

Dear child of God, are you *in sorrow now*? May the Holy Ghost take of the things of Christ, and show them unto you! There is an end to sorrow when you see Jesus, for sorrow itself is so sweetly sanctified by the companionship of Christ which it brings to you, that you will be glad to drink of his cup and to be baptized with his baptism.

Are you *in want*, without even a place where to lay your head? So, too, was he. "The Son of man hath not where to lay his head." Go to him with your trouble. He will help you to bear your poverty. He will help you to get out of it, for he is able to help you in temporal trials as well as in spiritual ones. Therefore go you to Christ. All power is given unto him in heaven and in earth. Nothing is too hard for the Lord. Go your way to him, and a sight of him will give you comfort.

Are you *persecuted?* Well, a sight of the thorn-crowned brow will take the thorn out of persecution. Are you very, very low? I think that you have all heard the story I am about to tell you, but some of you have, perhaps, forgotten it. Many years ago, when this great congregation first met in the Surrey Music Hall, and the terrible accident occurred when many persons were either killed or wounded in the panic, I did my best to hold the people together till I heard that some were dead, and then I broke down like a man stunned, and for a fortnight or so I had little reason left. I felt so broken in heart that I thought that I should never be able to face a congregation again; and I went down to a friend's house, a few miles away, to be very quiet and still. I was walking round his garden, and I well remember the spot, and even the time, when this passage came to me, "Him hath God exalted with his right hand to be a Prince and a Saviour;" and this thought came into my mind at once, "You are only a soldier in the great King's army, and you may die in a ditch; but it does not matter what becomes of you as long as your King is exalted. *He*—HE is glorious. God hath highly exalted him." You have heard of the old French soldiers when they lay a-dying. If the emperor came by, when they were ready to expire, they would just raise themselves up, and gave one more cheer for their beloved leader. "*Vive l'Empereur!*" would be their dying words. And so I just thought, "*He* is exalted. What matters it about me?" and in a moment my reason was perfectly restored. I was as clear as possible. I went into the house, had family prayer, and came back to preach to my congregation on the following Sabbath, restored only by having looked to Jesus, and having seen that he was glorious. If he is to the front, what does it matter what happens to us?

But now, lastly, *when Christ is glorified in the heart, he acts as a Comforter, too.* I believe that we should not have half the trouble that we have if we thought more of Christ. The fact is, that we think so much of ourselves that we get troubled. But someone says, "But I have so many troubles." Why should you not have a great many troubles? Who are you that you should not have troubles? "Oh, but I have had loss after loss which you do not know of!" Very likely. I do not know of your losses, but is it any wonder that you should have them? "Oh!" says one, "I seem to be kicked about like a foot-ball." Why should you not be? What are you? "Oh!" said one poor penitent to me the other night, "for me to come to Christ, sir, after my past life, seems so mean." I said, "Yes, so it is; but, then, you *are* mean. It was a mean business of the prodigal son to come home, and eat his father's bread and the fatted calf after he had spent his substance in riotous living." It was a mean thing, was it not? But, then, the father did not think it mean. He clasped him to his bosom, and welcomed him home. Come along, you mean sinners, you that have served the devil, and now want to run away from him! Steal away from Satan at once, for my Lord is ready to receive you. You have no idea how willing he is to welcome you. He is so ready to forgive, that you have not yet guessed how much sin he can forgive. "All manner of sin and blasphemy shall be forgiven unto men." Up to your necks in filth, in your very hearts saturated with the foulest iniquity; yet, if you come to Christ, he will wash you whiter than snow.

Have exalted ideas of Christ. Oh, if a man will but have great thoughts of Christ, he shall then find his troubles lessening, and his sins disappearing! You have been putting Christ on a wrong scale altogether, I see. Perhaps even you people of God have not thought of Christ as you ought to do. I have heard of a certain commander who had led his troops into a rather difficult position. He knew what he was at, but the soldiers did not all know; and there would be a battle on the morrow. So he thought that he would go round from tent to tent, and hear what the soldiers said. He listened, and there was one of them saying to his fellows, "See what a mess we are in now! Do you see, we have only so many cavalry, and so many infantry, and we have only a small quantity of artillery. And on the other side there are so many thousands against us, so strong, so mighty, that we shall be cut to pieces in the morning." And the general drew aside the canvas, and there they saw him standing, and he said, "How many do you count *me* for?" He had won every battle that he had ever been engaged in. He was the conqueror of conquerors. "How many do you count me for?" O souls, you have never counted Christ for what he is! You have put down your sins, but you have never counted what kind of a Christ he is who has come to save you. Rather do like Luther, who says that, when the devil came to him, he brought him a long sheet containing a list of his sins, or of a great number of them, and Luther said to him, "Is that all?" "No," said the devil. "Well, go and fetch some more, then." Away went Satan to bring him another long list, as long as your arm. Said Luther, "Is that all?" "Oh, no!" said the devil, "I have more yet." "Well, go and bring them all," said Luther. "Fetch them all out, the whole list of them." Then it was a very long black list. I think that I have heard that it would have gone round the world twice. I know that mine would. Well, what did Luther say when he saw them all? He said, "Write at the bottom of them, 'The blood of Jesus Christ his Son cleanseth us from all sin!'" It does not matter how long the list is when you write those blessed words at the end of it. The sins are all gone then. So, though your sins are very many,—if you have trusted Jesus,—your sins are all gone, drowned in the Red Sea of your Saviour's blood, and Christ is glorified in your salvation. May God the Holy Ghost bring every unsaved one here to repentance and faith in our Lord Jesus Christ! The Lord bless every one of you, for his name's sake!

X

THE INDWELLING AND OUTFLOWING OF THE HOLY SPIRIT

"He that believeth on me, as the scripture hath said, out of his belly shall flow rivers of living water. (But this spake he of the Spirit, which they that believe on him should receive: for the Holy Ghost was not yet given; because that Jesus was not yet glorified.)"—John 7: 38, 39.

"Nevertheless I tell you the truth; It is expedient for you that I go away: for if I go not away, the Comforter will not come unto you; but if I depart, I will send him unto you."—John 16: 7.

IT is essential that we should worship the living and true God. It will be ill for us if it can be said, "Ye worship ye know not what." "Thou shalt worship the Lord thy God, and him only shalt thou serve" (Matt. 4: 10). The heathen err from this command by multiplying gods, and making this and that image to be the object of their adoration. Their excess runs to gross superstition and idolatry. I fear that sometimes we who "profess and call ourselves Christians" err in exactly the opposite direction. Instead of worshipping more than God I fear we worship less than God. This appears when we forget to pay due adoration to the Holy Spirit of God. The true God is triune, Father, Son, and Holy Spirit; and though there be but one God yet that one God has manifested himself to us in the trinity of his sacred persons. If, then, I worship the Father and the Son, but forget or neglect to adore the Holy Spirit, I worship less than God. While the poor heathen in his ignorance goes far beyond and transgresses, I must take care lest I fall short and fail too. What a grievous thing it will be if we do not pay that loving homage and reverence to the Holy Spirit which is so justly his due. May it not be the fact that we enjoy less of his power and see less of his working in the world because the church of God has not been sufficiently mindful of him? It is a blessed thing to preach the work of Jesus Christ, but it is an evil thing to omit the work of the Holy Ghost; for the work of the Lord Jesus itself is no blessing to that man who does not know the work of the Holy Spirit. There is the ransom price, but it is only through the Spirit that we know the redemption: there is the precious blood, but it is as though the fountain had never been filled unless the Spirit of God lead us with repenting faith to wash therein.

You that are believers have the most forcible reasons to hold the Holy Ghost in the highest esteem; for what are you now without him? What were you, and what would you still have been, if it had not been for his gracious work upon you? He quickened you, else you had not been in the living family of God to-day. He gave you understanding that you might know the truth, else would you have been as ignorant as the carnal world is at this hour. It was he that awakened your conscience, convincing you of sin: it was he that gave you abhorrence of sin, and led you to repent: it was he that taught you to believe, and made you see that glorious Person who is to be believed, even Jesus, the Son of God. The Spirit has wrought in you your faith and love and hope, and every grace. There is not a jewel upon the neck of your soul which he did not place there.

Notwithstanding all that the Spirit of God has already done in us, it is very possible that we have missed a large part of the blessing which he is willing to give, for he is able to "do exceeding abundantly above all that we ask or think" (Eph. 3: 20). We have already come to Jesus, and we have drunk of the life-giving stream: our thirst is quenched, and we are made to live in him. Is this all? Now that we are living in him, and rejoicing to do so, have we come to the end of the matter? Assuredly not. We have reached as far as that first exhortation of the Master, "If any man thirst, let him come unto me and drink": but do you think that the generality of the church of God have ever advanced to the next, "He that believeth on me, as the Scripture hath said, out of his belly shall flow rivers of living water"? I think I am not going beyond the grievous truth if I say that only here and there will you find men and women who have believed up to that point.

Their thirst is quenched, as I have said, and they live, and because Jesus lives they shall live also, but health and vigour they have not: they have life, but they have not life more abundantly. They have little life with which to act upon others: they have no energy welling up and overflowing to go streaming out of them like rivers. They have not thought it possible perhaps, or thinking it possible they have not imagined it possible to themselves; or believing it possible to themselves they have not aspired to it, but they have stopped short of the fullest blessing.

Thus I introduce you to my texts, and by their guidance we will enter upon the further consideration of the operations of the Holy Spirit, especially of those to which we would aspire.

We will commence with the remark that THE WORK OF THE SPIRIT IS INTIMATELY CONNECTED WITH THE WORK OF CHRIST. It is a great pity when persons preach the Holy Spirit's work so as to obscure the work of Christ; and I have known some do that, for they have held up before the sinner's eye the inward experience of believers, instead of lifting up first and foremost the crucified Saviour to whom we must look and live. The gospel is not "Behold the Spirit of God" but "Behold the Lamb of God." It is an equal pity when Christ is so preached that the Holy Spirit is ignored; as if faith in Jesus prevented the necessity of the new birth, and imputed righteousness rendered imparted righteousness needless. Have I not often reminded you that in the third chapter of John, where Jesus taught Nicodemus the doctrine, "Except a man be born again of water and of the Spirit he cannot enter the kingdom of heaven," we also read those blessed words, "And as Moses lifted up the serpent in the wilderness, even so must the Son of man be lifted up: that whosoever believeth in him should not perish, but have eternal life. For God so loved the world, that he gave his only begotten Son, that whosoever believeth in him should not perish, but have everlasting life." The necessity for regeneration by the Spirit is there put very clearly, and so is the free promise that those who trust in Jesus shall be saved. This is what we ought to do: we must take care to let both these truths stand out most distinctly with equal prominence.

They are so joined together that, first of all, *the Holy Spirit was not given until Jesus had been glorified.* Carefully note our first text; it is a very striking one: "This spake he of the Spirit which they that believe on him should receive, for the Holy Ghost was not yet." The word "given" is not in the original: it is inserted by the translators to help out the sense, and they were perhaps wise in making such an addition, but the words are more forcible by themselves. How strong the statement, "For the Holy Ghost was not yet." Of course, we none of us dream that the Holy Spirit was not yet existing, for he is eternal and self-existent, being most truly God, but he was not yet in fellowship with man to the full extent in which he now is since Jesus Christ is glorified. The near and dear intercourse of God with man which is expressed by the indwelling of the Spirit could not take place till redeeming work was done and the Redeemer was exalted. As far as men were concerned, and the fulness of the blessing was concerned, indicated by the outflowing rivers of living water, the Spirit of God was not yet. "Oh," say you, "but was not the Spirit of God in the church in the wilderness, and with the saints of God in all former ages?" I answer, Certainly, but not in the manner in which the Spirit of God now resides in the church of Jesus Christ.

You read of the prophets, and of one and another gracious man, that the Spirit of God came upon them, seized them, moved them, spake by them; but he did not dwell in them. His operations upon men were a coming and a going: they were carried away by the Spirit of God, and came under his power, but the Spirit of God did not rest upon them or abide in them. Occasionally the sacred endowment of the Spirit of God came upon them, but they knew not "the communion of the Holy Ghost." As a French pastor very sweetly puts it, "He appeared unto men; he did not incarnate himself in man. His action was intermittent: he went and came, like the dove which Noah sent forth from the ark, and which went to and fro, finding no rest; while in the new dispensation he dwells, he abides in the heart, as the dove, his emblem, which John the Baptist saw descending and alighting upon the head of Jesus. Affianced of the soul, the Spirit went off to see his betrothed, but was not yet one with her; the marriage was not consummated until the Pentecost, after the glorification of Jesus Christ."

You know how our Lord puts it, "He dwelleth with you and shall be in you." That indwelling is another thing from being *with* us. The Holy Spirit was with the Apostles in the days when Jesus was with them; but he was not in them in the sense in which he filled them at and after the Day of Pentecost. The operations of the Spirit of God before our Lord's ascension were not according to the full measure of the Gospel, but now the

Spirit of God has been poured upon us from on high; now he has descended, and now he abides in the midst of the church, and now we enter into him and are baptized into the Holy Ghost, while he enters into us and makes our bodies to be his temples. Jesus said, "I will send you another Comforter, which shall abide with you for ever;" not coming and going, but remaining in the midst of the church. This shows how intimately the gift of the Holy Ghost is connected with our Lord Jesus Christ, inasmuch as in the fullest sense of his indwelling the Holy Ghost could not be with us until Christ had been glorified. It has been well observed that our Lord sent out seventy evangelists to preach the Gospel, even as he had aforetime sent out the twelve; and no doubt they preached with great zeal and produced much stir; but the Holy Ghost never took the trouble to preserve one of their sermons, or even the notes of one. I have not the slightest doubt that they were very crude and incomplete, showing more of human zeal than of divine unction, and hence they are forgotten; but no sooner had the Holy Spirit fallen than Peter's first sermon is recorded, and henceforth we have frequent notes of the utterances of apostles, deacons, and evangelists. There was an abiding fulness, and an overflowing of blessing, out of the souls of the saints after the Lord was glorified, which was not existing among men before that time.

Observe, too, that the Holy Spirit was given after the ascent of our divine Lord into his glory, partly *to make that ascent the more renowned.* When he ascended up on high he led captivity captive and gave gifts to men. These gifts were men in whom the Holy Spirit dwelt, who preached the gospel unto the nations. The shedding of the Holy Spirit upon the assembled disciples on that memorable day was the glorification of the risen Christ upon the earth. I know not in what way the Father could have made the glory of heaven so effectually to flow from the heights of the New Jerusalem and to come streaming down among the sons of men as by giving that chief of all gifts, the gift of the Holy Spirit when the Lord had risen and gone into his glory. With emphasis may I say of the Spirit of Pentecost that he glorified Christ by descending at such a time. What grander celebration could there have been? Heaven rang with hosannahs, and earth echoed the joy. The descending Spirit is the noblest testimony among men to the glory of the ascended Redeemer.

Was not the Spirit of God also sent at that time *as an evidence of our divine Master's acceptance?* Did not the Father thus say to the church, "My Son has finished the work, and has fully entered into his glory; therefore give I you of the Holy Spirit"? If you would know what a harvest is to come of the sowing of the bloody sweat and of the death wounds, see the first fruits. Behold how the Holy Spirit is given, himself to be the first fruits, the earnest of the glory which shall yet be revealed in us. I want no better attestation from God of the finished work of Jesus than this blazing, flaming seal of tongues of fire upon the heads of the disciples. He must have done his work, or such a boon as this would not have come from it.

Moreover, if you desire to see how the work of the Spirit comes to us in connection with the work of Christ, recollect that *it is the Spirit's work to bear witness of Jesus Christ.* He does not take of a thousand different matters and show them to us, but he shall take "of mine," saith Christ, "and he shall show them unto you." The Spirit of God is engaged in a service in which the Lord Jesus Christ is the beginning and the end. He comes to men that they may come to Jesus. Hence he comes to convince us of sin that he may reveal the great sacrifice of sin: he comes to convince us of righteousness that we may see the righteousness of Christ; and of judgment that we may be prepared to meet him when he shall come to judge the quick and dead. Do not think that the Spirit of God has come or ever will come among us to teach us a new gospel, or something other than is written in the Scriptures. Men come to me with their fudges and fancies, and tell me that they were revealed to them by the Holy Spirit. I abhor their blasphemous impertinence, and refuse to listen to them for a minute. They tell me this and that absurdity, and then father it upon the Spirit of wisdom. It is enough to try our patience to hear their foolish ravings; but to find the Holy Spirit charged with them is more than we can bear. We have tests and judgments by which to know whether they who claim to speak by the Holy Spirit do so or not: for the testimony of the Spirit is ever most honourable to our Lord Jesus Christ, and does not concern itself with the trifles of time and the follies of the flesh.

It is by the Gospel of Jesus Christ that the Spirit of God works in the hearts of men. "Faith cometh by hearing, and hearing by the word of God" (Rom. 10: 17): the Holy Spirit uses the hearing of the word of God for the conviction, conversion, consolation, and sanctification of men. His usual and ordinary method of operation is to fasten upon the mind the things of God, and to put life and force into the consideration of them. He revives in men's memories things that have long been forgotten, and he frequently makes these the means of affecting the heart and conscience. The men can hardly recollect hearing these truths, but still they were heard by them at some time or other. Saving truths are such matters as are contained in their substance in the word of God, and lie within the range of the teaching, or the person, or work, or offices of our Lord Jesus Christ. It is the Spirit's one business here below to reveal Christ to us and in us, and to that work he steadily adheres.

Moreover, *the Holy Spirit's work is to conform us to the likeness of Jesus Christ.* He is not working us to this or that human ideal, but he is working us into the likeness of Christ that he may be the first-born among many brethren. Jesus Christ is that standard and model to which the Spirit of God by his sanctifying processes is bringing us till Christ be formed in us the hope of glory.

Evermore it is for the glory of Jesus that the Spirit of God works. He works not for the glory of a church or of a community: he works not for the honour of a man or for the distinction of a sect: his one great object is to glorify Christ. "He shall glorify me" is our Saviour's declaration, and when he takes of the things of Christ and shows them unto us, we are led more and more to reverence and love and adore our blessed Lord Jesus Christ.

I will not detain you longer with this. You will see how the works of Jesus and of the Spirit are joined together indissolubly, so that we may neither set the work of Jesus before the work of the Spirit nor the work of the Spirit before the work of Jesus, but we are glad to joy in both and to make much of them. As we delight in the Father's love and the grace of our Lord Jesus, so do we equally rejoice in the communion of the Holy Ghost, and these three agree in one.

We will now advance another step, and here we shall need our second text. THE OPERATIONS OF THE HOLY SPIRIT ARE OF INCOMPARABLE VALUE. They are of such incomparable value that the very best thing we can think of was not thought to be so precious as these are. Our Lord himself says, "It is expedient for you that I go away: for if I go not away, the Comforter will not come unto you." The Presence of Jesus Christ was of inestimable value to his disciples, and yet it was not such an advantage to his servants as the indwelling of the Holy Spirit. Is not this a wonderful statement? Well might our Lord preface it by saying, "Now I tell you the truth," as if he felt that they would find it a hard saying, for a hard saying it is. Consider for a moment what Christ was to his disciples while he was here, and then see what must be the value of the Spirit's operations when it is expedient that they should lose all that blessing in order to receive the Spirit of God. Our Lord Jesus Christ was to them their teacher, they had learned everything from his lips: he was their leader, they had never to ask what to do, they had only to follow in his steps: he was their defender, whenever the Pharisees or Sadducees assailed them he was like a brazen wall to them: he was their comforter, in all times of grief they resorted to him, and his dear sympathetic heart poured out floods of comfort at once. What if I were to say that the Lord Jesus Christ was everything to them, their all in all? What a father is to his children, ay, what a mother is to her suckling, that was Jesus Christ to his disciples; and yet the Spirit of God's abiding in the church is better even than all this.

Now take another thought. What would you think if Jesus Christ were to come among us now as in the days of his flesh: I mean not as he will come, but as he appeared at his first advent. What joy it would give you! Oh, the delights, the heavenly joys, to hear that Jesus Christ of Nazareth was on earth again, a Man among men! Should we not clap our hands for joy? Our one question would be, "Master, where dwellest thou?" for we should all long to live just where he lived. We could then sympathize with the negroes when they flocked into Washington in large numbers to take up their residence there. Why, think you, did they come to live in that city? Because Massa Abraham Lincoln lived there who had set them free, and they thought it would be glorious to live as near as possible to their great friend. If Jesus lived anywhere, it would not matter where, if it were in the desert or on the bleakest of mountains, there would be a rush to the place. How would the spot be crowded; what rents they would pay for the worst of tenements if Jesus was but in the neighbourhood. But do you not see the difficulty? We could not all get near him in any literal or corporeal fashion. Now that the church is multiplied into millions of believers, some of the Lord's followers would never be able to see him, and the most could only hope to speak with him now and then. In the days of his flesh the twelve might see him every day, and so might the little company of disciples, but the case is altered now that multitudes are trusting in his name.

If our Lord were at this time living in the United States we should be much grieved to have an ocean between us and our leader: all the companies that could be formed would not be able to run enough boats to carry us over. If the Master personally came here to this little island, it would not hold all the vast company of the faithful who would flock to it. It is much better to have the Holy Spirit, because he is dwelling with us and in us. The difficulties of the bodily presence are too great, and so, though we would be thankful, like the apostles, if we had known Christ after the flesh, yet we do not marvel that they expressed little sorrow when they said that after the flesh they knew even him no more. The Comforter had filled the void caused by his absence, and made them rejoice because the Lord had gone unto his Father.

Are we not apt to think that if our Lord Jesus were here it would give unspeakable strength to the church? Would not the enemy be convinced if they saw him? No, they would not. If they hear not Moses and the prophets neither would they be converted though one rose from the dead. Jesus rose, but they did not therefore believe. If our Lord had lingered here all this while his personal presence would not have converted unbelievers, for nothing can do that but the power of the Holy Ghost.

"But," you say, "surely it would thrill the church with enthusiasm." Fancy the Lord himself standing on this platform in the same garb as when he was upon earth. Oh, what rapturous worship! What burning zeal! What enthusiasm! We should go home in such a state of excitement as we never were in before. Yes, it is even so, but then the Lord is not going to carry on his kingdom by the force of mere mental excitement, not even by such enthusiasm as would follow the sight of his Person. The work of the Holy Spirit is a truer work, a deeper work, a surer work, and will more effectually achieve the purposes of God than even would the enthusiasm to which we should be stirred by the bodily Presence of our well-beloved Saviour. The work is to be spiritual, and therefore the visible Presence has departed. It is better that it should be so. We must walk by faith, and by faith alone; how could we do this if we could see the Lord with these mortal eyes? This is the dispensation of the unseen Spirit, in which we render glory to God by trusting in his word, and relying upon the unseen energy. Now, faith works and faith triumphs though the world seeth not the foundation upon which faith is built; for the Spirit who works in us cannot be discerned by carnal minds: the world seeth him not, neither knoweth him.

Thus you see that the operations of the Holy Spirit must be inestimably precious. There is no calculating their value, since it is expedient that we lose the bodily Presence of Christ rather than remain without the indwelling of the Spirit of God.

Now go back to my first text again and follow me in the third head. Those operations of the Spirit of God, of which I am afraid some Christians are almost ignorant, are of wondrous power. The text says, "He that believeth on me, out of the midst of him shall flow rivers of living water." THESE OPERATIONS ARE OF MARVELLOUS POWER. Do you understand my text? Do rivers of living water flow out of you?

Notice, first, that this is to be *an inward work*: the rivers of living water are to flow out of the midst of the man. The words are according to our version, "Out of his belly"—that is, from his heart and soul. The rivers do not flow out of his mouth: the promised power is not oratory. We have had plenty of words, floods of words; but this is heart work. The source of the rivers is found in the inner life. It is an inward work at its fountain head. It is not a work of talent and ability, and show, and glitter, and glare: it is altogether an inward work. The life-flood is to come out of the man's inmost self, out of the bowels and essential being of the man. Homage is shown too generally to outward form and external observance, though these soon lose their interest and power; but when the Spirit of God rests within a man it exercises a home rule within him and he gives great attention to what an old divine was wont to call "the home department." Alas, many neglect the realm within which is the chief province under our care. O my brother in Christ, if you would be useful, begin with yourself. It is out of your very soul that a blessing must come. It cannot come out of you if it is not in you: and it cannot be in you unless God the Holy Ghost places it there.

Next, it is *life-giving* work. Out of the heart of the man, out of the centre of his life, are to "flow rivers of living water"; that is to say, he is instrumentally to communicate to others the divine life. When he speaks, when he prays, when he acts, he shall so speak and pray and act that there shall be going out of him an emanation which is full of the life of grace and godliness. He shall be a light by which others shall see. His life shall be the means of kindling life in other men's bosoms. "Out of his belly shall flow rivers of living water."

Note *the plenitude* of it. The figure would have been a surprising one, if it had said, "Out of him shall flow a river of living water"; but it is not so: it says "rivers." Have you ever stood by the side of a very abundant spring? We have some such not far from London. You see the water bubbling up from many little mouths. Observe the sand dancing as the water forces its way from the bottom; and there, just across the road, a mill is turned by the stream which has just been created by the spring, and when the water-wheel is turned you see a veritable river flowing forward to supply Father Thames. Yet this is only one river; what would you think if you saw a spring yielding such supplies that a river flowed from it to the north, and a river to the south, a river to the east, and a river to the west; this is the figure before us: rivers of living water flowing out of the living man in all directions? "Ah," say you, "I have not reached to that." A point is gained when you know, confess, and deplore your failure. If you say, "I have all things and abound," I am afraid you will never reach the fulness of the blessing; but if you know something of your failure, the Lord will lead you further. It may be that the spirit of life which comes forth of you is but a trickling brooklet, or even a few tiny drops; then be sure to confess it, and you will be on the way to a fuller blessing. What a word is this! "Rivers of living water"!! Oh that all professing Christians were such fountains.

See how *spontaneous* it is: "Out of the midst of him shall flow." No pumping is required; nothing is said about machinery and hydraulics; the man does not want exciting and stirring up, but, just as he is, influence of the best kind quietly flows away from him. Did you ever hear a great hubbub in the morning, a great outcry, a sounding of trumpets and drums, and did you ever ask, "What is it?" Did a voice reply, "The sun is about to rise, and he is making this noise that all may be aware of it"? No, he shines, but he has nothing to say about it; even so the genuine Christian just goes about flooding the world with blessing, and so far from claiming attention for himself, it may be that he himself is unconscious of what he is effecting. God so blesses him that his leaf does not wither, and whatsoever he doeth is prospering, for he is like a tree planted by the rivers of water that bringeth forth its fruit in its season: his verdure and fruit are the natural outcome of his vigorous life. Oh, the blessed spontaneity of the work of grace when a man gets into the fulness of it, for then he seems to eat and drink and sleep eternal life, and he spreads a savour of salvation all round.

And this is to be *perpetual,*—not like intermittent springs which burst forth and flow in torrents, and then cease—, but it is to be an everyday outgushing. In summer and winter, by day and by night, wherever the man is, he shall be a blessing. As he breathes, he shall breathe benedictions; as he thinks, his mind shall be devising generous things; and, when he acts, his acts shall be as though the hand of God were working by the hand of man.

I hope I hear many sighs rising up in the place! I hope I hear friends saying, "Oh that I could get to that." I want you to attain the fulness of the favour. I pray that we may all get it; for because Jesus Christ is glorified therefore the Holy Spirit is given in this fashion, given more largely to those in the kingdom of heaven than to all those holy men before the Lord's ascent to his glory. God gives no stinted blessing to celebrate the triumph of his Son: God giveth not the Spirit by measure unto him. On such an occasion heaven's grandest liberality was displayed. Christ is glorified in heaven above, and God would have him glorified in the church below by vouchsafing a baptism of the Holy Ghost to each of us.

So I close by this, which I hope will be a very comforting and inspiriting reflection:—

THESE OPERATIONS OF THE SPIRIT OF GOD ARE EASILY TO BE OBTAINED BY THE LORD'S CHILDREN. Did you say you had not received them? They are to be had, they are to be had at once. First, they are to be had by *believing in Jesus.* "This spake he of the Spirit, which they that believe on him should receive." Do you not see that it is faith which gives us the first drink and causes us to live, and this second more abundant blessing of being ourselves made fountains from which rivers flow comes in the same way? Believe in Christ, for the blessing is to be obtained, not by the works of the law, nor by so much of fasting, and striving, and effort, but by belief in the Lord Jesus for it. With him is the residue of the Spirit. He is prepared to give this to you, ay, to every one of you who believe on his name. He will not of course make all of you preachers; for who then would be hearers? If all were preachers the other works of the church would be neglected; but he will give you this favour, that out of you there shall stream a divine influence all round you to bless your children, to bless your servants, to bless the workmen in the house where you are employed, and to bless the street you live in. In proportion as God gives you opportunity these "rivers of living water" will flow in this channel and in that, and they will be pouring forth from you at all times, if you believe in Jesus for the full blessing, and can by faith receive it.

But there is another thing to be done as well, and that is *to pray;* and here I want to remind you of those blessed words of the Master, "Everyone that asketh receiveth; and he that seeketh findeth; and to him that knocketh it shall be opened. If a son shall ask bread of any of you that is a father, will he give him a stone? Or if he ask a fish, will he for a fish give him a serpent? Or if he shall ask an egg, will he offer him a scorpion? If ye then, being evil, know how to give good gifts unto your children: how much more shall your heavenly Father give the Holy Spirit to them that ask him?" (Luke 11: 10–13).

You see, there is a distinct promise to the children of God, that their heavenly Father will give them the Holy Spirit if they ask for his power; and that promise is made to be exceedingly strong by the instances joined to it. If there be a promise that God can break (which there is not), this is not the promise, for God has put it in the most forcible and binding way. I know not how to show you its wonderful force. Did you ever hear of a man who when his child asked for bread gave him a stone? Go to the worst part of London, and will you find a man of that kind? You shall, if you like, get among pirates and murderers, and when a little child cries, "Father, give me a bit of bread and meat," does the most wicked father fill his own little one's mouth with stones? Yet the Lord seems to say that this is what he would be doing if he were to deny us the Holy Spirit when we ask him for his necessary working: he would be like one that gave his children stones instead of bread. Do you think the Lord will ever bring himself down to that? But he says, "*How much more* shall your heavenly Father give the Holy Spirit to them that ask him?" He makes it a stronger case than that of an ordinary parent. The Lord must give us the Spirit when we ask him, for he has herein bound himself by no ordinary pledge. He has used a simile which would bring dishonour on his own name, and that of the very grossest kind, if he did not give the Holy Spirit to them that ask him. Oh, then, let us ask him at once, with all our hearts. Am I not so happy as to have in this audience some who will immediately ask? I pray that some who have never received the Holy Spirit at all may now be led, while I am speaking, to pray, "Blessed Spirit, visit me; lead me to Jesus." But especially those of you that are the children of God, to you is this promise especially made. Ask God to make you all that the Spirit of God can make you, not only a satisfied believer who has drunk for himself, but a useful believer, who overflows the neighbourhood with blessing.

XI

CARTE BLANCHE

"Then Jesus answered and said unto her, O woman, great
is thy faith: be it unto thee even as thou wilt."—Matt. 15: 28.

I MEAN to dwell specially upon those words at the end of the
verse, "Be it unto thee even as thou wilt;" but before we
consider them, I should like to remind you, that our Lord
admired this woman's faith. He said unto her, "O woman,
great is thy faith." She was humble, she was patient, she was
persevering, she was affectionate towards her child; but our
Saviour did not mention any of these things, for he was most of
all struck by her faith. What other good things she had, sprang
out of her faith; so the Lord Jesus went at once to the root of
the matter, and, as it were, held up his hands in astonishment,
and exclaimed, "O woman, great is thy faith."

Her faith really was great, extremely great, when you consider that she was a Gentile, and one of a race that had, ages
before, been doomed, the Canaanitish race, in whose nature
idolatry seemed to be ingrained; yet this woman showed that
she had greater faith than many a Jew. There are two cases of
extraordinary faith recorded in the early part of Matthew's
Gospel; and in both of these instances where our Saviour expressed his astonishment at the greatness of the faith, the
believers were Gentiles. Of the centurion at Capernaum he
said, "Verily I say unto you, I have not found so great faith, no,
not in Israel." It is a wonderful thing when persons who have
lived in ignorance and vice exhibit great faith. We are glad
when those who have been brought up religiously and morally
are led to believe in Christ; but we are often more astonished
when the immoral, those who have previously known nothing
of true godliness, are enabled by grace to exercise great faith in
Christ.

"O woman, great is thy faith," said our Lord, for it was great
even apart from her being a Gentile, for it had been sorely tried.

Trials of faith from disciples are often very severe, and the disciples had put her aside, and even besought their Lord to "Send her away." But trials of faith from the Master himself are still more severe. To have Christ's deaf ear and dumb lips— this was a trial indeed; and, worse than that, to have rough words from such a loving and tender Teacher as he was, and even to be called a dog by the great Shepherd of Israel, and to be told that it was not meet to give her the children's bread— these were heavy tests of her confidence; but she had such faith that she bore up under all, and still pressed her suit with the Son of David, the Lord of mercy. We cannot but feel that Christ did her justice when he said, "O woman, great is thy faith."

Our Saviour seems to have been specially struck with the ingenuity of her faith. Little faith always lacks ingenuity, it must have everything very plain or else it cannot move at all; but great faith makes crooked things straight, sees light in the midst of darkness, and gathers comfort out of discouragement. For this woman to turn Christ's work inside out, as it were, and when he said, "It is not meet to take the children's bread, and to cast it to dogs," for her to say, in effect, "I do not ask to have it cast to me; only let me have the crumbs which fall by accident from the children themselves when they have brought the dogs under the table"—this was indeed extraordinary faith and wonderful pleading. "If thou wilt heal my daughter, there will be none the less of thy marvellous power for the children of Israel, for thou canst heal them, too. If thou dost give me this that I ask, great as it is to me, it is only like a crumb to thee, thy table is so lavishly provided for by thine omnipotence of grace. Even this great boon that I ask of thee will be nothing more to thee than a chance crumb that falls from the children's table." This was splendid pleading, and the Saviour saw the force of it at once. He loves ingenuity on the part of those who come to him. He is so ingenious himself in devising means of bringing back his banished ones, that he is glad to see ingenuity in the banished ones themselves when they desire to come back to him. He therefore cries in holy astonishment, "O woman, great is thy faith."

Taking the case of the woman as a whole I think that it must have been her pertinacity, her firmness, that surprised the Lord.

Others are so easily put off, but she would not be put off. Others need encouragement, but she encouraged herself. When the door is shut in her face, she only knocks at it; and when Christ calls her "Dog," she only picks up what Christ has said, as a good dog will pick up his master's stick, and bring it right to his feet. There was no baffling her. If all the devils in hell had been about the business, not merely that terrible one that possessed her daughter, she would have beaten them all, for she had such faith—shall I not say?—such dogged faith in the Lord Jesus Christ, that she could even get comfort out of being called a dog. She had such resolute faith that she must have what she sought, and she would not go away without it. If she does not succeed at first, she will battle on until she does win the victory; she will continue pleading till she carries her suit.

Our Lord was not only, to speak after the manner of men, astonished at her faith; but with reverence we may say that he was conquered by it. He yielded to her faith, and he yielded unconditionally. He gave her much more than she asked, for she had not asked that her daughter might be healed the self-same hour. She had hardly got as far as the asking at all; and as to mentioning the details, she had only pleaded with him in general; but Christ gave her definitely what he knew she wished for, and gave it to her at once. And what is more, he did, as it were, hand her over the keys of his house. "There," said he, "my good woman, I so admire your faith that I say to you, Go and help yourself. You may have whatever you like. Whatever treasure of grace I have, is yours if you want it; be it unto thee even as thou wilt." He gave her the keys of the heavenly cash-box.

Some time ago, a lady wishing to help the Orphanage sent me a cheque, and she did a very unwise thing indeed, for she signed the cheque, but she did not fill up the amount. Never do that; you see, I might have put all her fortune down, and filled up the cheque to any amount that the lady had in the bank. She evidently trusted me very largely, but I sent her cheque back to her, saying that I did not know what amount to put down. Of course, she intended to give a guinea, or £5, or something of the kind, but she forgot to say how much; and that is a very dangerous plan indeed with most people. So, our Saviour gave this woman a blank cheque. "Fill it up for what you like," he said. "Great is thy faith; be it unto thee even as thou wilt. Whatever it is that you wish for, you shall have. Your faith has won from me this boon, that I now put at your disposal all my power to bless. Be it unto thee even as thou wilt."

I am going to talk specially about that point, and first, I will try to answer the question, *How far did this carte-blanche extend?* Then, secondly, *when is it safe for the Lord to give such a carte-blanche as that?* And, thirdly, *if he did give us such power, how would we use it?*

First, then, HOW FAR DID THIS CARTE-BLANCHE EXTEND when the Saviour said to the woman "Be it unto thee even as thou wilt"?

In answer to which I would say, first, that it went so far as *to baffle all the powers of hell.* This woman's child was grievously vexed with a devil, and we read, "her daughter was made whole from that very hour." "For this saying, go thy way;" said Christ, according to Mark's account, "the devil is gone out of thy daughter." Now, Satan is very mighty; there is not one of us, nor all of us put together, who can be equally matched with him. He takes small account of ten thousand men; he is more crafty and cunning than all the wise men, and more powerful than all the mighty men who ever came together, and yet the Saviour seems to say, "I have heard thee, good woman, I have seen thy faith; I will rebuke the demon, I will send the evil spirit back to his own place, and your child shall be snatched out of his cruel grasp." Beloved, if you have faith enough, Christ will give you power even to cast out devils. If you can only trust him, trust him without measure or stint, and believe in him as this woman did, he will give you power to make Satan fall like lightning from heaven, and flee before you. "Jesus I know," said the evil spirit at Corinth, "and Paul I know," and the devil still knows those who make him know them. Through faith in Jesus, they speak to him with authority, and he must flee from them. So, if you have faith, you shall resist the devil, and even he, powerful as he is, shall turn his back, and flee from you; and, as Luther said, though there were as many devils as the tiles upon the housetops, yet would faith in God give you grace to vanquish them all. Remember that glorious promise, "The God of peace shall bruise Satan under your feet shortly"

(Rom. 16:20). So this *carte-blanche*, when he said to the woman, "Be it unto thee even as thou wilt," meant, "The devils themselves are now subject to thy will."

Next, it meant that it was the will of the Lord *to heal her daughter completely*. She had come all the way from Syrophœnicia to the borders of the land of Israel that she might plead with Christ about her daughter, her dear child, perhaps her only child. This sorrow pressed very heavily on her heart, so she cried unto the Lord, "Have mercy on me." She so identified herself with her child that she did not know any difference between herself and her child. They had seemed to grow into one in the great trouble that they had at home. I have known many a mother who certainly would far rather have suffered herself than that her child should suffer, so completely had she identified herself with her child. Now, if you can plead with Christ with this woman's heroic faith, if you can fully believe in him, and not dare to doubt him, you shall have your children put at your disposal. He will deal graciously with them,— with the girl for whom you are pleading, with the boy over whom your heart is aching. He will say to you, dear mother, "O woman, great is thy faith; be it unto thee even as thou wilt." The boy shall repent, the girl shall believe, the children shall come to Jesus' feet, and become your comfort and joy through their early conversion to Christ. Is not this a great blessing?

Ay, and the woman had such faith in Christ that this blank cheque further meant her *to have this boon at once*. "Be it unto thee even as thou wilt, now, at once." So she willed at once, of course, that the devil should go out of her daughter, and out the devil had to go, for her will had become God's will, and Christ had infused into her will a mighty power which even Satan could not resist. Oh, if you have faith enough, you may get the blessing you desire even now! It may be that, while sitting here, breathing a prayer for your child, God may bless your child before you get home. If you can but have faith enough, he has power enough; and if he deigns to say, "Be it unto thee even as thou wilt," I know that it will be your will, not that your girl may be converted when she becomes a woman, not that your boy may be saved when he becomes a man, but that the blessed miracle may be wrought at once, even now. What parents want to let the devil have their children even for an hour? O Jesus, turn him out at once! Let us see our children, our children's children, our brothers and sisters and friends, converted now, for while now is the accepted time with God, now is the time which every earnest Christian will prefer for the conversion of those for whom he prays. A splendid promise is this concerning great blessings to be had, and to be had at once: "Be it unto thee even as thou wilt."

I must go a little further and say that I think our Lord, when he said to the woman, "Be it unto thee even as thou wilt," permitted her *to eat the children's bread*. She had before said, "The little dogs eat of the crumbs which fall from their master's table," and "then Jesus answered and said unto her, O woman, great is thy faith: be it unto thee even as thou wilt." I think this means that, instead of having the privilege to go and roam like a dog under the table, and eat what she could pick up, she was made into a child, and was permitted to sit at the table, and eat of all that the Lord had provided. O poor sinner, you came in here feeling like a whipped dog, did you not? You said to yourself, "There will not be anything for me in the sermon;" but, by-and-by, as you heard of the great grace of Christ to this poor woman, you thought that there might be hope even for you, and now you begin to think that there is a possibility that even you may be blessed. Well, I venture to say to you that, if you wish to eat the children's bread, you may. "Be it unto thee even as thou wilt." Lord, we do not ask of thee that we may be treated better than the rest of thy family! If any of you pray to God to make a distinction, and to give you more than he gives his other children, I do not think you are likely to get it; but if you say, "O Lord, thou art my God; I love thy people, let me fare as they do. I had rather be a doorkeeper in the house of my God than dwell in the tents of wickedness. I do not ask to be exempt from tribulation, for all the heirs of salvation have to endure it. I only ask that I may eat what thy children eat. If they have bread, Lord, I will be happy to have bread; I ask for no dainties. If they drink water from the rock, Lord, let me have a draught of the same; I ask for nothing more." Jesus says, "Be it unto thee even as thou wilt. If you are content to sit at the table with my children, come along with you. If you sigh after their bread, which came down from heaven, if you will take 'scot and lot' with them, there is nothing to hinder you. Be it unto thee even as thou wilt."

Surely, also, when the Saviour spoke thus to the Syrophœnician woman, he meant to make reference to her first prayer. She cried unto him, saying, "*Have mercy on me, O Lord, thou Son of David.*" "Yes," said he, "now be it unto thee even as thou wilt. I have mercy on thee. If thou hast sinned, I forgive thee. If thou art hard of heart, I will soften thy heart. If thou hast been an ignorant heathen, I will enlighten thee, and bring thee to my feet. I will be to thee the Son of David, and thou shalt be one of mine own chosen people, and I will care for thee, and protect thee, and deliver thee, as David did the many for whom he fought." O souls, if any one of you is crying, "Lord, have mercy upon me," if you have faith in Christ—and he deserves to be trusted; there is none like him; he deserves to be trusted without a single doubt, for he never failed anyone, and he never lied to anyone, therefore let no wicked mistrust come in to weaken thy faith,—if *thou canst* trust him, he says to thee, "Be it unto thee even as thou wilt." Take mercy; take mercy, and more mercy, and yet more mercy. Come to the table of love, and sit among the children of the Lord, and feed on heavenly bread. Put up thy prayer for thy child, pleading the promise to the jailor, "Believe on the Lord Jesus Christ, and thou shalt be saved, *and thy house.*" Come to Christ with all the torment thou hast felt from the devil's possession of thee, the horrible thoughts, the blasphemous insinuations, the desperate doubts; and hear the Saviour say to thee, "Be it unto thee even as thou wilt." The devil shall be made to depart from thee. Thy poor head shall lose the fever from the burning brow; thy heart shall beat at its even pace, and thou shalt be at peace again. The Lord shall rebuke thine adversary. In this confidence, say unto the demon even now, "Rejoice not against me, O mine enemy: when I fall, I shall arise."

Oh, this is a grand, grand word from our Lord's lips! It is a wonderful cheque, signed by our Saviour's own hand, and left in blank for faith to fill up. We might have half thought that he would have said, "O woman, your faith is too big for me to trust you with unlimited prayer. If you had only a little faith, I would go as far as your little faith would go, and keep pace with you." But no, no; that is not Christ's method of acting.

He says, "O woman, great is thy faith, and as thou canst trust *me*, I can trust *thee*. Cry as thou wilt, for so be it unto thee. Thou hast firmly resolved to have no doubt about my power and willingness, and to trust me without reserve; so I trust thee without reserve, be it unto thee even as thou wilt."

So now I pass to our second question, which is this: WHEN IS IT SAFE FOR THE LORD TO TRUST ANYBODY WITH SUCH A PROMISE AS THIS, "Be it unto thee even as thou wilt"?

It would be very unsafe thus to trust some of you. Why, there is one man here who, if it was said to him, "Be it unto thee even as thou wilt," would at once pray for—well, I do not know how many thousand pounds; and when he got home, he would be discontented, and say, "What a fool I was not to ask two or three times as much!" Ah! yes but the Lord does not trust greedy people in that way. Not while there is any idea of your own merit left, will Christ trust you at all. Not while there is a fraction of self-will left, will Christ trust you at all, and not while doubt remains. That must go, for the whole verse says, "O woman, great is thy faith: be it unto thee even as thou wilt." He trusts faith; he will not trust unbelief, he will not trust self-confidence, he will not trust human merit; but, where there is faith, there he gives over the keys of his treasury, and says, "Be it unto thee even as thou wilt."

When will the Lord thus trust us? Well, I think, first, *when we agree with Christ*, when we are like this woman who had no quarrel with the Saviour. Whatever he said was right in her eyes. If he called her a dog, she said, "Truth, Lord." When you and Christ agree, and there is no quarrel between you, then he says, "Be it unto thee even as thou wilt." If you do not yield to him, he will not yield to you; but when you just end all disputing, and say, "Lord, I have done with all quibbling and quarrelling; I will never raise another question, and never harbour another doubt. I believe thee. I believe thee. As a child believes its mother, I believe thee. When I cannot understand thee, when thou dost distress me, still I do believe thee." Ah! when you come to that point, then the Lord will say, "Be it unto thee even as thou wilt."

Next, *when our soul is taken up with proper desires*. This woman had no idea of asking for a hundred thousand shekels of silver, or a wedge of gold, or a goodly Babylonish garment. One thought alone possessed her, "My child! My child! Oh, that the devil might be cast out of my child!" "Now," says Christ, "be it unto thee even as thou wilt." And, when you have great desires for heavenly things, when your desires are such as God approves of, when you will what God wills, then you may will what you like. When it comes to this, that you have dropped your own desires of an inferior and grovelling kind, and you are taken up with desires for necessary things, desires that come to you from Christ himself, when you desire the bread, not from the devil's oven, but from Christ's table, when that is what you crave, then it shall be unto you even as you will.

Next, it shall be to us even as we will *when we see our Lord in his true offices.* This woman saw that Christ was a Healer, and she appealed to him as a Healer. If you see Christ as Prophet, Priest, and King, you may go and ask of him as a Prophet what a prophet is ordained to give, or as a Priest what a priest is intended to bestow, or as a King what a king is set upon the throne to do. You may go to Christ as he really is, and if you see that he is ordained for this purpose and for that, then keep in tune with what he is ordained to be, and you may ask what you will, and it shall be done unto you. You must not try to take Christ away from his offices. Christ is not sent of God to make you a rich man; he is sent of God to make you a saved man, so you may go to him as a Saviour, for that is his office. You may go to him as a Priest, for it is his office to cleanse, to offer sacrifice, to make intercession. Take Christ as God sets him forth, and then be it unto thee even as thou wilt.

Next, it will be to us even as we will *when we can believe about the distinct object that is before us.* This woman pleaded for her child. All her faith went out towards her child. I love the prayer that has in it faith concerning the thing for which it pleads. There are many Christian people who say they have faith about twenty things; but then the thing that they cannot believe about is the twenty-first. You must have a faith that can not only cover twenty-one things, but that can cover everything. We say, "Oh! I could believe if my trouble were like So-and so's." You could not believe at all unless you can believe about your present trouble; and you must believe about the object for which you are praying, that it can be given you, that it will be given you in answer to your prayer;

and then Jesus will say to you, "Be it unto thee even as thou wilt."

Again, we can have whatever we like *when our heart seeks only God's glory*; when what we pray for is not for wealth, nor with a desire for our own honour, but when even what we want for ourselves is asked with the higher motive that God may be glorified in us by our obtaining such-and-such a gift, or being delivered from such-and-such a trial. When God's glory is thy one aim, thou mayest ask what thou wilt, and it shall be given unto thee.

And above all, when we always keep to what I have already mentioned, *when we only ask for the children's bread*, then the Lord will give us what we crave. If you ask for what God gives his elect, for what Christ has bought for his redeemed, if you ask for what the Holy Ghost works in the minds of men converted by his power, if you ask for what God has promised, if you ask for what it is customary for God to bestow upon his waiting people, then "be it unto thee even as thou wilt." No wild fancy, no rhapsody, no whim that makes thee wish for this or that, is worthy to come within the compass of my text; but that which the Lord waits to give thee, that which he knows would be good for thee, that which will be an honour to him, and which will help thee to honour him, thou mayest ask without any stammering or fear; and thou shalt have it, for he says to thee, "Be it unto thee even as thou wilt."

I do not know; but I think that I am speaking personally to somebody here in trouble, who has been long pleading and praying, and has never got an answer yet. "Be it unto thee even as thou wilt." Hannah, the woman of a sorrowful spirit, sits in this house, bowed down in soul, and pouring out before the Lord her silent prayer. Let her take this message from the Lord's servant, or, better still, from the Lord himself, "Be it unto thee even as thou wilt." But then I only dare to say it to one to whom I could also say, "O woman, great is thy faith." If you have not any faith, how are you to have it? Here is a soup-kitchen opened for the poor, and they are told to bring their jugs, their mugs, their basins—anything they like. A woman comes, and says, "I have not a mug." "Have you a basin?" "No." Well, you say to her, "You can have the soup;" but then, you see, she cannot carry it home without a basin, or a jug. So, here is the mercy of God, and many lack it; here is a blessing rich and rare, and many cannot carry it home because they have no faith; but Christ could say to the Syrophœnician, "O woman, great is thy faith: be it unto thee even as thou wilt."

Now I finish by asking another question. Suppose this blank cheque to be given to us, HOW WILL IT BE USED?

Well, first, *I should use it upon that thing about which I have been praying most.* I will not say what it is. This woman had been praying most about her daughter, so, when the Saviour said, "Be it unto thee even as thou wilt," she did not say a single word, but she just willed in her mind that the devil should be driven out of her daughter. Oh, that you might have faith enough to be able to will the right thing! If Christ leaves his own will in your hands, and feels safe in doing so, oh, will strongly! It is for God, you know, to give a fiat; but Christ here gives a fiat to the woman. As I read the text, he says to her, "Be it unto thee"—"So let it be." "Be it so," says he, "as thou wilt." Behold, the fiat of God goes forth to thee, believer, to let it be even as thou dost will it to be. Now, can you not will for the child for whom you have been praying? Do you not will for the congregation that lies on your heart? Do you not will for that friend with whom you have been speaking in order to try to bring him to Christ? Will for the distinct object for which you have been praying; and then, may the will of the Lord be done, and may your will also be done because it is an echo of the will of the Lord!

Next, I think that, if we had this said to each one of us, "Be it unto thee even as thou wilt," *we should first will our own salvation.* Pray, as we sang just now—

> *With my burden I begin,*
> *Lord, remove this load of sin;*
> *Let thy blood, for sinners spilt,*
> *Set my conscience free from guilt.*
>
> *Lord! I come to thee for rest,*
> *Take possession of my breast;*
> *There thy blood-bought right maintain,*
> *And without a rival reign.*

Let each one of us pray, "Lord, save me! Lord, make sure work of it; save me from sin, save me from self, save me from everything that dishonours thee." I was talking, the other day, with a man who was saying that he attended a ministry where he heard very little about holy living. He thought that he was a believer, though he was living in sin, and continued to live in sin. He knows now that he was no believer, or else he could not have lived in sin as he did; and now he prays to God not for salvation while he is living in sin, but for salvation from sin. So, we will first ask of God our own full salvation, and we know that his answer will be, "Be it unto thee even as thou wilt."

Have we not all a prayer also *for our children, or our friends, or those who lie near to our hearts?* Then let us pray on, with great faith, till we hear Christ say, "Be it unto thee even as thou wilt;" and then let us go home, and expect to see the work of grace begun in our children. Watch for it, O parent; and carefully nurture it as soon as you see the first beginnings of it! About this matter also Jesus says, "Be it unto thee even as thou wilt."

I think that, if I were asked to pray now for something very special, and that I might have whatever I asked, my prayer would be, "Lord, make me grow in grace. Give me more faith. If I have great faith, give me more. If I have much love to thee, give me more love to thee. If I know my Lord, I pray that I may know more of him, and know him to a fuller and intenser degree." My prayer shall be—

> *Nearer, my God, to thee,*
> *Nearer to thee.*

Let that be the prayer of each one of you to whom it is left to fill up this blank cheque.

Then there is another prayer that I am sure I should remember, if nobody else here did, and that would be *concerning Christ's kingdom.* If it is to be unto me as I will, then I will it that God's truth should be preached everywhere, and that false doctrines should be made to fly like chaff before the wind. If our prayer be heard, and we are permitted to have what we will, our will is that God may send us Luthers and Calvins, and brave men like John Knox back again, men with bones in their backs, and fire on their lips, with hearts that burn and words that glow with holy fervour; we want them so badly now. The Lord have mercy upon the Free Church of Scotland, and give her back faithful covenanting men and women! The Lord have mercy upon our own poor denomination, and give us those who love the truth of God, and dare to stand up for it come what may! Oh, for such a prayer as that! Lord, revive thy Church! Lord, lift up a banner because of the truth! Lord, put thine adversaries to the rout!

> *Fight for thyself, O Jesus, fight,*
> *The travail of thy soul regain!*

Oh, to hear in our hearts this gracious word from the King himself, as we plead with him concerning his kingdom, "Be it unto thee even as thou wilt."

By-and-by, you and I shall lie sick and ill, and they will say, "His days are numbered." Then, if the Lord shall visit us in answer to our prayers, and whisper to us, "Be it unto thee even as thou wilt," oh then, the promise will read in a very different sense from what I can read it now! Then will the poor tent begin to be taken down; well, it never was worth much. Fearfully and wonderfully made is this mortal frame, but it is capable of bringing us great pain and much sorrow, and also of deadening our devotion, and hampering us in our work for God. "The spirit is willing, but the flesh is weak." "Ah, well!" says the Lord, "you shall be rid of your flesh one day. It shall be unto thee even as thou wilt." You have sung, sometimes—

> *Father, I long, I faint to see*
> *The place of thine abode;*
> *I'd leave thine earthly courts, and flee*
> *Up to thy seat, my God!*

"Be it unto thee even as thou wilt." A dear sister, who was buried to-day, said when they told her that she could not live another day, "Does it not seem wonderful? Is it not a grand thing to know that I am going to see the Lord Jesus Christ to-day?" And she lay on her bed saying this to all who came, "It seems too good to be true, that I should be so near that for which I have longed these many years; I am going to-day to see the King in his beauty."

Ah, thank God, we too shall come to that last day of our earthly life! Unless the Lord descend quickly, we too shall come to our dying bed, and then we shall hear our Saviour say, "Be it unto thee even as thou wilt," and oh! we shall will to see his face, and to be for ever with the Lord, and to praise him with infinite rapture for ever and ever. Blessed be his name, we have faith to believe that it will be even so. Then we will tell him what we cannot tell him now, how much we love him, how deeply we feel our indebtedness to him, and we will give all the glory of our salvation to his holy name for ever and ever. God grant that this may be the happy lot of every one of us, for our Lord Jesus Christ's sake!

XII

WORK FOR JESUS

"Son, go work to-day in my vineyard."—Matt. 21: 28.

I AM not going to confine myself to the connection of these words, nor to use them strictly after the manner in which they were first spoken. I may, perhaps, explain the parable very briefly at the close; but I take leave to withdraw these words from their immediate context, and use them as a voice which, I believe, sounds often in the ears of God's people, and sometimes sounds in vain. "Son, go work to-day in my vineyard."

It is certain that God still speaks to us. He has spoken to us in his word. There are his precepts and promises; his statutes and testimonies. He that hath ears to hear let him hear these sacred oracles. But beside this open revelation there are counsels and rebukes more closely and personally addressed to the conscience, voices, soft sometimes as whispers, at other times loud as the thunders that pealed from Sinai. The Lord has a way of speaking to men when "he openeth the ears of men and sealeth their instruction," as Elihu said. Thus he speaks when he calls them effectually by his grace in conversion. So he once called "Samuel, Samuel," till the child answered. So he said, "Matthew, follow me." So he called out, "Zaccheus, come down." So he cried out, "Saul, Saul, why persecutest thou me?" So he bid some of us till the divine accents were clear and irresistible. In like manner we have, many of us, heard him say, "Son, give me thy heart;" and we have given him our hearts: we could do no otherwise. That voice exerted such a charming spell and swayed us with such a divine power that we were subdued by it, and we yielded our hearts to the God of love.

Since then you who know the Lord must often have heard a voice speaking to you and bidding you seek his face in prayer. Perhaps you have been busy with the world, but you found an impulse of a mysterious kind coming over you, and you have been fain to withdraw yourself for a few minutes to the closet that you might speak with God. You know how it has been when you have been meditating alone, and yet not alone. One whose Presence you knew, whose face you could not see, was with you. You felt as if you must pray. It has not been any effort on your part. The exercise has been as easy as to breathe and as pleasant as to partake of your daily bread. You felt the Lord drawing you to the mercy-seat and saying in your soul, "My son, ask what thou wilt and it shall be done unto thee." You must have been conscious of such a voice as that.

And have you not at times, in the silence of your mind, heard the Lord call you to a closer communion with himself? Has not the sense, if not the words, of the spouse in the canticle been heard in your soul,—"Come, my beloved, let us see if the vines flourish. Come with me from Lebanon, my spouse, with me from Lebanon"? You have been up and away. You have gone into the secret places where Christ has shown you his love, till you sat under his shadow with great delight, and his fruit has been sweet to your taste. Our experience makes us know that there are heavenly voices that invite prayer and call to communion. And probably some of you have also been conscious of another voice which I earnestly desire we may all hear now, namely, the more martial and stirring call to service for the Lord Jesus Christ. Some of you have been obedient to the call these many years, and it calls louder and louder and louder still. You have been reaping and bearing the heat and burden of the day, but you cannot throw down your sickle, your hand cleaves to it. Yea, rather do you take more gigantic strides and sweep down more of the precious corn at every stroke you take. You feel that you can never cease from it till you do

> *Your body with your charge lay down,*
> *And cease at once to work and live.*

A voice divine seems calling thee and saying, "Follow me, and I will make thee a fisher of men. Behold I have made thee a chosen vessel to bear my name unto the Gentiles." You have heard that voice, and you are striving to obey it more and more.

Others either have never heard it, or hearing it have forgotten it. There are none so deaf as those who will not hear, and there are some who have a very deaf ear to any admonitions of this kind. They are like Issachar—a strong ass crouching down between two burdens, but yet lifting neither. I fear lest upon them should come the curse of Meroz, because they come not "to the help of the Lord—to the help of the Lord against the mighty" (cp. Judges 5: 23). Now, mayhap there are some Christian men or women here that shall feel as if the hand of the Crucified were laid upon them, and they hear him say to them, "Ye are not your own. Ye are bought with a price; wherefore glorify God in your bodies and in your spirits, which are his. Awake thou that sleepest and arise from the dead, and Christ shall give thee light."

The text, I hope, may be blest of God, to be such a voice as that. Listening to it, we notice four things.

First, then, THE CHARACTER UNDER WHICH IT CALLS US.

It appears to me to be a very powerful selection of terms. "Son, go work to-day in my vineyard." It puts work on a very gracious footing, when we are bidden to work for the Lord, not as slaves, nor as mere servants, but as sons. Moses speaks to us, and he says, "Servant, go and work for thy wages." But the Father in Christ speaks to us, and he says, "Son, go work to-day in my vineyard." No more as a servant, but as a son, shalt thou serve the Lord. The returning prodigal said "Make me as one of thy hired servants." That was not an evangelical prayer, and was not answered. The father said, "This my son was dead, and is alive again," and so he received him, not as a hired servant at all, but as a son. Oh, dear people of God, I trust you always draw the distinction very clearly between the covenant of works and the covenant of grace. When you work for God you do not work *for* life but *from* life. You do not try to serve Christ in order that you may be saved, but because you are saved. You do not obey his commands that you may become his children, but because you are his children, and therefore are imitators of God as dear children. You say "Abba, Father," because you feel the spirit of adoption within you, and you endeavour to obey the commands of your Father for the self-same reason. I do not, therefore, say to anyone here, "Go and work for God that you may be saved." I would not venture to put it on that footing. "Believe in the Lord Jesus Christ, and thou shalt be saved." But turning to those who are saved, the gospel exhortation is put after a gospel sort—"Son, go work to-day in my vineyard."

And it has all the more strength on this account, because, in addressing us as sons, it reminds us of the great love which has made us what we are. We were by nature heirs of wrath even as others, but, beloved, "Behold, what manner of love the Father hath bestowed upon us, that we should be called the sons of God" (1 John 3: 1). Think of the love which chose us when we were still aliens and enemies; the love which adopted us, and put us into the family, itself wondering while it did it, for the Lord is represented as saying, "How shall I put thee among the children?"—as if it were a strange thing that such as we are should ever be numbered among the children of God. The love which adopted us did not stay there, but having given us the rights of children, it gave us the nature of children, wherefore we were regenerated—"Begotten again unto a lively hope by the resurrection of Jesus Christ from the dead; being born again not of corruptible seed, but of incorruptible, by the word of God which liveth and abideth for ever" (1 Pet. 1: 3, 23). Now, just think of election, adoption, regeneration, and when the Lord addresses you by that term of "son," think of all that and say, "I owe to God an immeasurable debt of gratitude for having enabled me to become his son: giving me power and privilege to become a child of God. Therefore do I feel the claims of obligation, and I would endeavour to work in the vineyard because I am his child, his son, his daughter, made so by his grace."

This, you see, engages us to work in the vineyard all the more cogently, because we may reflect not only on the grace which has made us sons, but on the privileges which that same grace bestowed upon us in making us sons; for, if children of God, the Lord will provide for us, will clothe us, will heal us, will protect us, will guide us, will educate us, will make us meet to be partakers of the inheritance of the saints in light. Remember, too, that precious passage, "If children, then heirs; heirs of God, and joint-heirs with Christ; if so be that we suffer with him, that we may be also glorified together" (Rom. 8: 17). If heirs of God, how large is our inheritance, and if joint-heirs with Christ how sure that inheritance is; and we have been brought now to such an estate as this that the angels themselves might envy us.

In appealing thus to us under the name of son, it is supposed that we have some feelings within us correspondent to the condition to which our heavenly Father has called us. He says, "son." If any of you, being a son, hath a father, and if that father wished you to do something for him, and he addressed you as "my son," you would feel at once that whatever you could do you were bound to do because you were a son. It would awaken in you the filial feeling which is swift at once to yield obedience and love. And when the Lord looks upon thee, and says to thee "Son," it is supposed that there is in thy heart a child's nature given by his grace, and that this filial instinct prompts the quick response, "My Father, what dost thou say to me? Speak, Lord, speak, Father, for thy son heareth thee. I long to do thy will. I delight in it, for to me it is the greatest joy I know that thou art my Father and my God. Therefore, Lord, my heart stands ready now to listen to whatever thou hast to say, and my hand is ready to do it, as thy grace shall enable me, only strengthen me in thy ways." Son, daughter, go work to-day in my vineyard.

By the use of that term "son," also, it is supposed that you have something of the qualification that will fit you to do what he bids you. A man who has a vineyard naturally supposes that his son knows something about vineyards. The boy will have learned something through his sire, and you that know the Lord are the only people that can serve him in his vineyard—that is to say, in winning souls for Christ none can do this but those who are won themselves. If there be a lost child to be reclaimed, he shall be brought in by one of the children who has himself been found. Unto the wicked God saith, "What hast thou to do to declare my statutes?" but to you who are his sons and daughters he entrusts the gospel, putting you in trust with it that you may bear it to others and bring others to know and love his name. Oh, it must be a dreadful thing to be trying to save the souls of others while you yourselves are lost; and what an unhappy mortal must he be who has to preach the gospel that he never knew—to tell of promises that he has never believed, and to preach a Christ in whom his soul has never trusted! But when the Lord speaks to you as his son and his

F

daughter, the very fact that you stand in that relationship to him proves that you have some qualification for the service; and, therefore, you must not back out of it. You must not wrap your talent in a napkin, for you have got some talent in the very fact of being a child of God—a son or daughter of the Most High.

Well, now, secondly, let us turn to the next point, and that is, THE SERVICE TO WHICH THE LORD CALLS US—"Go work."

I know some Christians who do not like the name of work, and they look very black in the face if you say anything about duty. As for the matter of that, I do not mind how black they look, because there are some people who very much expose their own disposition by black looks and sullen moods; and when they turn sour they only manifest what is in their own nature. He that quarrels with the precept quarrels with God. Let him mind that. And he that does not like the practical part of Christianity may do what he likes with the doctrinal part of it, for he has neither part nor lot in this matter. The language of the true child of God is, "I delight myself in thy precepts"; and, as David put it, "Thy precepts have been my song in the house of my pilgrimage." He would even sing about the precepts of the gospel.

And now the text says, "Go work." That is something practical, something real. Go work. He does not say, "My son, go and think and speculate, and make curious experiments, and fetch out some new doctrines and astonish all thy fellow creatures with whims and oddities of thine own." "My son, go work." And he does not here say, "My son, go and attend conferences one after another all the year round and live in a perpetual maze of hearing different opinions and going from one public meeting and one religious engagement to another, and so feed thyself on the fat things full of marrow." All this is to be attended to in its proper proportion, but here it is, "Go work: go work." How many Christians there are that seem to read, "Go plan;" and they always figure in a way with some wonderful plan for the conversion of all the world, but they are never found labouring to convert a baby—never having a good word to say to the tiniest child in the Sunday School. They are always scheming, and yet never effecting anything. But the text says, "My son, go work." Oh, yes, but those who do not like to work themselves display the greatness of their talents in finding fault with those who do work, and a very clear perception they have of the mistakes and the crotchets of the very best of workers, whose zeal and industry are alike unflagging. Howbeit the text does not say, "My son, go and criticize;" what it distinctly says, is, "Go and work."

I remember that when Andrew Fuller had a very severe lecture from some Scotch Baptist brethren about the discipline of the church, he made the reply, "You say that your discipline is so much better than ours. Very well, but discipline is meant to make good soldiers. Now, my soldiers fight better than yours, and I think therefore that you ought not to say much about my discipline." So the real thing is not to be for ever calculating about modes of church government, and methods of management and plans to be adopted and rules to be laid down, which it shall be accounted a serious breach to violate. All well in their place, for order is good in its way. But come, now, let us go to work. Let us have something done.

I believe the very best working for God is often done in a very irregular manner. I get more and more to feel like the old soldier of Waterloo when he was examined about the best garment that could be worn by a soldier. The Duke of Wellington said to him, "If you had to fight Waterloo over again how would you like to be dressed?" The answer was, "Please, sir, I should like to be in my shirtsleeves." I think that is about the best. Get rid of everything superfluous, and get at it and hack away. I would to God that some Christians could do that, just strip to it, get rid of the superfluities of orderliness and propriety, and everything else which hampers them in trying to get back poor souls. There they are, going down to hell, and we are stickling about this mode and that, and considering the best way not to do it, and appointing committees to consider and debate, to adjourn and to postpone, and to leave the work in abeyance. The best way is to arise and do it, and let the committee sit afterwards. God grant we may. My son, go *work* to-day. Let it be something practical, something real, something actually done.

And by good work is meant something that will involve effort, toil, earnestness, self-denial, perhaps something that will want perseverance. In right earnest you will need to stick to it.

You will have heartily to yield yourself up to it, and give up a good deal else that might hinder you in doing it. Oh, Christian men and women, you will not glorify God much unless you really put your strength into the ways of the Lord, and throw your body, soul, and spirit—your entire manhood and womanhood—into the work of the Lord Jesus Christ. To do this you need not leave your families, or your shops, or your secular engagements. You can serve God in these things. They will often be vantage grounds of opportunity for you, but you must throw yourself into it. A man does not win souls to Christ while he is himself half asleep. The battle that is to be fought for the Lord Jesus must be fought by men who are wide awake and quickened by the Spirit of God. "My son, go work to-day." Do not go and play at teaching in Sunday Schools. Do not go and play the preacher. Do not go and play at exhorting people at the corners of streets, or even play at giving away tracts. "My son, go work." Throw thy soul into it. If it is worth doing it is worth doing well; and if it is worth doing well, it is worth doing better than you have ever done it yet; and even then it will be worth doing better still, for when you have done your best you have still to reach forward to a something far beyond; for the best of the best is all too little for such a God and for such a service. "My son, go work."

Well, now, such a claim as this may, perhaps, you think, sound rather hard; but I could tell you of many who would be very glad indeed if the Lord would say that to them. I might tell you of some who seldom leave their couches, some who can seldom sit upright through their weakness, to whom the nights are often full of pain, and the days are spent in weariness. They have learned, by God's teaching, to be content to suffer; but sometimes they cannot stifle an ardent wish; they wish the Lord would let them serve him. They do not envy, but yet there sometimes crosses over their minds the shadow of something like envy when they recollect what opportunities some of you have, who are full of health and strength. I have seen my brother minister laid aside, the voice perhaps gone, the lungs feeble, the heart prone to palpitate, and, oh, how he has wished that he could preach. With what fervour has he said, "Oh, if I had but those opportunities over again, how I would try to use them better than when I was favoured with them!" I tell you there are thousands of God's servants who would kiss the dust of his feet if he would only say to them, "Go work."

Besides, there is a great deal of honour in this work. You know how much your little boy wants to be a man. All boys do. When he first wears stick-up collars he congratulates himself upon the sign of anything like being a man. How proud he is of it! And if you, being a father, were to say to your boy, "My son, you are now of such an age that I can trust you to do some work for me"; see how the little man would begin to lift himself up: he is glad of it. And I am sure that if we look at it rightly, we who are the children of God ought to feel honoured by our heavenly Father saying to us, "You may do something for me." We must be very humble, for, after all, we cannot do anything except as he worketh in us to will and to do. But it is really very gratifying and ennobling to a poor mortal spirit to be allowed to do anything for God, ay, and to do what perfect saints above and holy angels cannot do; for there is no glorified spirit that can go down that back street and up that blind alley, and up those staircases that seem as if they would tumble down under your feet. Go and talk to that dying woman about Christ. You have a privilege which honoured Gabriel has not got: be thankful that you have it. There is no angel that can take that little child in the Sunday School class and tell it of "Gentle Jesus, meek and mild," and carry the little lamb for the Good Shepherd. The Lord sends you to do it. And it should be a point of thankfulness with us all that he has counted us worthy, and put us into the ministry—into any part or parcel of that ministry—to do something for his name's sake. Well, we are always receiving—always receiving, and it is very blessed; but still in this, as in other things, it is more blessed to give than to receive; and when we can give back to God some little trifle of service, stained with our tears because it is no better than it is, oh, it is a happy and a blessed thing. How grateful you ought to be that the Lord does say to you, "Son, go work to-day."

And remember, once more, on this point, that the work to which the Lord calls us is very varied, therefore there is a great deal of change in it; and, besides that, it suits the different temperaments, constitutions, dispositions, and abilities of his people. He says, "My son, go work to-day in my vineyards." But he does not give you to do my work, and he does not give me to do your work. Dear sister, you would like to do the work of such and such an excellent Christian woman, would not you? Yes, but that is naughty of you. Be satisfied to do your own. Suppose your housemaid always wanted to do the cook's work, the house would soon be in bad order. Better keep to your own place, dear sister. Ah, there is a brother here who says, "I think I could preach if I only had such and such a congregation." Very likely, brother, but you had better preach to your own and do what good you can there. Very likely I should do better with my own congregation, and you will do better with yours than I should. Every man had better keep to his own work in his own place. And how thankful we ought to be that if one can preach a sermon, yet another can offer a prayer, that if one can go and speak to thousands, yet another can speak to ones and twos. There is work in the school; there is work in the family; there is work in the street; there is work in the work-shop; there is work everywhere for Jesus if thou wilt but stretch out thy hand to find it and follow Solomon's good advice, "Whatsoever thy hand findeth to do, do it with thy might."

Now, THE TIME is the next thing. "My son, go work *to-day*." That means directly—now.

I will not say a word about what it is your duty to do to-morrow. Let the morrow take care of itself. I will have nothing to say about what it will be right for you to do in ten years' time. If you are alive, grace will be given to you for that. But what I have to say to you in God's name is, "Go work to-day," and as the sun has gone down, let it be, "Go work to-night in my vineyard," if there be opportunity, even to-night, ere another day's sun has dawned upon the world. "And why to-day?" Because, thy Father wants thee to be at it at once. "Why stand ye here all the day idle?" If thou hast done nothing for Christ thou hast wasted enough time. Do not rest to-day, but be at it now. He wants thee to do it now, because the vines are in a certain condition that just now require work. There is somebody in the world who is in a tender state of mind, to whom thou mayest speak successfully. There is a mourner here who wants comfort to-night. There is one struggling against his conscience, who wants urging on to-night in the right way. If the case be neglected to-night it will be like neglecting to trim the vines just at the proper time for taking away the superfluous wood. Now canst thou do it. Thou canst not do it on any other day. Therefore, "go work to-day."

"To-day," because there are certain dangers to which those whom thou art about to bless are just now exposed. The devil is tempting them: it is needful that thou go and help them against that temptation. They are just now in despair; it is needful that thou step in with the word of comfort from thy Master's mouth. They are, perhaps, this very night, before they go to their rest, about to commit a great sin. Mayhap the Lord means thee to interpose just now, ere that sin be done. Son, go work to-day; thou art wanted. There are very few labourers just now: many of them have gone. Son, do thou go to-day, while the others have gone out for their recreation—while the others are asleep and grown idle. There is a gap just now: it is at this moment. Many a brave deed of valour owed its success to being done at once. "Haste thee now, even now, and go work to-day in my vineyard." "To-day:" mark that.

It means work all the day: work as long as ever you live. Son, if once thou get into that vineyard do not come home again until the day is done. I am always sorry when I hear of Christian people beginning to give up some of their work before the infirmities of old age come on; although I think that many a minister, when he gets old, had better give up a charge for which he is not equal and take one smaller for which his strength would avail. But I know that some give up this work and that, and they say, "Let the young people come and take their turn." Yes, but suppose the sun were to stop shining and say, "There is a star over there; let him have a turn and shine instead of me." Suppose the moon were for ever to give up shining in the night watches, and say that she has had enough of being out at night; and suppose the earth were to say it has had enough of yielding harvests. "Why should I yield any more? Let the sea take its turn and grow corn." And so, dear Christian friends, keep on as long as you can. Who can blame dear old John Newton? When he got too feeble to get up the pulpit stairs of St. Mary Wool-noth, he was helped up, and then, leaning on his pulpit Bible he poured out his soul. A friend of his said to him, "Dear Mr. Newton, don't you think you ought to give up preaching?" "What!" said he, "shall the old African blasphemer ever give up praising the grace of God as long as there is breath in his body? Never." And so he went to his work again. Oh, for more of that spirit to persevere in the Master's service.

Only there is this thought: it is only a day. "Son, go work to-day." It will only be a day. The longest life is no more, and then the shadows of death will gather: but there will be no night, for instead thereof the day shall break and the shadows shall flee away, and then life's service here below will all be over. There will be no troublesome children to teach, no hard-hearted sinners to rebuke, no backsliding, lukewarm Christians to reprove, no deceivers to encounter, no sceptics to answer with the testimony that cannot be shaken, no scoffers to put up with, patiently bearing their contumely. It will be all over then; and then shall those who have served their Master behold him gird himself and sit down and serve them, and they shall feast at his table and enter into his joy. "My son, go work to-day," for thou shalt rest to-morrow. Work on, for there is rest enough in heaven: work on, for eternity shall well repay thee for the toils of time.

Then, as to THE PLACE WHERE THE LORD CALLS US TO THE WORK. "My son, go work to-day in *my vineyard*."

I like to think of this special sphere of labour, because it must be a pleasure to work in our Father's vineyard, for there every-thing that we do will be done for him. I trim this vine; it is my Father's vine. I dig this trench; but it is my Father's ground I turn. I gather out these stones; it is my Father's vineyard that I am engaged in clearing. I repair this fence; it is my Father's soil that I am thus hedging about. It is all done for him. Who would not do all that he could for the dear Redeemer, dying Lamb, and for the blessed Father of our spirits? "Go work to-day in my vineyard."

Then what interesting work it is, for it is our own vineyard because it is our Father's vineyard. All that belongs to him belongs to us. We are sons working in our Father's vineyard; so we can say, "This vine; why, I have an interest in it, for I am the heir of my Father's property. This ground that I endeavour to dig about and manure; it is my ground, it is my Father's. And this wall that I try to mend; it is mine, it is my Father's." It is always pleasant to work for ourselves, you know; and, in a blessed sense, when we are working for God we are working for ourselves. Ye are labourers, ye are God's husbandry, ye are God's people; and when ye are working for the Lord ye really are taking shares with him.

And what a work it is, too! "Go work to-day in my vineyard." One likes working in a vineyard, because it pays. Working in a desert may be thankless toil; but working in a vineyard where there will be clusters is very different. One can think already of those juicy grapes that will be ready for the winepress, and for the festival when the ruddy juice comes freely forth—when they make merry and joy in the vintage. And you will have the new wine, and the wine on the lees well refined. All sorts of pleasures await the man who serves the Lord.

"Go work in my vineyard." Does it not mean that the work is plentiful? There is always something to be done in a vineyard. If you ask those who keep vines they will tell you that there is much labour required. From one part of the year right on there is something still to be done, many dangers to be averted, and many enemies to be kept off from the vine; so there is plenty to do. Go work in the vineyard, where there will be need of all thy hands. It is close at hand, hard by you; for the heavenly Father did not say, "Son, take a ship and go to Tarshish, or to Ophir." He said, "My son, go work in my vineyard"; and the vineyard was just out of the back door there. Now, your heavenly Father's vineyard is close to you. Those streets where you live, the very house in which you dwell—perhaps the very chamber in which you sleep—is God's vineyard, where you are to work for him. It is your heavenly Father's own work, to be done by you in your heavenly Father's own strength. Oh, if I might set one young man on fire with love to Christ I should be glad. If I could but be the humble means of inspiring some Christian woman with the high mission of being useful in her day and generation, how much would my soul rejoice! There came into this Tabernacle one evening a young gentleman who was well known as being a great hand with his cricket bat. He was a Christian and full of earnestness in laying hold upon the great truths of revelation; but he had never served his God. He thought it right to spend his leisure time in manly exercises, and in such pursuits he sought recreation. But while I spoke a fire kindled within him, and he went home to begin to preach the Gospel in the street of the city where he lived, and now he is the pastor of a large and influential church which he has gathered together. Since then he has preached more than once in this place the Gospel of Jesus Christ. Oh, that some other believer who may happen to be in that condition—some young man of ability who is spending all his strength on the world without going into anything grossly wrong, but simply wasting his talent—might hear a voice saying to him, "My son, go work to-day in my vineyard."

After dwelling so long upon the practical admonition, I have but little time left for that brief explanation of the parable, or more properly the parables of the vineyard with which on the outset I promised to close. The occasion on which they were spoken is memorable. Assailed "*while he was teaching*," rudely interrupted by the legal sanhedrim of the Jews with the high priest in the forefront, they confronted our Lord as it were with a warrant and propounded to him two questions; one as to the authority or title by which he acted, and the other as to the source from which his authority was derived. You all know how skilfully he evaded his unscrupulous antagonists. "*I also will ask you one thing*," he said. Therewith he put to them a question that proved a poser, and left them to a ridiculous parley, for "*they reasoned among themselves*," went aside to whisper, and then drew back in sheer timidity declining an answer, for "*they feared the people*," or, as you may read it, they were afraid of the mob. The advantage our Lord thus gained he quickly followed up with a parable—in fact, with the parable we have been talking about.

He opened it thus: "*What think ye?*" putting a query about two sons, the one forward in profession, yet utterly disobedient, the other sullen in appearance though afterwards penitent in spirit and diligent in labour. The thing was so obvious that they answer without hesitation with a reply that nailed the censure to their own breasts. "Whether of these twain did the will of his father?" They say unto him, "The first." Read it, read the parable for yourselves. Realize the force of it if you can. The penitent harlot and the obdurate high priest are put in the scales. "*In the way of righteousness*"—according to the truthful caricature—the chief priests and elders themselves admit that "*the first*" of these twain did the will of our heavenly Father. Digest this parable, I pray you. Almost without a break "*the *vineyard*" supplied him yet again with another parable which he insisted on their hearing—a parable that brought out the character of the dispensation and "the signs of the times" so distinctly, that they could not fail to read it in the light of their own prophets, and at the same time it so exposed the treachery of their counsel and conspiracy that they recognized their own portrait at once and perceived that he spake of them. "The vineyard," you are all aware, was the constant symbol of the Jewish nation as a theocracy. The men that sat in Moses's seat were the stewards in charge of that vineyard which was Jehovah's special property. They, like the perverse rulers of every age, sought to shelter their evil designs under cover of syndicates and conferences. But the words and warnings of Jesus, his proverbs and parables, were keen enough to probe all their subtleties, and leave them to stand abashed without an excuse for the guile of their hearts or the guilt of their conduct. Now remember that the kingdom of God was taken from them and given to a nation bringing forth the fruits thereof. To what nation is it given? Is it not to the church which is called "a chosen generation, a royal priesthood, an holy nation, a peculiar people; that ye should shew forth the praises of him who hath called you out of darkness into his marvellous light"? (1 Pet. 2: 9). The vine is the express symbol of our Christian life, as all believers are incorporated with Christ. Well then, there is a vineyard of God's own planting; you believe that. He has let it out to husbandmen; you believe that. He will come seeking fruit of this vineyard; you believe that. You are the children of the husbandmen; you believe that, or else you would not presume to sit at his table and drink of his cup. He says therefore to you, "Son, go work in my vineyard." What answer do you give with your lips? What answer do you give with your life?

XIII

HARVEST PAST, AND MEN UNSAVED

"The harvest is past, the summer is ended, and we are not saved."—Jer. 8: 20.

THIS is a very mournful chapter, especially if we include in it, as we rightly should, the first verse of the ninth chapter: "Oh that my head were waters." The passage is full of lamentation and woe, and yet it is somewhat singular that the chief mourner here is not one who needed chiefly to be in trouble. Jeremiah was under the especial protection of God, and he escaped in the evil day. Even when Nebuchadnezzar was exercising his utmost rage, Jeremiah was in no danger, for the heart of the fierce monarch was kindly towards him. "Now Nebuchadnezzar king of Babylon gave charge concerning Jeremiah to Nebuzar-adan the captain of the guard, saying, take him, and look well to him, and do him no harm; but do unto him even as he shall say unto thee."

The man of God, who personally had least cause to mourn, was filled with heavy grief, while the people who were about to lose their all, and to lose their lives, still remained but half awakened; complaining, but not repenting; afraid, but yet not humbled before God. None of them uttered such a grievous lament as that which came from the heart and mouth of the prophet. Their heads were full of idle dreams, while his had become waters; their eyes were full of wantonness, while his were a fountain of tears. He loved them better than they loved themselves. Is it not strange that it should be so, that the physician should be more anxious than the sick man? Perhaps, however, it is not so singular that the shepherd should care more for the flock than the sheep care for themselves. When the sheep are men it is certainly an unreasonable thing! The weeping prophet cries, "For the hurt of the daughter of my people am I hurt;" he was more hurt than they were.

A preacher whom God sends will often feel more care for the souls of men than men feel for themselves or their own salvation. Is it not sad that there should be an anxious pain in the heart of one who is himself saved, while those who are unsaved, and are obliged to own it, feel little or no concern? To see a man in jeopardy of his life, and all around him alarmed for his danger, while he himself is half asleep, is a sad sight. See yonder man about to be condemned to die, standing at the bar, the judge putting on the black cap is scarcely able to pronounce the sentence for emotion, and all around him in the court break down with distress on his account, while he himself is brazen-faced and feels no more than the floor he stands upon! How hardened has he become! Pity is lost upon him, if pity ever can be lost.

Such a sad sight we constantly see in our congregations: those who are "condemned already" on account of sin are altogether indifferent to their awful peril, while their godly parents are greatly distressed for them, Christian people are pleading with them, and earnest messengers from God expostulating with them. Heaven and earth are moved for them, and yet they are unaffected. May none of you be hardened through the deceitfulness of sin. May God of his infinite mercy strike the rock, and make the waters of penitence to gush out from it. May his transforming hand turn stone into flesh, and cause a holy tenderness to banish all stubbornness and insensibility. Such is my agonising cry to the Holy Spirit.

Certainly there ought to be dismay, and even terror, in the heart of any who are compelled to use my text in reference to themselves. Those few words, "We are not saved!" sound like a peal of thunder. They should cut the soul as with a case of knives—"We are not saved!" What worse thing can men say of themselves? We are now under the abiding wrath of God, for "we are not saved!" We must soon stand before the judgment seat of God, and then we shall be condemned of the great Judge, for "we are not saved!" We shall ere long be driven from his Presence and from the glory of his power, for "we are not saved!" We shall then be shut out in outer darkness, where shall be weeping and wailing and gnashing of teeth, for "we are not saved!" Had men but reason, or having reason would they but use it upon the most important of all subjects, surely they would cry out in the bitterness of their souls, "Oh that our heads were water and our eyes fountains of tears, that we might weep day and night till we had found our Saviour and he had washed away our sin and saved us." How saddening to see the loaded waggons of harvest bearing no real blessing to us, and to watch the clusters on the vine ripen all unblessed! Alas for that summer which amid all its flowers yields us no perfume of peace or joy. On the other hand, how blessed to feel that the harvest is past, and the summer is ended, and blessed by God we are saved! Now let winter come with all its blasts, we have nothing to fear, for wrapped in our Saviour's righteousness, and hidden in the cleft of his side, we shall outlive every storm.

I earnestly pray the Lord to bless the words I am about to speak, that they may be rendered useful to many undecided persons to lead them to decision, and induce them to give themselves up to Christ at once. May the Holy Spirit work this blessed result in thousands. I have so long been silent that I am hungering to speak with power. Come Holy Spirit! Come!

First, I shall look at the text as *a complaint*—"We are not saved;" and, secondly, I shall suggest that out of it ought to come *consideration:* those who utter the complaint should be led thereby to solemn consideration.

First, we have before us the language of COMPLAINT. These Jews said, "The seasons are going by, the year is spending itself, the harvest is past, the vintage also is ended, and yet we are not saved." Some of them were captives in Babylon, and they fondly expected to be brought back from the distant land, but they were disappointed. They hoped that when the produce of the Nile had been reaped Egyptian troops would march against Nebuchadnezzar and break his power. Others of them had fled into the defenced cities, and taken refuge behind the walls of Jerusalem, and they also dreamed that the march of the Chaldeans would be stopped, and the land would be delivered from their invasion as soon as the summer heats were over. The rescue did not come; indeed, they could from Jerusalem hear the neighing of the Babylonian horses: "The snorting of his horses was heard from Dan: the whole land trembled at the sound of the neighing of his strong ones; for they are come, and have devoured the land, and all that is in it;

the city, and those that dwell therein." Therefore they complained that their hopes had failed. In effect they complained of God that he had not saved them, as if he was under some obligation to have done so, as if they had a kind of claim upon him to interpose: and so they spoke as if they were an ill-used people, a nation that had been neglected by their Protector. Husbandmen had gathered in the harvest, and vine-dressers had gleaned the grapes, yet they had not been cared for, but left to suffer: despite their hopes they were not saved. Certain persons fall into the same state of mind in these days. They know that they are not saved, but they do not blame themselves for it; they would not like to say where it does lie, but they will not own that it lies in themselves. They are not saved, and somebody should be blamed for it, or perhaps nobody, but they mention the fact, not as a confession of which they are ashamed, but as a misfortune for which they are to be pitied.

This complaint was a very unjust one, for there were many reasons why they were not saved and why God had not delivered them.

The first was *they had looked to the wrong quarter:* they expected that the Egyptians would deliver them. You remember that in the reign of Zedekiah the Jews revolted from their subjection to the Babylonians because they hoped that the king of Egypt would come up and fight with the Babylonian power. Those who were captives hoped that yet the great armies of the Pharaohs might break down the might of Chaldea, and so they looked to Egypt for help, an old fault with Israel and a gross folly, for why should they look to the house of bondage for succour? The same folly dwells in multitudes of men. They are not saved, and they never will be while they continue to look where they do look. All dependence upon ourselves is looking to Egypt for help, and leaning our weight upon a broken reed. Whether that dependence upon self takes the form of relying upon ceremonies, or depending upon prayers, or trusting in our own attempts to improve ourselves morally, it is still the same proud folly of self-dependence. Vain is all searching for legal righteousness, hoping to merit something of God, or to do something without help from on high, for the Lord himself has assured us that by the works of the law no flesh shall be justified. You may have been very earnest and serious about divine things, but if you have looked in any measure or degree to what you are, or can do, or what any man can do for you, it is no wonder that you are not saved, for there is no salvation there.

I am afraid some think that it is a great thing to sit under a faithful minister, that if the gospel be thoroughly preached they may naturally expect that if they take a seat at the place they will be saved. But all dependence upon ministers is only another form of superstitious confidence in priestcraft. All trust but that which is found in Jesus is a delusion and a falsehood. No man can help you. Though Noah, Samuel, and Moses prayed for you, their prayers could not avail unless you believed in the blood of Jesus; there is salvation nowhere else. Though the whole church were to unite in one protracted intercession, and determine that all its ministers should preach to you alone for the next seven years, there would be no more hope of your being saved then than now, unless you would believe in the Lord Jesus Christ, who alone is the salvation of the sons of men. The most fruitful of harvests may pass and the most genial of summers may smile upon you, but while you look to yourself no sunshine from God shall cause you to flourish. Eternal barrenness is the portion of those who trust in man and make flesh their arm. While men go about to establish their own righteousness, and will not submit themselves to the righteousness of Christ, they shall be like the woman who spent all her living upon physicians, and was nothing better, but rather grew worse.

Those people had *prided themselves upon their outward privileges;* they had presumed upon their favoured position, for they say in the nineteenth verse, "Is not the Lord in Zion? is not her king in her?" Because they belonged to the chosen nation, because the Lord had entrusted them with the sacred oracles, and manifested himself to their fathers, therefore they thought that they might sin with impunity, and reckon upon being delivered in the day of danger. I do not know how many of you here may be depending upon outward religiousness, or indulging some kind of thought that, apart from your personal faith in Christ, you will be saved by your pious connections and hallowed relationships; but if that is what you are depending upon, rest assured you will be deceived. Vain are the baptism or the confirmation of your youth: faith in Jesus is the one thing needful; vain is the fact that you were born of Christian parents: ye must be born again; vain is your sitting as God's people sit, and standing as they stand, in the solemn service of the sanctuary: your heart must be changed; vain is your observance of the Lord's Day, and vain your Bible reading and your form of prayer night and morning, unless you are washed in Jesus' blood; vain are all things without living faith in the living Jesus. Though you had been descended from an unbroken line of saints, though you had no unconverted relative, your ancestry and lineage would not avail you; the sons of God are born, not of blood, nor of the will of man, nor of the will of the flesh, but of God. All the external privileges that can be heaped upon you, though you had sermons piled up and Gospel services heaped on them, as the giants piled mountain upon mountain, Pelion upon Ossa, that they might climb to heaven, would be useless; there is no reaching to salvation by such means. If your reliance be upon external ordinances, of professions or privileges in any measure or degree, no wonder that the harvest is past, and the summer is ended, and you are not saved, for you never will be saved till doomsday while you look in that direction. Look like sinners to your Saviour and you shall be saved, but not else.

Thirdly, there was another and very powerful reason why these people were not saved, for, with all their religiousness and their national boast as to God's being among them, they *had continued in provoking the Lord*. He says in the nineteenth verse, "Why have they provoked me to anger with their graven images and with strange vanities?" They lived in sin, disobeying God to his face; they set up new idols, and imported false deities from foreign lands, and yet they said, "We are not saved." Would they have the Lord sanction their degrading idolatry by sending them deliverance? Do you know a man who goes frequently into ill company, and gets intoxicated, and yet comes to hear the gospel, and murmurs that he is not saved? Is he not mad? Let me speak plainly to him. Do you think that you are going to heaven to reel about the holy streets? Shall the pure heavens be polluted by your profanities? You are dreadfully mistaken if you fancy so. Another person indulges lust, lives an unclean life, and yet he comes in and listens to the word of God as one who has a loving ear for it, and he also complains that he is not saved. O unclean man, how canst thou dream of salvation whilst thou art defiled with filthiness? What, thou and thy harlot, members of Christ! Oh, thou knowest not my pure and holy Master. He receiveth sinners, but he rejecteth those who delight in their iniquities. Thou must have done with the indulgence of sin if thou wouldst be cleansed from the guilt of it. There is no going on in transgression, and yet obtaining salvation: it is a licentious supposition. Christ comes to save us from our sins, not to make it safe to do evil. That blood which washes out the stain brings with it also a hatred of the thing which made the stain. Sin must be relinquished, or salvation cannot be received.

I spoke very plainly just now, but some here of pure heart little know how plainly we must speak if we are to reach some men's consciences, for it shames me when I think of some who year after year indulge in secret sin, and yet they are regular frequenters of the house of God. You would think they surely were already converted, or soon would be when you saw them here, but if you followed them home you would quite despair of them. O lovers of sin do not deceive yourselves, you will surely reap that which you sow. How can grace reign in you while you are the slaves of your own passions? How can it be while you are anchored to a secret sin that you should be borne along by the current of grace towards the desired haven of safety? Either you must leave your sin or leave all hope of heaven; if you hold your sin hell will ere long hold you. Jesus was not sent to be the minister of sin; he never came into the world to bleed and die to make the way of the transgressors easy by enabling them to be vicious without risk. The friend of sinners is the enemy of sin. There is a religion that will let you pay a shilling or two and purchase priestly absolution, but this we protest against. Such a faith may well breed iniquity. What can it be but like Egypt's Nile, when in the days of Moses it became the fruitful mother of ten thousand unclean frogs? Under the religion of Christ absolution for the past is only to be obtained through faith in Jesus, and that faith brings with it repentance for former offences, and a change of life for days to come. Wherefore do men say "We are not saved" when they are still hugging their iniquities? They may as well hope to gather grapes of thorns or figs of thistles, as to find salvation while they abide in sin. May God deliver us all from the love of sin, for such a deliverance is salvation.

Again, there was another reason why they were not saved, and that was because *they made being saved from trouble the principal matter.* Many make a great mistake about salvation; they mistake the meaning of the term, and to them salvation means being delivered from going down into the pit of hell, just as to these Jews it meant rescue from Nebuchadnezzar. Now, the right meaning of salvation is purification from evil. These people never thought of this: they never said, "We are not cleansed, we are not made holy," but "we are not saved." If their cry had been, "The harvest is past, the summer is ended, and we have not yet conquered sin," that would have been a mark of something good and true, but they showed no trace of it. There is not much in a man's desiring to be saved if he means by that an escape from the punishment of his offences. Was there ever a murderer yet who did not wish to be saved from the gallows? When a man is tied up to be flogged for a deed of brutal violence, and his back is bared for the lash, depend upon it he repents of what he did; that is to say, he repents that he has to suffer for it; but that is all, and a sorry all too. He has no sorrow for the agony which he inflicted on his innocent victim; no regret for maiming him for life.

What is the value of such a repentance? Here is the point: do you wish to have new hearts? If you do you shall have them. Do you wish to leave the sins you have loved? Do you desire to live as Christ lived? Do you wish to keep the commandments of God? Do you sigh for purity of life? Do you wish henceforth to be as God would have you to be, just, loving, kind, chaste, after the example of the great Redeemer? If so, then truly the desire you have cometh of God; but if all you want is to be able to die without dread, that you may wake up in the next world and not be driven down to the bottomless pit, if that is all, there is nothing gracious in it, and it is no wonder that you should say, "The harvest is past, the summer is ended, and I am not saved." You do not know what being saved means. God teach you to love holiness, and there shall not pass another harvest, nay not another day, before you shall be saved; indeed, that very love is the dawn of salvation. Seek salvation as the kingdom of God within you, seek it first and seek it now, and you shall not be denied.

Again, there was another reason why these people were not saved and could not be. Read the ninth verse, and see their fault and folly: "Lo, *they have rejected the word of the Lord*, and what wisdom is in them?" We hear persons complain that they are not saved, though they neglect the saving word. They go to a place of worship and therefore wonder that they are not saved; how can they be when that which they hear is not the object of their heart's attention? Do you read your Bible privately? Did you ever read it with an earnest prayer that God would teach you what you really are, and make you to be a true believer in Christ? Have you done that just as earnestly as you studied a book when you were trying to pass an examination? I do not know what calling you follow, but I will suppose, for instance, that you wish to be a chemist; if so, you go through a course of studies, and you acquaint yourself with certain books, in order that you may pass an examination. You stick to your work, for you know that you will not pass unless you are well informed as to the matters needful to your profession. Do you show the same diligence in reference to your soul and your God? Have you ever read your Bible with anything like the same intensity with which a man must study a class-book in order to pass his examinations? Have you read it with regard to yourself, asking God to teach you its meaning, and to make the sense of it press upon your conscience? Do you reply, "I have not done that"? Why then do you wonder that you are not saved? To put a slighter test than the former: when you hear the Gospel, do you always enquire, "What has this to do with me?" or do you listen to it as a general truth with which you have no peculiar concern?

What a difference is perceptible in hearers! Numbers of persons have come hither at this time merely to hear Spurgeon preach, and form an estimate of him. Is this a fit errand for God's day, and for an assembly gathered for worship? Do not imagine that we are flattered by such attentions. We do not covet such hearers. What care I about their estimate? A poor soul that wants to find Christ is a diamond in my eyes, but he who comes to hear me because of public talk is a common pebble that one might sling away, only it is well that even he should hear the word if perchance God might bless him. Many of you Christian people hear sermons that you may remember well-turned sentences and pithy sayings, or that you may gauge the preacher's earnestness, and judge whether he is likely to be useful. Hearing for others is a very common amusement. There is a deal of difference between walking through a baker's shop when you are well filled and counting all the loaves upon the shelves, and rushing in at the door to get a bit of bread at once, for fear of dying of starvation. Water seen as a picturesque object by a traveller is one thing, but a living draught swallowed by one dying of thirst is quite a different matter.

O that men would treat the Gospel as a necessary of life, which they must each one feed upon or perish. That is the style of hearing when a man prays that the word of God may search him, and try him. It is well when the hearer bares his bosom and cries, "Lord cut this cancer out of my soul, I pray thee. I beseech thee, let me live!" That kind of hearing ends in saving. "Incline your ear," saith the great Lord, "and come unto me; hear, and your soul shall live" (Isa. 55 : 3). "Hearken diligently unto me," saith he again; and in so doing he certifies that diligent hearkening shall bring a blessing with it. Alas, with the bulk of hearers the word goes in at one ear and out at the other. The noise of God's voice is drowned by the din of the world's traffic, the six days crush the influence of the seventh, and it is no wonder that January comes and December goes, and yet worldlings are not saved. They never will be while they slumber as they do.

There is a further reason why some men are not saved, and that is because *they have a great preference for slight measures.* They love to hear the flattering voice whispering—"Peace, peace, where there is no peace"; and they choose those for leaders who will heal their hurt slightly. They wish for something very comfortable, and in their folly they prefer poisoned sweets to healthful salts. "I felt so miserable," said one, "when I left that place that I said I would never enter it again." It was a foolish vow. He who is wise will go where the word has most power, both to kill and to make alive. Do you want a physician when you call upon him to please you with a flattering opinion? Must he needs say, "My dear friend, it is a very small matter; you want nothing but pleasant diet, and you will soon be all right"? If he talks thus smoothly when he knows that a deadly disease is commencing its work upon you, is he not a deceiver? Do you not think you are very foolish if you pay such a man your guinea, and denounce his neighbour who tells you the plain truth? Do you want to be deluded? Are you eager to be duped? Do you want to dream of heaven, and then wake up in hell? Have I such an idiot here? May heaven save him from his ruinous folly.

For my part, I should like to know the worst of my case, and things must be very bad with any one of you who cannot say the same. When a merchant dares not face his books, you know where he is. When he says to his clerk, "No, no, I do not want to know on which side the balance stands. I cannot bear to be worried. I dare say money will come in as well as go out, and my credit will raise me another loan. Things will come round, and the less we dive into difficulties the better." We shall hear of that gentleman very speedily in the Bankruptcy Court, I think. He is in the same condition spiritually who does not dare to face himself, but would rather not be troubled with questions and examinations. What, dare you not look yourself in the face? Have you covered up the looking-glass? Have you hid the word of God from yourselves, and dare not see how you look? Ay, then be sure you are in an evil plight. While men will not have the thorough-going truth preached to them, while they like some siren strain, while they would fain listen to soft music and float upon gentle streams that bear them down to destruction, there is little hope but what harvests and summers will come and go, and they will not be saved.

All this while these people have wondered that they were not saved, and yet *they never repented of their sin*. The Lord himself witnesses against them, "I hearkened and heard, but they spake not aright: no man repented him of his wickedness, saying, What have I done? Every one turned to his course, as the horse rusheth into the battle." "Were they ashamed when they had committed abomination? Nay, they were not at all ashamed, neither could they blush." Repentance was a jest with them, they had not grace enough even to feel shame, and yet they made a complaint against God, saying, "The harvest is past, the summer is ended, and we are not saved." What monstrous folly was this! Where has the Lord given half a promise to those who will not confess and forsake their sins? How can impenitent sinners hope that they should be forgiven?

We have said enough upon this unjustifiable complaint. Now, may the Spirit of God help us while we would lead unconverted persons into the CONSIDERATION of this matter.

First consideration, *"we are not saved."* I do not want to talk, I want you to think. "We are not saved." Put it in the personal, first person singular. Will everyone here only do me the favour of saying that to himself if it is true, "I am not saved! I am not saved! I am not saved from sin, I love it still. I am not saved from guilt, I am condemned for my failure to keep the law. I am not saved from wrath, I am not saved from judgment, I am not saved from the eternal curse. I am not saved! My dear child in heaven is for ever happy, but I am not saved. My dear wife is a happy Christian, but I am not saved. I am one of a family where many have been converted, but I am not saved. I am a grey-headed old man, and I am not saved. I am beloved in my family by my dear mother, for I am yet a child, but though she prays for me I am not saved." "I am a member of a church and am not saved." Are you obliged to say that, any of you? Be honest, then. Do not cover up the truth, however terrible it may be; better far to face it. What if some one must confess, "I am a preacher of the Gospel, but I am not saved." Oh, my heart, what terror is here! It is an awful thing if anybody here has to say, "I am a teacher in a Sunday School, and this afternoon the little ones will gather round me, but I am not saved. People respect me, they say I have all things good about me, but I have not the one thing needful, I am not saved." Teachers, does this touch any one of you? I pray you let it have its due influence. Now you down here in the area, and you in these galleries, will you do one of the two things; either say "By God's grace I have believed in Jesus and I am saved," or else just sigh out silently in your soul, "I am not saved." It will do you good to end all questions, and know once for all whether you are in Christ or not.

Furthermore, not only am I not saved, but *I have been a long time not saved.* Let me put language into the mouths of those who are ruining themselves by delay. "Time flies. How quickly it is gone! I was a young man a very little while ago, now I am getting into middle age, getting a little bald, grey hairs are upon me here and there. Why, dear me, here are grandchildren come—it seems but yesterday that I was married. Yes, harvests have passed, vintages have been gathered, and I am not saved. Twenty years ago I sat listening to this same preacher, and I was not saved then; and I remember how he touched my conscience, but all those years have gone, and I am not saved. The world has had its opportunities and used them; they sowed and they reaped their harvests. The vine-dresser used the knife and the vine was pruned, and in due season he gathered the clusters, but I have had no harvest, I have known no vintage. I have made money, I have got on in business, or at least I have just paid my way and supported my family, but I have had no spiritual harvest; no, for I never sowed. I have had no spiritual vintage, for I was never pruned. I never went to the great Husbandman and asked him to dig about me and make me fruitful to his name. What opportunities I had! I have been through revivals, but the sacred power passed over me; I remember several wonderful occasions when the Spirit of God was poured out, and yet I am not saved."

Worse still, *habits harden*. "If I was not saved during the last twenty or thirty years I am less likely to be impressed now. I do not feel as I once did. Sometimes the vile unbelief which now taints the very air creeps over me, and I am half a sceptic. Considerations that used to thrill me, and make my flesh creep, are now put before me, but I seem like a piece of steel—nay, I do not even rust under the word, I am unimpressible. Harvests have dried me, summers have parched me, age has shrivelled my soul: my moisture is turned into the drought of summer, I am getting to be old hay, or as withered weeds fit for the burning." It is a dreadful consideration for a man to turn over in his mind, but it is a very needful one, for it is an undoubted fact that every year fixes the character and engraves the lines of evil deeper in the nature. Harvests and summers leave us worse if they do not see us mend. As true as you are alive, unless God of infinite mercy arouse you out of your present condition to seek and immediately find Christ, and obtain everlasting life, some of you will settle down into a condition which will be the eternal state of your hearts. O for grace to repent at once, ere yet the wax has cooled and the seal is set for ever.

The last summer will soon come, and the last harvest will soon be reaped, and you must go to your long home. I will apply it mainly to myself: I must go up stairs for the last time, and I must lay me down upon the bed from which I shall never rise again; if I am unsaved my room will be a prison chamber to me, and the bed will be hard as a plank, if I have to lie there and know that I must die, that a few more days or hours must end this struggle for existence, and I am bound to stand before God. O my God, save me from an unready death-bed! Save these people from dying and passing into hell! You will have no doubts about it then, you know; you will see clearly that you are bound to stand before God. This naked spirit of mine, disrobed of its body, must appear before the Judge! What shall I do? What shall I say? Before my Maker's burning eyes, stripped naked to my shame, oh! what shall I do? And when I speechless stand before him, by my silence owning to my guilt, what shall I do? The gate of heaven is shut, I cannot enter there. I have not the password; I have rejected the way thither; I have rejected Christ, who is the King of the place; oh! whither must I go? I will not paint the picture. Souls, I charge you by everything that is rational within you, escape for your lives, and seek to find eternal salvation for your undying spirits. You are not dogs nor cats, nor horses nor cattle, as men tell you; you are nobler things, and an immortality awaits you, and you shall make to-day that immortality the most awful curse that can fall upon you, or a privilege infinite, unutterable. It is a grand alternative. God help us by his infinite mercy to choose eternal holiness and everlasting joy, and choose it now.

Come, let us consider a little longer a few practical truths which may be of service. It is quite clear that, if you are to get right, you must not go on in the old way. The harvest is past, and the summer is ended, and by the way in which you have been going on you are not saved. There must be a change of tactics. Salvation must be thought of in another light, and sought for in another spirit. Come, if you are to find salvation you must be more earnest about it, you must be more intense about it; there must be a greater valuing of this salvation, and a more solemn resolve that if heaven or earth or hell can yield it to you, you will have it, for "the kingdom of heaven suffereth violence, and the violent take it by force" (Matt. 11: 12). Never did a man sleep himself into eternal life. Salvation is all of grace, but sluggards have no grace. The Lord does not work in us to sleep and to slumber, but to will and to do. Men reach the Celestial City, not by drowsiness, but by their spirits being stirred to feel that there is nothing else that is worth a thought compared with going on pilgrimage to glory.

There is one thing certain, that, as the harvests have past and the summer is ended and we have not been saved, we must have been looking in the wrong place. Very likely we have been looking to something on earth for salvation. If so, we have not found it, because it is not there. The prophet enquires: "Is there no balm in Gilead: is there no physician there?" (Jer. 8: 22). He knew that there was none in that region which could meet his people's dreadful hurt. There was a balm in Gilead, but it was the resin of a tree; there were physicians there, but they were mostly quacks that duped the people. If there had been any true balm and any real physician there, the health of the daughter of his people would have been recovered. No, there is "no balm in Gilead" for you. The "balm of Gilead" was only good for certain bodily wounds and sores, but not for cuts and wounds and sores like these, for these are in the soul. The physicians of Gilead could only heal some few complaints, and seldom enough did they heal even these, but all the physicians of Gilead in a row cannot heal *your complaint*. I will tell you of another and better health-resort than Gilead—it is Calvary. Where Jesus bled you will find a balm; where Jesus lives you will find a physician.

Another thing must have suggested itself to you while I have been preaching, if you have listened in earnest; and it is this, that the great point must be that if I am to be saved *I must get rid of sin*. I will again speak for those whom I address. "I have been thinking that I should undergo some strange transformation, and some kind of mysterious shock, or have a vision or see some strange sight, and that then I should say I am a converted man. I discover that the main point is to get rid of sin; it must be driven out of my heart. I have not only to leave off the act of it, and the thought of it, but all love to it must go. I cannot be a saved man unless that is the case." If you have kept pace with the preacher so far, I think the next thought will come: "Then this is deep water; this is a place where my own strength utterly fails me. If I must have a new heart—well, I cannot make myself a new heart. If the very love of sin has to go, I cannot accomplish that; I can stop outside the theatre, but I cannot prevent my wanting to go in. I can renounce dishonesty, but I cannot help having an itching palm. Even if I dare not transgress yet I may feel the wish to do so if the punishment could be escaped."

This makes the matter too hard for unaided nature; since it is true that unless the love of sin is gone nothing is done. God must help me, or this will never be accomplished. This is the centre of the truth. Your great Creator must come and make you over again. His dear Son must come and end your captivity to the power of evil. He has come, he has died. Nothing can ever take out the stains of your past sin but the blood of the Son of God. Nothing can take from you the love of sin but the application of the atoning blood, and the work of the Spirit upon your entire nature, creating you anew in Christ Jesus. "Oh," saith one, "I see it all now. I seem to have come up against a wall of rock, and I can go no further. I wonder not that the summers have gone and the harvests have ended, when it is like this; for now I am brought up before a dread impossibility. What can I do?" Thou canst do this. God helping you, trust Christ to do it all. Throw thyself down at his feet. "Saviour, Saviour, from the highest heaven look down, here is a sinner in his blood. I read of others that when they were in their blood thou saidst to them, Live! Say that to me. Here is one condemned, and near to die; save him, forgive him, impute thy righteousness, make me to be accepted in the Beloved. I trust thee!"

Do you indeed trust Jesus? Is it true that you believe on him? Then you are saved! His merit is yours, his blood has cleansed you the moment you believe in him, it is done: you shall not love sin again. You shall be tempted, and often have to groan because of secret listings that will linger there; but you have a new life now, for you have believed in Jesus, and that new life will abhor sin, and will fight it, and will conquer it, and God will help you, and the Spirit will dwell in you, and you shall get sin more and more under your feet—yea, you shall bruise Satan under your feet ere long, and you shall triumph, and one day you shall burst this shell which holds you in, and you shall shine in the image of Christ, "without spot or wrinkle, or any such thing."

Yes, you, sinful man, shall be made perfectly holy, even you, now full of iniquity, transgression, and sin. You are a God-provoking rebel now, but if you trust in Christ Jesus you shall be washed and made God-pleasing this very day: black as hell to-day, you shall by infinite mercy be made as bright as a seraph before God, and all that because you trust the Saviour. O God, grant us thy saving grace for Jesus' sake.

XIV

THANKSGIVING TO THE FATHER

"Giving thanks unto the Father, which hath made us meet
to be partakers of the inheritance of the saints in light: who
hath delivered us from the power of darkness, and hath translated us into the kingdom of his dear Son."—Col. 1: 12, 13.

THIS passage is a mine of riches. I can anticipate the
difficulty in preaching, and the regret in concluding, we
shall experience now because we are not able to dig out all the
gold which lies in this precious vein. We lack the power to
grasp and the time to expatiate upon that volume of truths
which is here condensed into a few short sentences.

We are expected to "give thanks unto the Father." This
counsel is at once needful and salutary. I think we scarcely
need to be told to give thanks unto the Son. The remembrance
of that bleeding body hanging upon the cross is ever present to
our faith. The nails and the spear, his griefs, the anguish of
his soul, and his sweat of agony, make such tender touching
appeals to our gratitude—these will prevent us always from
ceasing our songs, and sometimes fire our hearts with rekindling
rapture in praise of the *man* Christ Jesus. Yes, we *will* bless
thee, dearest Lord; our souls are all on fire. As we survey the
wondrous cross, we cannot but shout—

> *O for this love let rocks and hills*
> *Their lasting silence break,*
> *And all harmonious human tongues*
> *The Saviour's praises speak.*

It is in a degree very much the same with the Holy Spirit. I
think we are compelled to feel every day our dependence upon
his constant influence. He abides with us as a present and personal Comforter and Counsellor. We, therefore, do praise the
Spirit of Grace, who hath made our heart his temple, and who

189

works in us all that is gracious, virtuous, and well-pleasing in the sight of God. If there be any one Person in the Trinity whom we are more apt to forget than another in our praises, it is God the Father. In fact there are some who even get a wrong idea of Him, a slanderous idea of that God whose name is LOVE. They imagine that love dwelt in Christ, rather than in the Father; and that our salvation is rather due to the Son and the Holy Spirit, than to our Father God. Let us not be of the number of the ignorant, but let us receive this truth. We are as much indebted to the Father as to any other Person of the Sacred Three. He as much and as truly loves us as any of the adorable Three Persons. He is as truly worthy of our highest praise as either the Son or the Holy Spirit.

In order to excite your gratitude to God the Father, I propose to dilate a little upon this passage, as God the Holy Spirit shall enable me. If you will look at the text, you will see two blessings in it.

The first blessing introduced to our notice is this—"God the Father has made us meet to be partakers of the inheritance of the saints in light." It is a PRESENT BLESSING. Not a mercy laid up for us in the covenant, which we have not yet received, but it is a blessing which every true believer already has in his hand. Those mercies in the covenant of which we have the earnest now while we wait for the full possession, are just as rich, and just as certain as those which have been already with abundant lovingkindness bestowed on us; but still they are not so precious in our enjoyment. The mercy we have in store, and in hand, is after all, the main source of our present comfort. And oh what a blessing this! "Made meet for the inheritance of the saints in light."

The true believer is fit for heaven; he is meet to be a partaker of the inheritance—and that now, at this very moment. What does this mean? Does it mean that the believer is perfect; that he is free from sin? No, where shall you ever find such perfection in this world? If no man can be a believer but the perfect man, then what has the perfect man to believe? Could he not walk by sight? When he is perfect, he may cease to be a believer. No, it is not such perfection that is meant, although perfection is implied, and assuredly will be given as the result. Far less does this mean that we have a right to eternal life from any doings of our own. We have a fitness for eternal life, a meetness for it, but we have no desert of it. We deserve nothing of God even now, in ourselves, but his eternal wrath and his infinite displeasure. What, then, does it mean? Why, it means just this: we are so far meet that we are accepted in the Beloved, adopted into the family, and fitted by divine approbation to dwell with the saints in light. There is a woman chosen to be a bride; she is fitted to be married, fitted to enter into the honourable state and condition of matrimony; but at present she has not on the bridal garment, she is not like the bride adorned for her husband. You do not see her yet robed in her elegant attire, with her ornaments upon her, but you know she is fitted to be a bride, she is received and welcomed as such in the family of her destination.

So Christ has chosen his Church to be married to him; she has not yet put on her bridal garment, and all that beautiful array in which she shall stand before the Father's throne, but, notwithstanding, there is such a fitness in her to be the bride of Christ, when she shall have bathed herself for a little while, and lain for a little while in the bed of spices—there is such a fitness in her character, such a grace-given adaptation in her to become the royal bride of her glorious Lord, and to become a partaker of the enjoyments of bliss—that it may be said of the church as a whole, and of every member of it, that they are "meet for the inheritance of the saints in light."

The Greek word, moreover, bears some such meaning as this; though I cannot give the exact idiom, it is always difficult when a word is not used often. This word is only used twice, that I am aware of, in the New Testament. The word may be employed for "suitable," or, I think, "sufficient." "He hath made us meet"—"sufficient"—"to be partakers of the inheritance of the saints in light." But I cannot give my idea without borrowing another figure. When a child is born, it is at once endowed with all the faculties of humanity. If those powers are wanting at first, they will not come afterwards. It has eyes, it has hands, it has feet, and all its physical organs. These of course are as it were in embryo. The senses though perfect at first, must be gradually developed, and the understanding gradually matured. It can see but little, it cannot discern distances; it can hear, but it cannot hear distinctly enough at first to know from what direction the sound comes; but you never find a new leg, a new arm, a new eye, or a new ear growing on that child. Each of these powers will expand and enlarge, but still there is the whole man there at first, and the child is *sufficient* for a man. Let but God in his infinite providence cause it to feed, and give it strength and increase, it has *sufficient* for manhood. It does not want either arm or leg, nose or ear; you cannot make it grow a new member; nor does it require a new member either; all are there. In like manner, the moment a man is regenerated, there is every faculty in his new creation that there shall be, even when he gets to heaven. It only needs to be developed and brought out: he will not have a new power, he will not have a new grace, he will have those which he had before, developed and brought out. Just as we are told by the careful observer, that in the acorn there is in embryo every root and every bough and every leaf of the future tree, which only requires to be developed and brought out in their fulness, so, in the true believer, there is a sufficiency or meetness for the inheritance of the saints in light. All that he requires is, not that a new thing should be implanted, but that that which God has put there in the moment of regeneration, shall be cherished and nurtured, and made to grow and increase, till it comes unto perfection and he enters into "the inheritance of the saints in light." This is, as near as I can give it to you, the exact meaning and literal interpretation of the text, as I understand it.

But you may say to me, "In what sense is this meetness or fitness for eternal life the work of God the Father? Are we already made meet for heaven? How is this the Father's work?" Look at the text a moment, and I will answer you in three ways.

What is heaven? We read, it is an *inheritance*. Who are fit for an inheritance? Sons. Who makes us sons? "Behold what manner of love *the Father* hath bestowed upon us, that we should be called the sons of God." A son is fitted for an inheritance. The moment the son is born he is fitted to be an heir. All that is wanted is that he shall grow up and be capable of possession. But he is fit for an inheritance at first. If he were not a son he could not inherit as an heir. Now, as soon as ever we become sons we are meet to inherit. There is in us an adaptation, a power and possibility for us to have an inheritance. This is the prerogative of the Father, to adopt us into his family, and to "beget us again unto a lively hope by the resurrection of Jesus Christ from the dead." And do you not see, that as adoption is really the meetness for inheritance, it is the Father who hath "made us meet to be partakers of the inheritance of the saints in light?"

Again, heaven is an inheritance; but whose inheritance is it? It is an inheritance of the *saints*. It is not an inheritance of sinners, but of saints—that is, of the holy ones,—of those who have been made saints by being sanctified. Turn, then, to the Epistle of Jude, and you will see at once who it is that sanctifies. You will observe the moment you fix your eye upon the passage that it is God the Father. In the first verse you read, "Jude, the servant of Jesus Christ, and brother of James, to them that are sanctified by God the Father." It is an inheritance for saints: and who are saints? The moment a man believes in Christ, he may know himself to have been truly set apart in the covenant decree; and he finds that consecration, if I may so speak, verified in his own experience, for he has now become "a new creature in Christ Jesus," separated from the rest of the world, and then it is manifest and made known that God has taken him to be his son for ever. The meetness which I must have, in order to enjoy the inheritance of the saints in light, is my becoming a son. God hath made me and all believers sons, therefore we are meet for the inheritance; so then that meetness has come from the Father. How meetly therefore doth the Father claim our gratitude, our adoration and our love!

You will however observe, it is not merely said that heaven is the inheritance of the saints, but that it is "the inheritance of the saints *in light.*" So the saints dwell in light—the light of knowledge, the light of purity, the light of joy, the light of love, pure ineffable love, the light of everything that is glorious and ennobling. There they dwell, and, if I am to appear meet for that inheritance, what evidence must I have? I must have light shining into my own soul. But where can I get it? Do I not read that "every good gift and every perfect gift is from above, and cometh down"—yea verily, but from whom? From the Spirit? No—"from the Father of lights, with whom is no variableness, neither shadow of turning." The preparation to enter into the inheritance in light is light; and light comes from the Father of lights; therefore, my meetness, if I have

G

light in myself, is the work of the Father, and I must give him praise.

A few general observations here. I am persuaded that if an angel from heaven were to come to-day and single out any one believer from the crowd here assembled, there is not one believer that is unfit to be taken to heaven. You may not be ready to be taken to heaven now; that is to say, if I foresaw that you were going to live, I would tell you you were unfit to die, in a certain sense. But were you to die now in your pew, if you believe in Christ, you are fit for heaven. You have a meetness even now which would take you there at once, without being committed to purgatory for a season. You are even now fit to be "partakers of the inheritance of the saints in light." You have but to gasp out your last breath and you shall be in heaven, and there shall not be one spirit in heaven more fit for heaven than you, nor one soul more adapted for the place than you are. You shall be just as fitted for its element as those who are nearest to the eternal throne.

Ah! this makes the heirs of glory think much of God the Father. When we reflect upon our state by nature, and how fit we are to be fire-brands in the flames of hell—yet to think that we are, at this very moment, if Jehovah willed it, fit to sweep the golden harps with joyful fingers, that this head is fit to wear the everlasting crown, that these loins are fit to be girded with that fair white robe throughout eternity, I say, this makes us think gratefully of God the Father; this makes us clap our hands with joy, and say, "Thanks be unto God the Father, who hath made us meet to be partakers of the inheritance of the saints in light."

Do you remember the penitent thief? It was but a few minutes before that he had been cursing Christ. I doubt not that he had joined with the other, for it is said, "*They* that were crucified with him reviled him." Not one, but both; *they* did it. And then a gleam of supernatural glory lit up the face of Christ, and the thief saw and believed. And Jesus said unto him, "Verily I say unto thee, this day," though the sun is setting, "*this day* shalt thou be with me in Paradise." No long preparation required, no sweltering in purifying fires. And so shall it be with us. We may have been in Christ Jesus to our own knowledge but three weeks, or we may have been in him for ten years, or three-score years and ten—the date of our conversion makes no difference in our meetness for heaven, in a certain sense. True indeed the older we grow the more grace we have tasted, the riper we are becoming, and the fitter to be housed in heaven; but that is in another sense of the word, the Spirit's meetness which he gives. But with regard to that meetness which the Father gives, I repeat, the blade of corn, the blade of gracious wheat that has just appeared above the surface of conviction, is as fit to be carried up to heaven as the full-grown corn in the ear. The sanctification wherewith we are sanctified by God the Father is not progressive, it is complete at once; we are now adapted for heaven, now fitted for it, and we shall be by-and-by completely ready for it, and shall enter into the joy of our Lord.

The second mercy is A MERCY THAT LOOKS BACK. We sometimes prefer the mercies that look forward, because they unfold such a bright prospect. "Sweet fields beyond the swelling flood." But here is a mercy that looks backward; turns its back, as it were, on the heaven of our anticipation, and looks back on the gloomy past, and the dangers from which we have escaped. Let us read the account of it—"Who hath delivered us from the power of darkness, and hath translated us into the kingdom of his dear Son." This verse is an explanation of the preceding, as we shall have to show in a few minutes. But just now let us survey this mercy by itself. Ah! what a description have we here of what manner of men we used to be. We *were* under "the power of darkness." Since I have been musing on this text, I have turned these words over and over in my mind —"the power of darkness." It seems to me one of the most awful expressions that man ever attempted to expound. I think I could deliver a discourse from it, if God the Spirit helped me, which might make every bone in your body shake.

"The power of darkness." We all know that there is a *moral* darkness which exercises its awful spell over the mind of the sinner. Where God is unacknowledged the mind is void of judgment. Where God is unworshipped the heart of man becomes a ruin. The chambers of that dilapidated heart are haunted by ghostly fears and degraded superstitions. The dark places of that reprobate mind are tenanted by vile lusts and noxious passions, like vermin and reptiles, from which in open daylight we turn with disgust.

And even *natural* darkness is tremendous. If one of you were to be taken to-night and led into some dark cavern, and left there, I can imagine that for a moment, not knowing your fate, you might feel a child-like kind of interest about it; there might be, perhaps, a laugh as you find yourselves in the dark; there might for the moment, from the novelty of the position, be some kind of curiosity excited. There might, perhaps, be a flush of silly joy. In a little time you might endeavour to compose yourself to sleep; possibly you might sleep; but, if you should awake, and still find yourself down deep in the bowels of earth, where never a ray of sun or candle light could reach you; do you know the next feeling that would come over you? It would be a kind of idiotic thoughtlessness. You would find it impossible to control your desperate imagination. Your heart would say, "O God I am alone, alone, alone, in this dark place." How would you cast your eyeballs all around, and never catching a gleam of light, your mind would begin to fail. Your next stage would be one of increasing terror. You would fancy that you saw something, and then you would cry, "Ah! I would I could see something, were it foe or fiend!" You would feel the dark sides of your dungeon. You would begin to "scribble on the walls," like David before king Achish. Agitation would seize hold upon you, and, if you were kept there much longer, delirium and death would be the consequence.

In a report lately written by the Chaplain of Newgate, there are some striking reflections upon the influence of darkness in a way of *discipline*. Its first effect is to shut the culprit up to his own reflections, and make him realize his true position in the iron grasp of the outraged law. Methinks the man that has defied his keepers, and come in there cursing and swearing, when he has found himself alone in darkness, where he cannot even hear the rattling of carriages along the streets, and can see no light whatever, is presently cowed; he gives in, he grows tame. "The power of darkness" literally is something awful. We cannot properly describe it, even in this world. The sinner is plunged into the darkness of his sins, and he sees nothing, he knows nothing. Let him remain there a little longer, and that joy of curiosity, that hectic joy which he now has in the path of sin, will die away, and there will come over him a spirit of slumber. Sin will make him drowsy, so that he will not hear the voice of the ministry, crying to him to escape for his life. Let him continue in it, and it will by-and-by make him spiritually an idiot. He will become so set in sin, that common reason will be lost on him. All the arguments that a sensible man will receive, will be only wasted on him. Let him go on, and he will proceed from bad to worse, till he acquires the raving mania of a desperado in sin; and let death step in, and the darkness will have produced its full effect; he will come into the delirious madness of hell.

Now, all of us were under this power once. It is but a few months—a few weeks with some of you—since you were under the power of darkness and of sin. Some of you had only got as far as the curiosity of it; others had got as far as the sleepiness of it; a good many of you had got as far as the apathy of it; and I do not know but some of you had got almost to the terror of it. You had so cursed and swore; so yelled ye out your blasphemies, that you seemed to be ripening for hell; but, praised and blessed be the name of the Father, he has "translated you from the power of darkness, into the kingdom of his dear Son."

Having thus explained this term, "the power of darkness," to show you what you were, let us take the next word, "and hath translated us." What a singular word this "translated" is. I dare say you think it means the process by which a word is interpreted, when the sense is retained, while the expression is rendered in another language. That is one meaning of the word "translation," but it is not the meaning here. The word is used by Josephus in this sense—the taking away of a people who have been dwelling in a certain country, and planting them in another place. This is called a "translation." We sometimes hear of a bishop being translated or removed from one see to another. Now, if you want to have the idea explained, give me your attention while I bring out an amazing instance of a great translation. The children of Israel were in Egypt under task-masters that oppressed them very sorely, and brought them into iron bondage. What did God do for these people? There were two million of them. He did not temper the tyranny of the tyrant; he did not influence his mind, to give them a little more liberty; but he translated his people; he took the whole two millions bodily, with a high hand and outstretched arm, and led them through the wilderness, and translated them into the kingdom of Canaan; and there they were settled. What an achievement was that, when, with their flocks and their herds, and their little ones, the whole host of Israel went out of Egypt, crossed the Jordan, and came into Canaan! The whole of it was not equal to the achievement of God's powerful grace, when he brings one poor sinner out of the region of sin into the kingdom of holiness and peace. It was easier for God to bring Israel out of Egypt, to split the Red Sea, to make a highway through the pathless wilderness, to drop manna from heaven, to send the whirlwind to drive out the kings; it was easier for Omnipotence to do all this, than to translate a man from the power of darkness into the kingdom of his dear Son. This is the grandest achievement of Omnipotence.

The sustenance of the whole universe, I do believe, is even less than this—the changing of a bad heart, the subduing of an iron will. But thanks be unto the Father, he has done all that for you and for me. He has brought us out of darkness; he has translated us, taken up the old tree that has struck its roots never so deep—taken it up, blessed be God, roots and all, and planted it in a goodly soil.

But where are we now? Into what place is the believer brought, when he is brought out of the power of darkness? He is brought into the kingdom of God's dear Son. Into what other kingdom would the Christian desire to be brought? A republic may sound very well in theory, but in spiritual matters, the last thing we want is a republic. We want a kingdom. I love to have Christ an absolute Monarch in the heart. I do not want to have a doubt about it. I want to give up all liberty to him, for I feel that I never shall be free till my self-control is all gone; that I shall never have my will truly free till it is bound in the golden fetters of his sweet love. We are brought into a kingodm —he is Lord and Sovereign, and he has made us "kings and priests unto our God," and we shall reign with him. The proof that we are in this kingdom must consist in our obedience to our King. Here, perhaps, we may raise many causes and questions, but surely we can say after all, though we have offended our King many times, yet our heart is loyal to him. "Oh, thou precious Jesus! we would obey thee and yield submission to every one of thy laws; our sins are not wilful and beloved sins, but though we fall we can truly say that we would be holy as thou art holy, our heart is true towards thy statutes; Lord, help us to run in the way of thy commandments."

Upon the third point, I shall be as brief as possible; it is to SHOW THE CONNECTION BETWEEN THE TWO VERSES.

When I get a passage of Scripture to meditate upon, I like, if I can, to see its drift; then I like to examine its various parts, and see if I can understand each separate clause; and then I want to go back again, and see what one clause has to do with another. I looked and looked again at this text, and wondered what connection there could be between the two verses. "Giving thanks unto God the Father, who hath made us meet to be partakers of the inheritance of the saints in light." Well, that is right enough; we can see how this is the work of God the Father, to make us meet to go to heaven. But has the next verse, the 13th, anything to do with our meetness?—"Who hath delivered us from the power of darkness, and hath translated us into the kingdom of his dear Son." Well, I looked it over, and I said I will read it in this way. I see the 12th verse tells me that the inheritance of heaven is the inheritance of light. Is heaven light? Then I can see my meetness for it as described in the 13th verse.—He "hath delivered me from the power of darkness." Is not that the same thing? If I am delivered from "the power of darkness," is not that being made meet to dwell in light? If I am now brought out of darkness into light, and am walking in the light, is not that the very meetness which is spoken of in the verse before? Then I read it again. It says they are "saints." Well, the saints are a people that obey the Son. Here is my meetness then in the 13th verse, where it says "He hath translated me from the power of darkness into the kingdom of his dear Son." So that I not only have the light, but the sonship too, for I am in "the kingdom of his dear Son." But how about the "inheritance"? Is there anything about that in the 13th verse? It is "an inheritance"; shall I find anything about a meetness for it there? Yes, I find that I am in "the kingdom of his dear Son." How came Christ to have a kingdom? Why, by inheritance. Then it seems I am in his inheritance; and, if I am in his inheritance here, then I am meet to be in it above, for I am in it already. I am even now part of it and partner of it, since I am in the kingdom which he inherits from his Father, and therefore there is the meetness.

Having thus shown the connection between these verses, I propose now to close with a few general observations. I like so to expound the Scripture, that we can draw some practical inferences from it. Of course the first inference is this: let us never omit God the Father in our praises. I think I have said this already six times over in the sermon. There are some truths, I believe, that need to be said over and over again, either because our silly hearts will not receive, or our treacherous memories will not hold them. Sing, I beseech you, habitually, the praises of the Father in heaven, as you do the praises of the Son hanging upon the Cross.

Yet another inference arises. Are you conscious that you are not now what you once were? Are you sure that the power of darkness does not now rest upon you, that you love divine knowledge, that you are panting after heavenly joys? Are you sure that you have been "translated into the kingdom of God's dear Son"? Then never be troubled about thoughts of death, because, come death whenever it may, you are meet to be a "partaker of the inheritance of the saints in light." Let no thought distress you about death's coming to you at an unseasonable hour. Should it come to-morrow, should it come now, if your faith is "fixed on nothing less than Jesu's blood and righteousness," you shall see the face of God with acceptance. I have that consciousness in my soul, by the witness of the Holy Spirit, of my adoption into the family of God, that I feel that though I should never preach again, but should lay down my body and my charge together, ere I should reach my home, and rest in my bed, "I know that my Redeemer liveth," and more, that I should be a "partaker of the inheritance of the saints in light."

One more reflection lingers behind. There are some of you here that cannot be thought by the utmost charity of judgment, to be "meet for the inheritance of the saints in light." If a wicked man should go to heaven without being converted, heaven would be no heaven to him. Heaven is not adapted for sinners; it is not a place for them. If you were to take a Hottentot who has long dwelt at the equator up to where the Esquimaux are dwelling, and tell him that you would show him the aurora, and all the glories of the North Pole, the poor wretch could not appreciate them; he would say, "It is not the element for me; it is not the place where I could rest happy!" And you, sinner, nothing makes you happy but sin; you do not want too much psalm singing, do you? Sunday is a dull day to you; you like to get it over, you do not care about your Bible; you would as soon there should be no Bible at all. You find that going to a meeting-house or a church is very dull work indeed. Oh then you will not be troubled with that in eternity; do not agitate yourself. If you love not God, and die as you are, you shall go to your own company, those who have been your mates on earth shall be your mates for ever; but you shall go to the Prince of those good fellows, unless you repent and be converted. Where God is you cannot come. What is to be done then? You must have a new nature. I pray God to give it to you. Remember if now you feel your need of a Saviour, that is the beginning of the new nature. "Believe on the Lord Jesus Christ"; cast yourselves simply on him, trust in nothing but his blood, and then the new nature shall be expanded, and you shall be made meet by the Holy Spirit's operations to be a "partaker of the inheritance of the saints in light."

The Second Advent

XV

"HE COMETH WITH CLOUDS"

> "Behold, he cometh with clouds; and every eye shall see
> him, and they also which pierced him: and all kindreds of the
> earth shall wail because of him. Even so, Amen."—Rev. 1:7.

IN reading the chapter we observed how the beloved John
saluted the seven churches in Asia with, "Grace and peace be
unto you." Blessed men scatter blessings. When the *benediction*
of God rests on us we pour out benediction upon others.

From benediction John's gracious heart rose into *adoration* of
the great King of Saints. As our hymn puts it, "The holy to
the holiest leads." They that are good at blessing men will be
quick at blessing God.

It is a wonderful doxology which John has given us: "Unto
him that loved us, and washed us from our sins in his own blood,
and hath made us kings and priests unto God and his Father; to
him be glory and dominion for ever and ever. Amen." I like
the Revised Version for its alliteration in this case, although I
cannot prefer it for other reasons. It runs thus: "Unto him
that *loveth* us, and *loosed* us from our sins by his blood." Truly
our Redeemer has loosed us from sin; but the mention of his
blood suggests washing rather than loosing. We can keep the
alliteration and yet retain the meaning of cleansing if we read
the passage, "Unto him that loved us, and laved us." *Loved*
us, and *laved* us: carry those two words home with you: let
them lie upon your tongue to sweeten your breath for prayer
and praise. "Unto him that loved us, and laved us, be glory
and dominion for ever and ever."

Then John tells of the dignity which the Lord hath put upon
us in making us kings and priests, and from this he ascribes
royalty and dominion unto the Lord himself. John had been
extolling the Great King, whom he calls, "The Prince of the
kings of the earth." Such indeed he was, and is, and is to be.

When John had touched upon that royalty which is natural to our divine Lord, and that dominion which has come to him by conquest, and by the gift of the Father as the reward of all his travail, he then went on to note that he has "made us kings." Our Lord's royalty he diffuses among his redeemed. We praise him because he is in himself a king, and next, because he is a King-maker, the Fountain of honour and majesty. He has not only enough of royalty for himself, but he hands a measure of his dignity to his people. He makes kings out of such common stuff as he finds in us poor sinners. Shall we not adore him for this? Shall we not cast our crowns at his feet? He gave our crowns to us; shall we not give them to him? "To him be glory and dominion for ever and ever. Amen." King by thy divine nature! King by filial right! King-maker, lifting up the beggar from the dunghill to set him among princes! King of kings by the unanimous love of all thy crownèd ones! Thou art he whom thy brethren shall praise! Reign thou for ever and ever! Unto thee be hosannas of welcome and hallelujahs of praise. Lord of the earth and heaven, let all things that be, or ever shall be, render unto thee all glory in the highest degree. Do not your souls take fire as you think of the praises of Immanuel? Fain would I fill the universe with his praise. Oh for a thousand tongues to sing the glories of the Lord Jesus! If the Spirit who dictated the words of John has taken possession of our spirits, we shall find adoration to be our highest delight. Never are we so near to heaven as when we are absorbed in the worship of Jesus, our Lord and God. Oh, that I could now adore him as I shall do when, delivered from this encumbering body, my soul shall behold him in the fulness of his glory!

It would seem from the chapter that the adoration of John was increased by his *expectation* of the Lord's second coming; for he cries, "Behold, he cometh with clouds." His adoration awoke his expectation, which all the while was lying in his soul as an element of that vehement heat of reverent love which he poured forth in his doxology. "Behold, he cometh," said he, and thus he revealed one source of his reverence. "Behold, he cometh," said he, and this exclamation was the result of his reverence. He adored until his faith realized his Lord, and became a second and nobler sight.

I think, too, that his reverence was deepened and his adoration was rendered more fervent by his conviction of the speediness of his Lord's coming. "Behold, he cometh," or is coming: he means to assert that he is even now on his way. As workmen are moved to be more diligent in service when they hear their master's footfall, so, doubtless, saints are quickened in their devotion when they are conscious that he whom they worship is drawing near. He has gone away to the Father for a while, and so he has left us alone in this world; but he has said, "I will come again and receive you unto myself," and we are confident that he will keep his word. Sweet is the remembrance of that loving promise. That assurance is pouring its savour into John's heart while he is adoring; and it becomes inevitable, as well as most meet and proper, that his doxology should at its close introduce him to the Lord himself, and cause him to cry out, "Behold, he cometh." Having worshipped among the pure in heart, he sees the Lord: having adored the King, he sees him assume the judgment-seat, and appear in the clouds of heaven. When once we enter upon heavenly things we know not how far we can go, nor how high we can climb. John who began with blessing the churches now beholds his Lord.

May the Holy Ghost help us reverently to think of the wondrous coming of our blessed Lord, when he shall appear to the delight of his people and the dismay of the ungodly!

There are three things in the text. They will seem common-places to some of you, and, indeed, they are the common-places of our divine faith, and yet nothing can be of greater import-ance. The first is, *our Lord Jesus comes:* "Behold he cometh with clouds." The second is, *our Lord Jesus Christ's coming will be seen of all:* "Every eye shall see him, and they also which pierced him." And, in the third place, *this coming will cause great sorrow:* "All kindreds of the earth shall wail because of him."

May the Holy Spirit help us while, in the first place, we remember that OUR LORD JESUS CHRIST COMES!

This announcement is thought worthy of a note of admira-tion. As the Latins would say, there is an "*Ecce*" placed here— "*Behold*, he cometh." As in the old books the printers put hands in the margin pointing to special passages, such is this "be-hold!" It is a *Nota Bene* calling upon us to note well what we are reading. Here is something which we are to *hold* and *behold*.

We now hear a voice crying, "Come and see!" The Holy Spirit never uses superfluous words, nor redundant notes of exclamation: when he cries, "Behold!" it is because there is reason for deep and lasting attention. Will you turn away when he bids you pause and ponder, linger and look? Oh, you that have been beholding vanity, come and behold the fact that Jesus cometh. You that have been beholding this, and beholding that, and thinking of nothing worthy of your thoughts; forget these passing sights and spectacles, and for once behold a scene which has no parallel. It is not a monarch in her jubilee, but the King of kings in his glory. That same Jesus who went up from Olivet into heaven is coming again to earth in like manner as his disciples saw him go up into heaven. Come and behold this great sight. If ever there was a thing in the world worth looking at, it is this. Behold and see if there was ever glory like unto his glory! Hearken to the midnight cry, "Behold, the bridegroom cometh!" It has practically to do with you. "Go ye forth to meet him." This voice is to you, O sons of men. Do not carelessly turn aside; for the Lord God himself demands your attention: he commands you to "Behold!" Will you be blind when God bids you behold? Will you shut your eyes when your Saviour cries, "Behold"? When the finger of inspiration points the way, will not your eye follow where it directs you? "Behold, he cometh." Look hither, I beseech you.

If we read the words of our text carefully, this "Behold" shows us first, that *this coming is to be vividly realized.* I think I see John. He is in the spirit; but on a sudden he seems startled into a keener and more solemn attention. His mind is more awake than usual, though he was ever a man of bright eyes that saw afar. We always liken him to the eagle for the height of his flight and the keenness of his vision; yet on a sudden, even he seems startled with a more astounding vision. He cries out, "Behold! Behold!" He has caught sight of his Lord. He says not, "He will come by-and-by," but, "I can see him; he is now coming." He has evidently realized the second advent. He has so conceived of the second coming of the Lord that it has become a matter of fact to him; a matter to be spoken of, and even to be written down.

"Behold, he cometh!" Have you and I ever realized the coming of Christ so fully as this? Perhaps we believe that he will come. I should hope that we all do *that*. If we believe that the Lord Jesus has come the first time, we believe also that he will come the second time; but are these equally assured truths to us? Peradventure we have vividly realized the first appearing: from Bethlehem to Golgotha, and from Calvary to Olivet we have traced the Lord, understanding that blessed cry, "Behold the Lamb of God, which taketh away the sin of the world!" Yes, the Word was made flesh and dwelt among us, and we beheld his glory, the glory as of the Only-begotten of the Father, full of grace and truth. But have we with equal firmness grasped the thought that he comes again without a sin-offering unto salvation? Do we now say to each other, as we meet in happy fellowship, "Yes, our Lord cometh"? It should be to us not only a prophecy assuredly believed among us, but a scene pictured in our souls, and anticipated in our hearts. My imagination has often set forth that dread scene: but better still, my faith has realized it. I have heard the chariot-wheels of the Lord's approach, and I have endeavoured to set my house in order for his reception. I have felt the shadow of that great cloud which shall attend him, damping the ardour of my worldliness. I hear even now in spirit the sound of the last trumpet, whose tremendous blast startles my soul to serious action, and puts force into my life. Would God that I lived more completely under the influence of that august event!

To this realization I invite you. I wish that we could go together in this, until as we went out of the house we said to one another, "Behold, he cometh!" One said to his fellow, after the Lord had risen, "The Lord has risen indeed." I want you to feel just as certain that the Lord is coming indeed, and I would have you say as much to one another. We are sure that he will come, and that he is on the way; but the benefit of a more vivid realization would be incalculable.

This coming is to be zealously proclaimed, for John does not merely calmly say, "He cometh," but he vigorously cries, "Behold, he cometh." Just as the herald of a king prefaces his message by a trumpet blast that calls attention, so John cries, "Behold!" As the old town-crier was wont to say, "O yes! O yes! O yes!" or to use some other striking formula by which he called upon men to note his announcement, so John stands in the midst of us, and cries, "Behold, he cometh!" He calls attention by that emphatic word "Behold!" It is no ordinary message that he brings, and he would not have us treat his word as a common-place saying. He throws his heart into the announcement. He proclaims it loudly, he proclaims it solemnly, and he proclaims it with authority: "Behold, he cometh."

No truth ought to be more frequently proclaimed, next to the first coming of the Lord, than his second coming; and you cannot thoroughly set forth all the ends and bearings of the first advent if you forget the second. At the Lord's Supper, there is no discerning the Lord's body unless you discern his first coming; but there is no drinking into his cup to its fulness, unless you hear him say, "Until I come." You must look forward, as well as backward. So must it be with all our ministries; they must look to him on the Cross and on the Throne. We must vividly realize that he, who has once come, is coming yet again, or else our testimony will be marred and one-sided. We shall make lame work of preaching and teaching if we leave out either advent.

And next, *it is to be unquestionably asserted*. "Behold, he cometh." It is not, "Perhaps he will come"; nor, "Peradventure he may yet appear." "Behold, he cometh" should be dogmatically asserted as an absolute certainty, which has been realized by the heart of the man who proclaims it. "Behold, he cometh." All the prophets say that he will come. From Enoch down to the last that spoke by inspiration, they declare, "The Lord cometh with ten thousands of his saints." You shall not find one who has spoken by the authority of God, who does not, either directly or by implication, assert the coming of the Son of man, when the multitudes born of woman shall be summoned to his bar, to receive the recompense of their deeds. All the promises are travailing with this prognostication, "Behold, he cometh." We have his own word for it, and this makes assurance doubly sure. He has told us that he will come again. He often assured his disciples that if he went away from them, he would come again to them; and he left us the Lord's Supper as a parting token to be observed until he comes. As often as we break bread we are reminded of the fact that, though it is a most blessed ordinance, yet it is a temporary one, and will cease to be celebrated when our absent Lord is once again present with us.

What is there to hinder Christ from coming? When I have studied and thought over this word, "Behold, he cometh," yes, I have said to myself, indeed he does; who shall hold him back? His heart is with his church on earth. In the place where he fought the battle he desires to celebrate the victory. His delights are with the sons of men. All his saints are waiting for the day of his appearing, and he is waiting also. The very earth in her sorrow and her groaning travaileth for his coming, which is to be her redemption. The creation is made subject to vanity for a little while; but, when the Lord shall come again, the creation itself also shall be delivered from the bondage of corruption into the glorious liberty of the children of God. We might question whether he would come a second time if he had not already come the first time; but, if he came to Bethlehem, be assured that his feet shall yet stand upon Olivet. If he came to die, doubt not that he will come to reign. If he came to be despised and rejected of men, why should we doubt that he will come to be admired in all them that believe? His sure coming is to be unquestionably asserted.

This fact that he will come again, *is to be taught as demanding our immediate interest.* "Behold, he cometh with clouds." Behold, look at it; meditate on it. It is worth thinking of. It concerns yourself. Study it again and again. "He cometh." He will so soon be here that it is put in the present tense: "He cometh." That shaking of the earth; that blotting out of sun and moon; that fleeing of heaven and earth before his face—all these are so nearly here that John describes them as accomplished. "Behold, he cometh."

There is this sense lying in the background, that *he is already on the way.* All that he is doing in providence and grace is a preparation for his coming. All the events of human history, all the great decisions of his august majesty whereby he ruleth all things—all these are tending towards the day of his appearing. Do not think that he delays his coming, and then upon a sudden he will rush hither in hot haste. He has arranged for it to take place as soon as wisdom allows. We know not what may make the present delay imperative; but the Lord knows, and that suffices. You grow uneasy because near two thousand years have passed since his ascension, and Jesus has not yet come; but you do not know what had to be arranged for, and how far the lapse of time was absolutely necessary for the Lord's designs. Those are no little matters which have filled up the great pause: the intervening centuries have teemed with wonders. A thousand things may have been necessary in heaven itself ere the consummation of all things could be arrived at. When our Lord comes it shall be seen that he came as quickly as he could, speaking after the manner of his infinite wisdom; for he cannot behave himself otherwise than wisely, perfectly, divinely. He cannot be moved by fear or passion so as to act hastily as you and I too often do. He dwells in the leisure of eternity, and in the serenity of omnipotence. He has not to measure out days, and months, and years, and to accomplish so much in such a space or else leave his life-work undone; but according to the power of an endless life he proceeds steadily on, and to him a thousand years are but as one day. Therefore be assured that the Lord is even now coming. He is making everything tend that way. All things are working towards that grand climax. At this moment, and every moment since he went away, the Lord Jesus has been coming back again. "Behold, he cometh!" He is on the way! He is nearer every hour!

And we are told that *his coming will be attended by a peculiar sign*. "Behold, he cometh *with clouds*." We shall have no need to question whether it is the Son of man who has come, or whether he is indeed come. This is to be no secret matter: his coming will be as manifest as yonder clouds. In the wilderness the presence of Jehovah was known by a visible pillar of cloud by day, and an equally visible pillar of fire by night. That pillar of cloud was the sure token that the Lord was in his holy place, dwelling between the cherubim. Such is the token of the coming of the Lord Christ.

> *Every eye the cloud shall scan,*
> *Ensign of the Son of man.*

So it is written, "And then shall appear the sign of the Son of man in heaven: and then shall all the tribes of the earth mourn, and they shall see the Son of man coming in the clouds of heaven with power and great glory." I cannot quote at this time all those many passages of Scripture in which it is indicated that our Lord will come either sitting upon a cloud, or "with the clouds," or "with the clouds of heaven;" but such expressions are abundant. Is it not to show that his coming will be *majestic?* He maketh the clouds his chariots. He cometh with hosts of attendants, and these of a nobler sort than earthly monarchs can summon to do them homage. With clouds of angels, cherubim and seraphim, and all the armies of heaven he comes. With all the forces of nature, thunder-cloud and blackness of tempest, the Lord of all makes his triumphant entrance to judge the world. The clouds are the dust of his feet in that dread day of battle when he shall ease him of his adversaries, shaking them out of the earth with his thunder, and consuming them with the devouring flame of his lightning. All heaven shall gather with its utmost pomp to the great appearing of the Lord, and all the terrible grandeur of nature shall then be seen at its full. Not as the Man of sorrows, despised and rejected of men, shall Jesus come; but as Jehovah came upon Sinai in the midst of thick clouds and a terrible darkness, so shall he come, whose coming shall be the final judgment.

The clouds are meant to set forth the *might*, as well as the majesty, of his coming. "Ascribe ye strength unto God: his excellency is over Israel, and his strength is in the clouds." This was the royal token given by Daniel the prophet in his seventh chapter, at the thirteenth verse, "I saw in the night visions, and, behold, one like the Son of man came with the clouds of heaven." Not less than divine is the glory of the Son of God, who once had not where to lay his head. The sublimest objects in nature shall most fitly minister to the manifest glory of the returning King of men. "Behold, he cometh;" not with the swaddling-bands of his infancy, the weariness of his man-hood, the shame of his death, but with all the glorious tapestry of heaven's high chambers. The hanging of the divine throne-room shall aid his state.

The clouds, also, denote *the terror of his coming to the ungodly.* His saints shall be caught up together with him in the clouds, to meet the Lord in the air; but to those that shall remain on earth the clouds shall turn their blackness and horror of dark-ness. Then shall the impenitent behold this dread vision—the Son of man coming in the clouds of heaven. The clouds shall fill them with dread, and the dread shall be abundantly justified, for those clouds are big with vengeance, and shall burst in judgment on their heads. His great white throne, though it be bright and lustrous with hope to his people, will with its very brightness and whiteness of immaculate justice strike dead the hopes of all those who trusted that they might live in sin and yet go unpunished. "Behold, he cometh. He cometh with clouds."

I am in happy circumstances, because my subject requires no effort of imagination from me. To indulge fancy on such a theme would be a wretched profanation of so sublime a subject, which in its own simplicity should come home to all hearts. Think clearly for a moment, till the meaning becomes real to you. Jesus Christ is coming, coming in unwonted splendour. When he comes he will be enthroned far above the attacks of his enemies, the persecutions of the godless, and the sneers of sceptics. He is coming in the clouds of heaven, and we shall be among the witnesses of his appearing. Let us dwell upon this truth.

Our second observation is this: OUR LORD'S COMING WILL BE SEEN OF ALL. "Behold, he cometh with clouds, *and every eye shall see him, and they also which pierced him.*"

I gather from this expression, first, that *it will be a literal appearing, and an actual sight.* If the second advent was to be a spiritual manifestation, to be perceived by the minds of men, the phraseology would be, "Every mind shall perceive him." But it is not so: we read, "Every eye shall see him." Now, the mind can behold the spiritual, but the eye can only see that which is distinctly material and visible. The Lord Jesus Christ will not come spiritually, for in that sense he is always here; but he will come really and substantially, for every eye shall see him, even those unspiritual eyes which gazed on him with hate, and pierced him. Go not away and dream, and say to yourself, "Oh, there is some spiritual meaning about all this." Do not destroy the teaching of the Holy Ghost by the idea that there will be a spiritual manifestation of the Christ of God, but that a literal appearing is out of the question. That would be altering the record. The Lord Jesus shall come to earth a second time as literally as he has come a first time. The same Christ who ate a piece of a broiled fish and of a honeycomb after he had risen from the dead; the same who said, "Handle me, and see; for a spirit hath not flesh and bones, as ye see me have"

—this same Jesus, with a material body, is to come in the clouds of heaven. In the same manner as he went up he shall come down. He shall be literally seen. The words cannot be honestly read in any other way.

"Every eye shall see him." Yes, I do literally expect to see my Lord Jesus with these eyes of mine, even as that saint expected who long ago fell asleep, believing that though the worms devoured his body, yet in his flesh he should see God, whom his eyes should see for himself, and not another. There will be a real resurrection of the body, though the moderns doubt it: such a resurrection that we shall see Jesus with our own eyes. We shall not find ourselves in a shadowy, dreamy land of floating fictions, where we may perceive, but cannot see. We shall not be airy nothings, mysterious, vague, impalpable; but we shall literally see our glorious Lord, whose appearing will be no phantom show, or shadow dance. Never day more real than the day of judgment; never sight more true than the Son of man upon the throne of his glory. Will you take this statement home, that you may feel the force of it? We are getting too far away from facts nowadays, and too much into the realm of myths and notions. "Every eye shall see him," in this there shall be no delusion.

Note well that *he is to be seen of all kinds of living men:* every eye shall see him: the king and the peasant, the most learned and the most ignorant. Those that were blind before shall see when he appears. I remember a man born blind who loved our Lord most intensely, and he was wont to glory in this, that his eyes had been reserved for his Lord. Said he, "The first whom I shall ever see will be the Lord Jesus Christ. The first sight that greets my newly-opened eyes will be the Son of man in his glory." There is great comfort in this to all who are now unable to behold the sun. Since "every eye shall see him," you also shall see the King in his beauty. Small pleasure is this to eyes that are full of filthiness and pride: you care not for this sight, and yet you must see it whether you please or do not please. You have hitherto shut your eyes to good things, but when Jesus comes you *must* see him. All that dwell upon the face of the earth, if not at the same moment, yet with the same certainty, shall behold the once crucified Lord. They will not be able to hide themselves, nor to hide him from their eyes.

They will dread the sight, but it will come upon them, even as the sun shines on the thief who delights in the darkness. They will be obliged to own in dismay that they behold the Son of man: they will be so overwhelmed with the sight that there will be no denying it.

He will be seen of those who have been long since dead. What a sight that will be for Judas, and for Pilate, and for Caiaphas, and for Herod! What a sight it will be for those who, in their lifetime, said that there was no Saviour, and no need of one; or that Jesus was a mere man, and that his blood was not a propitiation for sin! Those that scoffed and reviled him have long since died, but they shall all rise again, and rise to this heritage among the rest—that they shall see him whom they blasphemed sitting in the clouds of heaven. Prisoners are troubled at the sight of the judge. The trumpet of assize brings no music to the ears of criminals. But thou must hear it, O impenitent sinner! Even in thy grave thou must hear the voice of the Son of God, and live, and come forth from the tomb, to receive the things done in thy body, whether they were good or bad. Death cannot hide thee, nor the vault conceal thee, nor rottenness and corruption deliver thee. Thou art bound to see in thy body the Lord who will judge both thee and thy fellows.

It is mentioned here that *he will especially be seen by those that pierced him.* In this is included all the company that nailed him to the tree, with those that took the spear and made the gash in his side; indeed, all that had a hand in his cruel crucifixion. It includes all of these, but it comprehends many more besides. "They also who pierced him" are by no means a few. Who have pierced him? Why those that once professed to love him, and have gone back to the world. Those that once ran well, "What did hinder them?" And now they use their tongues to speak against the Christ whom once they professed to love. They also have pierced him whose inconsistent lives have brought dishonour upon the sacred name of Jesus. They also have pierced him, who refused his love, stifled their consciences, and refused his rebukes. Alas, that so many of you should be piercing him now by your base neglect of his salvation! They that went every Sunday to hear of him, and that remained hearers only, destroying their own souls rather than yield to his infinite love: these pierced his tender heart. I wish I could plead effectually with you now, so that you would not continue any longer among the number of those that pierced him. If you will look at Jesus now, and mourn for your sin, he will put your sin away; and then you will not be ashamed to see him in that day. Even though you did pierce him, you will be able to sing, "Unto him that loved us, and washed us from our sins in his own blood." But, remember, if you persevere in piercing him, and fighting against him, you will still have to see him in that day, to your terror and despair. He will be seen by you and by me, however ill we may behave. And what horror will that sight cost us!

We never know how soon we may be cut off, and then we are gone for ever from the opportunity of benefiting our fellow-men. It were a pity to be taken away with one opportunity of doing good unused. So would I earnestly plead with you under the shadow of this great truth: I would urge you to make ready, since we shall both behold the Lord in the day of his appearing. Yes, I shall stand in that great throng. You also will be there. How will you feel? You are not accustomed, perhaps, to attend a place of worship; but you will be there, and the spot will be very solemn to you. You may absent yourself from the assemblies of the saints, but you will not be able to absent yourself from the gathering of that day. You will be there, one in that great multitude; and you will see Jesus the Lord as truly as if you were the only person before him, and he will look upon you as certainly as if you were the only one that was summoned to his bar.

Will you kindly think of all this as I close this second head? Silently repeat to yourself the words, "Every eye shall see him, and they also that pierced him."

And now I must close with the third head, which is a painful one, but needs to be enlarged upon: HIS COMING WILL CAUSE GREAT SORROW. What does the text say about his coming? "All kindreds of the earth shall wail because of him."

"All kindreds of the earth." Then *this sorrow will be very general*. You thought, perhaps, that when Christ came, he would come to a glad world, welcoming him with song and music. You thought that there might be a few ungodly persons who would be destroyed with the breath of his mouth, but that the bulk of mankind would receive him with delight. See how different—"All kindreds of the earth," that is, all sorts of men that belong to the earth; all earth-born men, men out of all nations and kindreds and tongues shall weep and wail, and gnash their teeth at his coming. This is a sad outlook! We have no smooth things to prophesy. What think you of this?

And, next, *this sorrow will be very great*. They shall "*wail*." I cannot put into English the full meaning of that most expressive word. Sound it at length, and it conveys its own meaning. It is as when men wring their hands and burst out into a loud cry; or as when eastern women, in their anguish, rend their garments, and lift up their voices with the most mournful notes. All the "kindreds of the earth shall wail": wail as a mother laments over her dead child; wail as a man might wail who found himself hopelessly imprisoned and doomed to die. Such will be the hopeless grief of all the kindreds of the earth at the sight of Christ in the clouds: if they remain impenitent, they shall not be able to be silent; they shall not be able to repress or conceal their anguish, but they shall wail, or openly give vent to their horror. What a sound that will be which will go up before high heaven when Jesus sits upon the cloud, and in the fulness of his power summons them to judgment! Then "they shall wail because of him."

Will your voice be heard in that wailing? Will your heart be breaking in that general dismay? How will you escape? If you are one of the kindreds of the earth, and remain impenitent, you will wail with the rest of them. Unless you now fly to Christ, and hide yourself in him, and so become one of the kindred of heaven, one of his chosen and blood-washed ones—who shall praise his name for washing them from their sins—unless you do this, there will be wailing at the judgment-seat of Christ, and you will be in it.

Then it is quite clear that men will not be universally converted when Christ comes; because, if they were so, they would not wail. Then they would lift up the cry, "Welcome, welcome, Son of God!" The coming of Christ would be as the hymn puts it—

> *Hark, those bursts of acclamation!*
> *Hark, those loud triumphant chords!*
> *Jesus takes the highest station.*
> *Oh, what joy the sight affords!*

These acclamations come from his people. But according to the text the multitude of mankind will weep and wail, and therefore they will not be among his people. Do not, therefore, look for salvation to some coming day, but believe in Jesus now, and find in him your Saviour at once. If you joy in him now, you shall much more rejoice in him in that day; but if you will have cause to wail at his coming, it will be well to wail at once.

Note one more truth. It is quite certain that when Jesus comes in those latter days *men will not be expecting great things of him.* You know the talk they have nowadays about "a larger hope." To-day they deceive the people with the idle dream of repentance and restoration after death, a fiction unsupported by the least tittle of Scripture. If these "kindreds of the earth" expected that when Christ would come they would all die out and cease to be, they would rejoice that thereby they escaped the wrath of God. Would not each unbeliever say, "It were a consummation devoutly to be wished"? If they thought that at his coming there would be a universal restoration and a general jail delivery of souls long shut up in prison, would they wail? If Jesus could be supposed to come to proclaim a general restoration they would not wail, but shout for joy. Ah, no! It is because his coming to the impenitent is black with blank despair that they will wail because of him. If his first coming does not give you eternal life, his second coming will not. If you do not hide in his wounds when he comes as your Saviour, there will be no hiding place for you when he comes as your Judge. They will weep and wail because, having rejected the Lord Jesus, they have turned their backs on the last possibility of hope.

Why do they wail *because of him*? Will it not be because they will see him in his glory, and they will recollect that they slighted and despised him? They will see him come to judge them, and they will remember that once he stood at their door with mercy in his hands and said, "Open to me," but they would not admit him. They refused his blood: they refused his righteousness: they trifled with his sacred name; and now they must give an account for this wickedness. They put him away in scorn, and now, when he comes, they find that they can trifle with him no longer. The days of child's-play and of foolish delay are over; and now they have solemnly to give in their life's account. See, the books are opened! They are covered with dismay as they remember their sins, and know that they are written down by a faithful pen. They must give an account; and unwashed and unforgiven they cannot render that account without knowing that the sentence will be, "Depart, ye cursed." This is why they weep and wail because of him.

O souls, my natural love of ease makes me wish that I could preach pleasant things to you; but they are not in my commission. I need scarce wish, however, to preach a soft gospel, for so many are already doing it to your cost. As I love your immortal souls, I dare not flatter you. As I shall have to answer for it in the last great day, I must tell you the truth.

> *Ye sinners seek his face*
> *Whose wrath ye cannot bear.*

Seek the mercy of God now. I have come here in pain to implore you to be reconciled to God. "Kiss the Son lest he be angry, and ye perish from the way, when his wrath is kindled but a little. Blessed are all they that put their trust in him" (Ps. 2: 12).

But if you will not have my Lord Jesus, he comes all the same for that. He is on the road now, and when he comes you will wail because of him. Oh that you would make him your friend, and then meet him with joy! Why will ye die? He gives life to all those who trust him. Believe, and live.

XVI

THE STAR AND THE WISE MEN

"Now when Jesus was born in Bethlehem of Judea in the days of Herod the king, behold, there came wise men from the east to Jerusalem, saying, Where is he that is born King of the Jews? for we have seen his star in the east, and are come to worship him.

When they had heard the king, they departed; and, lo, the star, which they saw in the east, went before them, till it came and stood over where the young child was. When they saw the star, they rejoiced with exceeding great joy."—Matt. 2 : 1, 2, 9, 10.

SEE the glory of our Lord Jesus Christ, even in his state of humiliation! He is born of lowly parents, laid in a manger and wrapped in swaddling bands; but, lo! the principalities and powers in the heavenly places are in commotion. First, one angel descends to proclaim the advent of the new-born King, and suddenly there is with him a multitude of the heavenly host singing glory unto God. Nor was the commotion confined to the spirits above; for in the heavens which overhang this earth there is a stir. A star is deputed on behalf of all the stars, as if he were the envoy and plenipotentiary of all worlds to represent them before their King. This star is put in commission to wait upon the Lord, to be his herald to men afar off, his usher to conduct them to his Presence, and his body-guard to sentinel his Cradle.

Earth, too, is stirred. Shepherds have come to pay the homage of simple-minded ones: with all love and joy they bow before the mysterious child; and after them from afar come the choice and flower of their generation, the most studious minds of the age. Making a long and difficult journey, they too at last arrive, the representatives of the Gentiles. Lo! the kings of Seba and Sheba offer gifts—gold, frankincense, and myrrh. Wise men, the leaders of their peoples, bow down before him, and pay homage to the Son of God. Wherever Christ is he is honourable. "Unto you that believe he is honour." In the day of small things, when the cause of God is denied entertainment, and is hidden away with things which are despised, it is still most glorious. Christ, though a child, is still King of kings; though among the oxen, he is still distinguished by his star.

If wise men of old came to Jesus and worshipped, should not we come also? My intense desire is that we all may pay homage to him of whom we sing, "Unto us a child is born; unto us a son is given." Let those of us who have long worshipped worship anew with yet lowlier reverence and intenser love. And God grant—oh, that he would grant it!—that some who are far off from him spiritually, as the Magi were far off locally, may come to-day and ask, "Where is he that is born King of the Jews? for we have come to worship him." May feet that have been accustomed to broad roads, but unaccustomed to the narrow path, this day pursue that way till they see Jesus, and bow before him with all their hearts, finding salvation in him. These wise men came naturally, traversing the desert; let us come spiritually, leaving our sins. These were guided by the sight of a star; let us be guided by faith in the divine Spirit, by the teaching of his word and all those blessed lights which the Lord uses to conduct men to himself. Only let us come to Jesus. It was well to come unto the babe Jesus, led by the feeble beams of a star; you shall find it still more blessed to come to him now that he is exalted in the highest heavens, and by his own light reveals his own perfect glory. Delay not, for this day he cries, "Come unto me, all ye that labour and are heavy laden, and I will give you rest" (Matt. 10 : 28).

Let us try to do three things. First, let us *gather light from this star;* secondly, let us *gather wisdom from these wise men;* and thirdly, let us *act as wise men helped by our own particular star.*

First, then, LET US GATHER LIGHT FROM THIS STAR. May the Spirit of the Lord enable us so to do.

I suppose you have each one his own imagination as to what this star was. It would seem to have been altogether supernatural, and not a star, or a comet of the ordinary kind. It was not a constellation, nor a singular conjunction of planets: there is nothing in the Scriptures to support such a conjecture. In all probability it was not a star in the sense in which we now speak of stars: for we find that it moved before the wise men, then suddenly disappeared, and again shone forth to move before them. It could not have been a star in the upper spheres like others, for such movements would not have been possible. Some have supposed that the wise men went in the direction in which the star shone forth in the heavens, and followed the changes of its position: but it could not in that case have been said that it stood over the place where the young child was. If the star was at its zenith over Bethlehem, it would have been in its zenith over Jerusalem too; for the distance is so small that it would not have been possible to observe any difference in the position of the star in the two places.

It must have been a star occupying quite another sphere from that in which the planets revolve. We believe it to have been a luminous appearance in mid-air; probably akin to that which led the children of Israel through the wilderness, which was a cloud by day and a pillar of fire by night. Whether it was seen in the daylight or not we cannot tell. Chrysostom and the early fathers are wonderfully positive about many things which Scripture leaves in doubt, but as these eminent divines drew upon their imagination for their facts, we are not under bonds to follow them. They aver that this star was so bright as to be visible all day long. If so, we can imagine the wise men travelling day and night; but if it could be seen only by night, the picture before us grows far more singular and weird-like as we see these easterns quietly pursuing their star-lit way, resting *perforce* when the sun was up, but noiselessly hurrying at night through slumbering lands. These questions are not of much importance to us, and therefore we will not dwell long upon them.

Only here is a first lesson: *if it should ever be that men should fail to preach the Gospel, God can conduct souls to his Son by a star.* Ah! say not only by a star, but by a stone, a bird, a blade of grass, a drop of dew.

> *Remember that Omnipotence*
> *Has servants everywhere.*

Therefore, despond not when you hear that one minister has ceased to preach the Gospel, or that another is fighting against the vital truth of God. Their apostasy shall be to their own loss rather than to the hurt of Jesus and his church; and, sad though it be to see the lamps of the sanctuary put out, yet God is not dependent upon human lights, he is the Shekinah light of his own holy place. Mortal tongues, if they refuse to preach his word, shall have their places supplied by books in the running brooks and sermons in stones. The beam shall cry out of the wall, and the timber shall answer it. When chief priests and scribes have all gone out of the way, the Lord puts stars into commission, and once more in very deed the heavens are telling the glory of God, and the firmament is showing his handiwork. Sooner than lack speakers for the incarnate God, mountains and hills shall learn eloquence and break forth into testimony. Jehovah's message shall be made known to the utmost ends of the earth. God shall save his own elect; he shall give to Christ to see of the travail of his soul and to be satisfied. His counsel shall stand, and he will do all his pleasure. Hallelujah!

Now, when the Lord does use a star to be his minister, what is the order of his ministry? We may learn by this enquiry what kind of ministry God would have ours to be if we are stars in his right hand. We also shine as lights in the world: let us see how to do it.

We notice, first, that star-preaching is *all about Christ*. We do not know what the colour of the star was, nor the shape of the star, nor to what magnitude it had attained; these items are not recorded, but what is recorded is of much more importance: the wise men said: "We have seen *his* star." Then the star which the Lord will use to lead men to Jesus must be Christ's own star. The faithful minister, like this star, belongs to Christ; he is Christ's own man in the most emphatic sense. Before we can expect to be made a blessing, we must ourselves be blessed of the Lord. If we would cause others to belong to Jesus, we must belong wholly to Jesus ourselves. Every beam in that star shone forth for Jesus. It was *his* star, always, and only, and altogether. It shone not for itself, but only as *his* star: as such it was known and spoken of—"we have seen his star." As I have already said, there is no note taken of any peculiarity that it had except this one, that it was the star of the King. I wish that you and I, whatever our eccentricities or personalities may be, may never make so much of them as to attract men's attention to them. May people never dwell upon our attainments or our deficiencies, but may they always observe this one thing, that we are men of God, that we are ambassadors of Christ, that we are Christ's servants, and do not attempt to shine for ourselves, or to make ourselves conspicuous; but that we labour to shine for him, that his way may be known upon earth, his saving health among all people.

It is well for us to forget ourselves in our message, to sink ourselves in our Master. We know the names of several of the stars, yet they may each one envy that star which remains anonymous, but can never be forgotten because men who sought the King of Israel knew it as *"his* star." Though you be but a very little star, twinkling for Jesus; however feeble your light may be, be it plain that you are *his* star, so that if men wonder *what* you are, they may never wonder whose you are, for on your very forefront it shall be written, "Whose I am and whom I serve." God will not lead men to Christ by us unless we are Christ's heartily, wholly, unreservedly. In his temple our Lord uses no borrowed vessels; every bowl before the altar must be his own. It is not consistent with the glory of God for him to use borrowed vessels. He is not so poor as to come to that. This lesson is worthy of all acceptation. Are you in a hurry to preach, young man? Are you sure you are Christ's? Do you think it must be a fine thing to hold a company of people listening to your words? Have you looked at it in another light? Have you weighed the responsibility of having to speak as Christ would have you speak, and of yielding yourself in your entire personality to the utterance of the mind of God? You must be consecrated and concentrated if you hope to be used of the Lord. If you have one ray, or ten thousand rays, all must shine with the one design of guiding men to Jesus. You have nothing now to do with any object, subject, design, or endeavour, but Jesus only: in him, and for him, and to him must you live henceforth, or you will never be chosen of the Lord to conduct either wise men or babes to Jesus. See ye well to it that perfect consecration be yours.

Note, next, that true star-preaching *leads to Christ*. The star was Christ's star itself, but it also led others to Christ. It did this very much because it moved in that direction. It is a sad thing when a preacher is like a sign-post pointing the way but never following it on his own account. Such were those chief priests at Jerusalem: they could tell where Christ was born, but they never went to worship him; they were indifferent altogether to him and to his birth. The star that leads to Christ must always be going to Christ. Men are far better drawn by example than driven by exhortation. Personal piety alone can be owned of God to the production of piety in others. "Go," say you: but they will not go. Say "come," and lead the way: then they will come. Do not the sheep follow the shepherd? He who would lead others to Christ should go before them himself, having his face towards his Master, his eyes towards his Master, his steps towards his Master, his heart towards his Master. We are so to live that we may without boasting exhort those around us to have us for an example. Oh, that all who think themselves to be stars would themselves diligently move towards the Lord Jesus. The star in the east led wise men to Christ because it went that way itself: there is a wisdom in example which truly wise men are quick to perceive. This star had such an influence upon the chosen men that they could not but follow it: it charmed them across the desert. Such a charm may reside in you and in me, and we may exercise a powerful ministry over many hearts, being to them as loadstones, drawing them to the Lord Jesus.

Happy privilege! We would not merely show the road, but induce our neighbours to enter upon it. We read of one of old, not that they told him of Jesus, but that "they brought him to Jesus." We are not only to tell the story of the Cross, but we are to persuade men to fly to the Crucified One for salvation. Did not the king in the parable say to his servants, "Compel them to come in"? Assuredly he girds his own messengers with such a compelling power that men cannot hold out any longer, but must follow their lead and bow at the King's feet. The star did not draw, "as it were with a cart rope," nor by any force, material and physical; yet it drew these wise men from the remote east right to the manger of the new-born Child. And so, though we have no arm of the law to help us, nor patronage, nor pomp of eloquence, nor parade of learning, yet we have a spiritual power by which we draw to Jesus thousands who are our joy and crown.

The man sent of God comes forth from the divine presence

permeated with a power which makes men turn to the Saviour and live. Oh! that such power might go forth from all God's ministers, yea, from all God's servants engaged in street-preaching, in Sunday Schools, in tract-visitation, and in every form of holy service. God uses those whose aim and intent it is to draw men to Christ. He puts his Spirit into them, by which Spirit they are helped to set forth the Lord Jesus as so lovely and desirable that men run to him and accept his glorious salvation. It is a small thing to shine, but it is a great thing to draw. Any cast-away may be brilliant; but only the real saint will be attractive for Jesus. I would not pray to be an orator, but I do pray to be a soul-winner. Do not aim at anything short of leading men to Jesus. Do not be satisfied to lead them to orthodox doctrine, or merely to bring them to a belief in those views which you hold to be Scriptural, valuable as that may be. It is to the Person of the incarnate God that we must bring them: to his feet we must conduct them that they may worship him: our mission is not accomplished, it is a total failure, unless we conduct our hearers to the house where Jesus dwells, and then stand over them, keeping watch over their souls for Jesus' sake.

Once more, the star which God used in this case was a star that *stopped at Jesus:* it went before the wise men till it brought them to Jesus, and then it stood still over the place where the young child was. I admire the manner of this star. There are remarkable stars in the theological sky at the present time: they have led men to Jesus, so they say, and now they lead them into regions beyond, of yet undeveloped thought. The gospel of the Puritans is "old-fashioned"; these men have discovered that it is unsuitable for the enlarged intellects of the times; and so these stars would guide us further still. To this order of wandering stars I do not belong myself, and I trust I never shall. Progress beyond the Gospel I have no desire for. "God forbid that I should glory save in the cross of our Lord Jesus Christ" (Gal. 6: 14). When the star had come to the place where the young child was, it stood still: and so should the gracious mind become settled, fixed, immovable. The wise men knew where to find that star, and where to find the young child by it: so be it with us. Oh, you that have hitherto been diligent in leading souls to Christ, never indulge for a single moment the notion that you need a broader philosophy or a deeper spirituality than are to be found in Jesus. Abide in him. Cry, "O God, my heart is fixed; my heart is fixed."

There is nothing beyond Christ which is worth a moment's thought. Do not lose your paradise in Christ for another taste of that tree of knowledge-of-good-and-evil which ruined our first parents. Stick you to the old points: your one subject Christ, your one object to bring men to Christ, your one glory the glory of Christ. Standing by your Lord, and there alone, from this day to the last day, you will secure a happy, honoured and holy life. They said of Greece after her fall that it had become so ruined that you might search for Greece in Greece and fail to find it: I fear I must say that some professed preachers of the gospel have roamed so far away from it that you cannot find the gospel in their gospel, nor Christ himself in the Christ they preach. So far have some diverged from the grand essential soul-saving truth beyond which no man ought to dare to think of going, that they retain nothing of Christianity but the name. All that is beyond truth is a lie; anything beyond revelation is at best a minor matter, and most probably is an old wives' fable, even though he may be of the masculine gender who invented it. Stand you to your colours, you who hope to be used of the Lord. Abide so that men shall find you in twenty years' time shining for Jesus and pointing to the place where the Saviour is to be found, even as you are doing now. Let Jesus Christ be your ultimatum. Your work is done when you bring souls to Jesus, and help to keep them there, by being yourself "steadfast, unmovable." Be not carried away from the hope of your calling; but hold fast even the form of sound words, for it may be that in letting go the form you may lose the substance also.

Now that we have somewhat rejoiced in the light of the star, let us see if we can GATHER WISDOM FROM THE WISE MEN. Perhaps you have heard the "much speaking" of tradition as to who they were, whence they came, and how they travelled. In the Greek church, I believe, they know their number, their names, the character of their retinue, and what kind of ornaments were on their dromedaries' necks. Details which are not found in the word of God you may believe or not, at your pleasure, and you will be wise if your pleasure is not to believe

H

too much. We only know that they were Magi, wise men from the East, possibly of the old Parsee religion, watchers if not worshippers of the stars. We will not speculate about them, but learn from them.

They did not content themselves with admiring the star and comparing it with other stars, and taking notes as to the exact date of its appearance, and how many times it twinkled, and when it moved, and all that; but *they practically used the teaching of the star*. Many are hearers and admirers of God's servants, but they are not wise enough to make fit and proper use of the preaching. They notice the peculiarity of the preacher's language, how much he is like one divine, how much he is unlike another; whether he coughs too often or speaks too much in his throat; whether he is too loud or too low; whether he has not a provincial tone, whether there may not be about him a commonness of speech approaching to vulgarity; or, on the other hand, whether he may not be too florid in his diction. Such fooleries as these are the constant observations of men for whose souls we labour. They are perishing, and yet toying with such small matters.

With many it is all they go to the house of God for: to criticise in this paltry fashion. I have even seen them come to this place with opera glasses, as if they came hither to inspect an actor who lived and laboured to amuse their leisure hours. Such is the sport of fools; but these were wise men, and therefore practical men. They did not become star-gazers and stop at the point of admiring the remarkable star; but they said, "Where is he that is born King of the Jews? for we have seen his star in the east, and are come to worship him." They set out at once to find the new-born King, of whose coming the star was the signal. Oh, how I wish that you were all wise in this same manner! I would sooner preach the dullest sermon that was ever preached than preach the most brilliant that was ever spoken if I could by that poor sermon lead you quite away from myself to seek the Lord Jesus Christ. That is the one thing I care about. Will you never gratify me by enquiring after my Lord and Master? I long to hear you say, "What is the man talking about? He speaks about a Saviour; we will have that Saviour for ourselves. He talks about pardon through the blood of Christ; he speaks about God coming down among men to save them; we will find out if there is any reality in this pardon, any truth in this salvation. We will seek Jesus and find for ourselves the blessings which are reported to be laid up in him.'' If I heard you all saying this I should be ready to die of joy.

Is not this a good day on which to set out to find your Saviour? Some of you that have postponed it long, would it not be well to set out at once ere this expiring year has seen its last day? These wise men appear to have set out as soon as they discovered the star: they were not among those who have time to waste in needless delays. ''There is the star,'' said they; ''away we go beneath its guidance. We are not satisfied with a star, we go to find the King whose star it is!'' And so they set out to find Christ immediately and resolutely.

Being wise men, *they persevered in their search after him*. We cannot tell how far they journeyed. Travelling was extremely difficult in those times. There were hostile tribes to avoid, the broad rivers of the Tigris and the Euphrates to cross, and trackless deserts to penetrate; but they made nothing of difficulty or danger. They set out for Jerusalem, and to Jerusalem they came, seeking the King of the Jews. If it be true that God has taken upon himself our nature, we ought to resolve to find him, let it cost what it may. If we must circumnavigate the globe to find a Saviour, the distance and the expense ought to be nothing so long as we may but reach him. Were the Christ in the bowels of the earth, or in the heights of heaven we ought not to rest till we come at him. Everything that was necessary for their expedition the wise men soon gathered together, regardless of expense; and off they went following the star that they might discover the Prince of the kings of the earth.

At length they came to Jerusalem, and here new trials awaited them. It must have been a great trouble to them when they asked, ''Where is he that is born King of the Jews?'' and the people shook their heads as if they thought the question an idle one. Neither rich nor poor in the metropolitan city knew anything of Israel's King. The ribald multitude replied, ''Herod is king of the Jews. Mind how you speak of another king, or your head may have to answer for it. The tyrant brooks no rival.'' The wise men must have been more astonished still when they found that Herod was troubled. They were glad to think that he **was born** who was to usher in the age of gold; but

Herod's face grew blacker than ever at the bare mention of a king of the Jews. His eyes flashed, and a thunder-cloud was upon his brow; a dark deed of murder will come of it, though for the moment he conceals his malice. There is tumult all through the streets of Jerusalem, for no man knows what grim Herod may do now that he has been roused by the question, "Where is he that is born King of the Jews?" Thus there was a ferment in Jerusalem, beginning at the palace; but this did not deter the wise men from their search for the promised Prince. They did not pack up their bales and go back and say, "It is useless to try to discover this questionable personage who is unknown even in the country of which he is King, and who appears to be terribly unwelcome to those who are to be his subjects. We must leave to another day the solution of the question: "Where is he that is born King of the Jews?"

These earnest-minded seekers were not dispirited by the clergy and the learned men when they came together. To the chief priests and scribes the question was put, and they answered the enquiry as to where Christ would be born, but not a mother's son among them would go with the wise men to find this new-born King. Strange apathy! Alas, how common! Those who should have been leaders were no leaders; they would not even be followers of that which is good, for they had no heart towards Christ. The wise men rose superior to this serious discouragement. If the clergy would not help them they would go to Jesus by themselves. Oh, if you are wise you will say, "I will find Christ alone if none will join me: if I dig to the centre, I will find him; if I fly to the sun, I will find him; if all men put me off, I will find him; if the ministers of the gospel appear indifferent to me, I will find him: the kingdom of heaven of old suffered violence, and the violent took it by force, and so will I." The first Christians had to leave all the authorized teachers of the day behind, and to come out by themselves: it will be no strange thing if you should have to do the same. Happy will it be if you are determined to go through floods and flames to find Christ; for he will be found of you. Thus these men were wise because, having started on the search, they persevered in it till they found the Lord and worshipped him.

Notice that they were wise because, when they again saw the star, *"they rejoiced with exceeding great joy."* While enquiring among the priests at Jerusalem they were perplexed, but when the star shone out again, they were at ease and full of joy: this joy they expressed, so that the evangelist recorded it. In these days very wise people think it necessary to repress all emotion, and appear like men of stone or ice. No matter what happens, they are stoical, and raised far above the enthusiasm of the vulgar. It is wonderful how fashions change, and folly stands for philosophy. But these wise men were children enough to be glad when their perplexity was over, and the clear light shone forth. It is a good sign when a man is not ashamed to be happy because he hears a plain, unmistakable testimony for the Lord Jesus. It is good to see the great man come down from his pedestal, and, like a little child, rejoice to hear the simple story of the Cross. Give me the hearer who looks not for fineries, but cries out, "Lead me to Jesus. I want a guide to Jesus, and nothing else will suit me." Why, truly, if men did but know the value of things they would rejoice more to see a preacher of the gospel than a king. If the feet of the heralds of salvation be blessed, how much more their tongues when they tell out the tidings of a Saviour. These wise men, with all their mystic learning, were not ashamed to rejoice because a little star lent them its beams to conduct them to Jesus. We unite with them in rejoicing over a clear Gospel ministry. For us all else is darkness, sorrow, and vexation of spirit; but that which leads us to our own glorious Lord is spirit, and light, and life. Better the sun should not shine than that a clear Gospel should not be preached. We reckon that a country flourishes or decays according as Gospel light is revealed or withdrawn.

Now follow these wise men a little further. They have come to the house where the young child is. What will they do? Will they stand looking at the star? No: *they enter in*. The star stands still, but they are not afraid to lose its radiance, and behold the Sun of righteousness. They did not cry, "We see the star, and that is enough for us; we have followed the star, and it is all we need to do." Not at all. They lift the latch, and enter the lowly residence of the babe. They see the star no longer, and they have no need to see it, for there is he that is born King of the Jews. Now the true Light has shone upon them from the face of the child; they behold the incarnate God. Oh how wise you will be if, when you have been led to Christ by any man, you do not rest in his leadership, but must see Christ for yourselves. How much I long that you may enter into the fellowship of the mystery, pass through the door, and come and behold the young child, and bow before him. Our woe is that so many are so unwise. We are only their guides, but they are apt to make us their end. We point the way, but they do not follow the road; they stand gazing upon us. The star is gone; it did its work, and passed away: Jesus remains, and the wise men live in him. Will any of you be so foolish as to think only of the dying preacher, and forget the ever-living Saviour? Come, be wise, and hasten to your Lord at once.

These men were wise, last of all—and I commend their example to you—because when they saw the child *they worshipped*. Theirs was not curiosity gratified, but devotion exercised. We, too, must worship the Saviour, or we shall never be saved by him. He has not come to put away our sins, and yet to leave us ungodly and self-willed. Oh you that have never worshipped the Christ of God, may you be led to do so at once! He is God over all, blessed for ever, adore him! Was God ever seen in such a worshipful form before? Will you not worship God when he thus comes down to you and becomes your brother, born for your salvation? Here nature itself suggests worship: Oh, may grace produce it! Let us hasten to worship where shepherds and wise men and angels have led the way.

Here let my sermon come to a pause even as the star did. Enter the house and worship! Forget the preacher. Let the starlight shine for other eyes. Jesus was born that you might be born again. He lived that you might live. He died that you might die to sin. He is risen, and to-day he maketh intercession for transgressors that they may be reconciled to God through him. Come, then; believe, trust, rejoice, adore! If you have neither gold, frankincense, nor myrrh, bring your faith, your love, your repentance, and falling down before the Son of God pay him the reverence of your hearts.

And now I turn to my third and last point, which is this: LET US ACT AS WISE MEN UNDER THE LIGHT OF OUR STAR. We too have received light to lead us to the Saviour: I might say that for us many stars have shone to that blessed end. I will, however, on this point content myself with asking questions.

Do you not think that there is some light for you in your particular vocation, some call from God in your calling? Listen to me, and then listen to God. These men were watchers of the stars; therefore a star was used to call them. Certain other men soon after were fishermen, and by means of an amazing take of fish the Lord Jesus made them aware of his superior power, and then he called them to become fishers of men. For a star-gazer a star; for a fisherman a fish. The Master-Fisher hath a bait for each one of his elect, and oftentimes he selects a point in their own calling to be the barb of the hook. Were you busy yesterday at your counter? Did you hear no voice saying "Buy the truth and sell it not"? When you closed the shop last night did you not bethink yourself that soon you must close it for the last time? Do you make bread? and do you never ask yourself, "Has my soul eaten the bread of heaven?" Are you a farmer? do you till the soil? Has God never spoken to you by those furrowed fields and these changing seasons, and made you wish that your heart might be tilled and sown? Listen! God is speaking! How I wish that your common vocation would be viewed by you as concealing within itself the door to your high vocation. Oh that the Holy Spirit would turn your favourite pursuits into opportunities for his gracious work upon you.

I wish that those of you who conclude that your calling could never draw you to Christ would make a point of seeing whether it might not be so. We are to learn from ants, and swallows, and cranes, and conies; surely we need never be short of tutors. It did seem that a star was an unlikely thing to head a procession of eastern sages, and yet it was the best guide that could be found; and so it may seem that your trade is an unlikely thing to bring you to Jesus, and yet the Lord may so use it. There may be a message from the Lord to thee in many a left-handed providence; a voice for wisdom may come to thee from the mouth of an ass; a call to a holy life may startle thee from a bush, a warning may flash upon thee from a wall, or a vision may impress thee in the silence of night when deep sleep falleth upon men. Only be thou ready to hear and God will find a way of speaking to thee. Answer the question as the wise men would have answered it, and say, "Yes, in our calling there is a call to Christ."

Then, again, *what should you and I do better in this life than seek after Christ?* The wise men thought all other pursuits of small account compared with this. "Who is going to attend to that observatory and watch the rest of the stars?" They shake their heads, and say they do not know: these things must wait; they have seen *his* star, and they are going to worship him. But who will attend to their wives and families, and all besides, while they make this long journey? They reply that every lesser thing must be subordinate to the highest thing. Matters must be taken in proportion, and the search after the King of the Jews, who is the desire of all nations, is so out of all proportion great that all the rest must go. Are not you, also, wise enough to judge in this sensible fashion? If you were to take a week, and give it wholly to your own soul, and to seeking Christ, would it not be well spent? How can you live with your soul in jeopardy? Oh that you would say, "I must get this matter right; it is an all-important business, and I must see it secure." This would be no more than common-sense. If you are driving, and a trace is broken, do you not stop the horse, and set the harness right? How, then, can you go on with the chariot of life when all its harness is out of order, and a fall means eternal ruin? If you will stop driving to arrange a buckle for fear of accident, I would beg of you to stop anything and everything to see to the safety of your soul.

See how the engineer looks to the safety-valve: are you content to run more desperate risks? If your house were not insured, and you carried on a hazardous trade, the probability is you would feel extremely anxious until you had arranged that matter: but your soul is uninsured, and it may burn for ever; will you not give heed to it? I beseech you be just to yourself; be kind to yourself. Oh! see to your eternal well-being.

When we do come near to Jesus, let us ask ourselves this question, "*Do we see more in Jesus than other people do?*" for if we do, we are God's elect, taught of God, illuminated by his Spirit. We read in the Scriptures that when these wise men saw the young child they fell down and worshipped him. Other people might have come in and seen the child, and said, "Many children are as interesting as this poor woman's babe." Ay, but as these men looked, they saw: all eyes are not so blessed. Eyes that see are gifts from the All-seeing One. Carnal eyes are blind; but these men saw the Infinite in the infant; the Godhead gleaming through the manhood; the glory hiding beneath the swaddling bands. Undoubtedly there was a spiritual splendour about this matchless Child! We read that Moses' father and mother saw that he was a "goodly child"; they saw he was "fair unto God," says the original. But when these elect men saw that holy thing which is called the Son of the Highest, they discovered in him a glory all unknown before. Then was his star in the ascendant to them: he became their all in all, and they worshipped with all their hearts. Have you discovered such glory in Christ? "Oh!" says one, "you are always harping upon Christ and his glory. You are a man of one idea!" Precisely so. My one idea is that he is "altogether lovely," and that there is nothing out of heaven nor in heaven that can be compared with him even in his lowest and weakest estate. Have you ever seen as much as that in Jesus? If so, you are the Lord's; go you, and rejoice in him. If not, pray God to open your eyes until, like the wise men, you see and worship.

Lastly, learn from these wise men that when they worshipped they did not permit it to be a mere empty-handed adoration. Ask yourself, "*What shall I render unto the Lord?*" Bowing before the young Child, they offered "gold, frankincense and myrrh," the best of metals and the best of spices; an offering to the King of gold; an offering to the priest of frankincense; an offering to the child of myrrh. Wise men are liberal men. Consecration is the best education. To-day it is thought to be wise to be always receiving; but the Saviour said, "It is more blessed to give than to receive." God judges our hearts by that which spontaneously comes from them: hence the sweet cane bought with money is acceptable to him when given freely. He doth not tax his saints or weary them with incense; but he delights to see in them that true love which cannot express itself in mere words, but must use gold and myrrh, works of love and deeds of self-denial, to be the emblems of its gratitude. You will never get into the heart of happiness till you become unselfish and generous; you have but chewed the husks of religion which are often bitter, you have never eaten of the sweet kernel until you have felt the love of God constraining you to make sacrifice.

XVII

THE LAST SERMON OF THE YEAR

"Give an account of thy stewardship; for thou mayest be no longer steward."—Luke 16: 2.

THE first part of this text applies to us all; the second part will apply to each one of us before long. "Give an account of thy stewardship," is a command that may be addressed to the ungodly. They are accountable to God for all that they have, or ever have had, or ever shall have. The law of the Lord is not relaxed because they have sinned; they still remain responsible to God, even though they attempt to cast off the yoke of the Almighty. As creatures formed by the divine hand and sustained by divine power, they are bound to serve God; and, if they do not and will not, his claims upon them do not cease, and to each of them he saith, "Give an account of thy stewardship."

This text may also be applied to the children of God, to the godly, in a different sense, however, and after another fashion. For, first of all, the godly are God's children, they are accounted as standing in Christ. They are no longer merely God's subjects; for what they owed to God as sinners has all been discharged by Jesus Christ their Substitute and Saviour. They have, therefore, been placed on a different footing from other men; but, having been saved by grace and adopted into God's family, they have had entrusted to them talents which they are to use to his honour and glory. Being the Lord's children, and being saved, they become his servants, and as his servants they are under responsibility to God, and they will all have to give to him an account of their stewardship.

Look at Eli; I have no doubt that he was a saved man, but God made him a steward over his own family as well as a prophet to Israel, and he had to give an account of his stewardship, and because he had not been faithful in it, although he was not condemned eternally, yet he was made most miserably to suffer when he was told that the whole of his house should be swept away, and also when he heard of the deaths of his sons, and as the direst news of all learned that the ark of God was taken by the Philistines. God visited him in his capacity of steward, made him give in his account, and awarded him in this life a heavy penalty for his unfaithfulness; and I do not doubt that many a child of God, who has been saved at the last, yet, being found unfaithful as a steward, has had to suffer much, has lost much of honour and much of fellowship with God, and much of high advancement in the way of grace which he might otherwise have obtained.

David also was another such a steward. He was not a lost soul, I have no doubt that he is among the saved and blessed saints in heaven; but as a steward he was not found faithful. You remember how grievously he sinned, and from that moment his family was full of rebellion, his kingdom was full of trouble, and he went with broken bones all the way down to his grave. Hence I may say to you, children of God, who are not under the law,—and I do not address you at all in a legal strain when I so speak to you—you also have a stewardship. Give an account of it, or else perhaps you may be no longer spared; or, being spared, yet still you may have tokens of your Lord's displeasure, which you may carry with you even to your tomb. Thank God, you shall leave them there! But it would be more for God's glory, and for your own comfort, not to have them at all.

I desire, on this last day of another year, not so much to speak to you, as to get you to talk to yourselves. So, first, we will together think upon *the reasonable demand* made in our text: "Give an account of thy stewardship." Next, we will examine *some reasons why we should at once give an account of our stewardship;* and, lastly, we will consider *the weighty reason in the text*, which will come with force to each of us sooner or later: "Thou mayest be no longer steward."

First, then, let us consider this REASONABLE DEMAND, and let each one of us try to comply with it: "Give an account of thy stewardship." Thou man of God, thou Christless soul, thou aged man, thou young sister, "Give an account of thy steward-ship."

First, give an account of the stewardship of *thy time*. How hast thou spent it? Have not many hours been allowed to run to waste, or worse than waste, in frivolity and sin? Hast thou lived as a dying man should live? Hast thou employed thine hours as remembering that they are very few, and more precious than the diamonds in an emperor's crown? What about thy time? Has there not been much of it spent in indolence, in frothy talk, or that did not minister to edification? Thou needest not accuse thyself for time spent in lawful recreation that may sustain thy body, and fit it better for the Lord's service. It is well that thou shouldst have such recreation; but how much time is utterly wasted by some people, neither used for the good of this world, nor of that which is to come, but wholly frittered away in the service of sin, and self, and Satan! Where, for instance, did some of you spend yesterday, and how did you employ its precious hours? I will but bring that one day to your remembrance: was it a well-spent day? Is that hour well spent that is passed in the company of drunkards? Call you that day well spent that is given up to riotings, or that night that is defiled with wantonness? I charge you now to answer this question. For every moment that God has lent to you, he will ask for an account of what you did with it.

"Give an account of thy stewardship," next, as to *thy talents*. We all vary in our natural gifts and in our acquirements; one has the tongue of eloquence, another has the pen of a ready writer, and a third has the artistic eye that discerns beauty; but, whichever of these gifts we may have, they belong to God, and ought to be used in his service. Some have only such gifts as qualify them to earn their daily bread by manual labour; they have but little mental power, yet for that little they must give an account, and also for the physical strength with which God has blessed them. There is no person here without a talent of some sort or other; there is no one individual here without some form of power either given by nature or acquired by education. We are all endowed in some degree or other, and we must each one give an account for that talent. What an account must some give, who have been endowed with ten talents, but have wasted them all! What must be the account rendered by a Napoleon? What must be the reckoning given in by a Voltaire, with all the splendour of his intellect laid at the feet of Satan, and desecrated to the damnation of mankind? Yet, while you think of these great ones of the earth, do not forget yourselves. What has been your special gift? You can speak well enough in some companies; have you ever spoken for Christ? You can write well, you judge that you have no mean gift in that direction; has your pen never written a line that will bring your fellow-men to the service of the Saviour?

Next, give an account of *thy substance*. We vary greatly as to our temporal circumstances. I suppose there are a few present to whom God has entrusted great wealth, more to whom he has given considerable substance, and that to most of us he has given somewhat more than is absolutely necessary for our actual wants; but whether it is much or little, we must give an account for it all. I do not know what some rich professors will have to say concerning that which they give to the cause of God. It is no tithe of their substance; nay, it is, as it were, but the cheese-parings, and the candle-ends, and these they only give for the sake of appearance, because it would not look respectable if they were altogether to withhold them. The church's coffers could never be so empty as they are if it were not that some of the stewards in the church are not faithful to their trust. It is very sad to think of some of the great men in our own country, who have incomes which, in a single month, would furnish a competent support for an entire family during their whole lives. I wonder what sort of reckoning theirs will be when they have to give an account of hundreds of thousands or even millions of pounds. With some of them, all that they can say will be, "So much lost on the race-course, so much spent upon a paramour, so much paid for diamonds, so much squandered in this form of waste, and so much in that." But for the poor and needy, who are perishing in our streets, the multitudes who crave even necessary bread, some of them have done nothing at all. There are grand exceptions, names that shall live as long as philanthropy is prized amongst mankind; but the exceptions are so terribly few, that when the rich men of England are indicted at the bar of God, as they certainly will be, the account of their stewardship will be a truly terrible one. Yet what are you, and what am I, to judge thus, if we cannot say that we have been faithful with our little? I ask you if you have, and I pray you to make a reckoning in your mind now of your stewardship of the gold, or the silver, or the copper, with which God has entrusted you.

We must give an account, in the next place, of *our influence*. Everybody has some kind of influence. The mother who never leaves the nursery has a wondrous influence over those little children of hers, though no neighbour feels the force of her influence, and no one but her own little ones is affected by her faithfulness. And who knows but that she is pressing to her bosom, perhaps a Whitefield, who will thunder out the Gospel through the length and breadth of the land; or perhaps, on the other hand, an infidel, whose dreadful blasphemies shall ruin multitudes? There is an influence that the mother has for which she must give an account to God. And the father's influence,—oh! fathers, you cannot shake off your obligations to your children by sending them to school, whether to a Sunday School or a boarding-school. They are your children, and you must give an account of your stewardship concerning your own offspring. Ay, and even the nurse girl, though she seems of small note in the commonwealth, yet she also has an influence over her little charge, which she must use for Christ. Not only he who thrills a senate with his oratory, but he also who speaks a word from the carpenter's bench, each has his influence, and each must use it, and give an account of it; not merely the man who, by refusing to lend his millions, could prevent the horrors of war, but the man who with a smile might help to laugh at sin or with a word of rebuke might show that he abhorred it. There is no one of you without influence, and I ask you now how you have used it. Has it always been on the side of the Lord? "Give an account of thy stewardship," for that influence will not always last.

We might pass on to consider all the other things that God has entrusted to us, but time would fail us; so I would remind you, with much affection, that the account which you will have to render, and which I ask you to render now, is *not an account concerning other people*. Oh, how nice it would be if we had to do that, would it not? With what gusto some, would undertake the task if they had to give in a report upon other people's characters! How easily each of us can play the detective upon our fellows! How ready we are to say of this man, "Oh, yes! he gives away a good deal of money, but it is only out of ostentation," or of that woman, "Yes, she appears to be a Christian, but you do not know her private life," or of that minister of the Gospel, "Yes, he is very zealous; but he makes a good thing out of his ministry." We like thus to reckon up our fellow-creatures, and our arithmetic is wonderfully accurate —at least, so we think; but when other people cast us up according to the same rule, the arithmetic seems terribly out of order, and we cannot believe it to be right. Ah! but at the great judgment we shall not be asked to give an account for others, neither will I ask any of you now to be thinking about the conduct of others. What if others are worse than you are, does that make you the better, or the less guilty? What if others are not all they seem to be, perhaps neither are you; at any rate, their hypocrisy shall not make your pretence to be true. Judge yourselves, that ye be not judged. Let each man thrust the lancet into his own wound, and see to the affairs of his own soul, for each one must give account of himself to God.

Remember, too, that *you are not called upon to give an account to others.* Alas! there are many people who seem to live only that they may win the esteem of their fellows. There is somebody to whom we look up; if we do but have that somebody's smile, we think all is well. Perhaps some here are broken-hearted because that smile has vanished, and they have been misjudged and unjustly condemned. It is a small matter to be judged of man's judgment; and who is he that judges another man's servant? To his own Master the servant shall stand or fall, and not to this interloping judge. When the opinion of one leans this way, and of another goes the other way, when we see public opinion to be as restless and changing as the vane upon the church steeple, swinging round with every wind that blows, we may well bid defiance to it all, and thank God that the last bar is not swayed by the follies of the times, and that the Great Judge will not give his verdict according to the whimsies of an hour, but according to the rule of absolute equity. Yet remember that, if it be hard to be judged of man, it will be sterner still to be judged of God. If, weighed even in the balances of men, some of us are found wanting, how shall we bear to be put into the unerring scales adjusted by the divine hand, to be adjudged by him who cannot err, and to have our destiny fixed for all eternity, either in heaven or in hell? Recollect this, and be ready to give an account of thy stewardship, not to thy fellow-creature, but to the great Creator and Judge of all.

Remember also, that the account to be rendered will be from every man, *from every man personally concerning himself;* and whatever another man's account may be, it will not affect him. Some men will not have been any better than others of you have been; yet if you perish as they perish, a numerous company will not make hell any the cooler. If some men shall have been worse than others of you have been, it certainly will not diminish your punishment if you know that their doom is heavier than your own. Forget, for a while, that there are any other men in the world, and stand individually and separately before those awful eyes which are searching you through and through, for God will judge each of you as if there were no other men to judge, and read your inmost heart, as if he had not another object to look upon. Give an account, then, of thy stewardship.

Now let us examine SOME REASONS WHY WE SHOULD AT ONCE GIVE AN ACCOUNT OF OUR STEWARDSHIP.

It was a maxim of Pythagoras that each of his disciples should, every eventide, give in a record of the actions of the day. I think it is well to do so; for we cannot too often take a retrospect of the past. But since, perhaps, some of you may have been lax in this duty, let me remind you that *we have come, as it were, to the eventide of the year*, and it seems to be most suitable that, before we cross into another year of grace, we should in our heart and conscience take stock, and give an account of our stewardship. Sit down a while, pilgrim; sit down a while. Here is the milestone marked with the end of another year; sit down upon it, put thine hand to thy brow and think, and lay thine hand upon thy heart, and search and see what is there. This last Sabbath evening in the year is a most fitting time for giving in this account, and I ask you to use it in making up the account which you have to present before God; and if you feel unwilling to do it, I shall the more earnestly press you to do it. There are no persons who so dislike to look into their account-books as those who are insolvent. Those who keep no books, when they come before the court, are understood to be rogues of the first water; and men who keep no mental memoranda of the past, and bring up no recollections with regard to their sins, having tried to forget them all, may depend upon it that they are deceiving themselves. If you dare not search your hearts, I am afraid there is a reason for that fear, and that above all others you ought to be diligent in this search.

Permit me to remind you that, *if all should be wrong with you, it is best for you to know it.* It is only the most reckless seaman who would rather not know whether there is a rock in the course that he is sailing. Are you like the ostrich that, having covered its head in the sand and shut its eyes to the hunter, thinks it is all secure? I pray you, seek to know the worst of your case. It seems to me that any honest and sane man would want to do this. There is nothing a wise man hates more, when he is sick, than to have a doctor attending him, who will always, if he can, give a flattering report, but will never speak the truth about his patient. Let not your heart flatter you any longer, but say to it, "My soul, make out an honest account, see what and where thou art, and whether thou art God's servant or not, doing as God would have thee do."

Believer in Christ, it will be well for you to make out this account, because you will find that *it will help you to prize your Saviour more.* I never look into my own heart without first feeling shame, and afterwards feeling greater love to him who has eternally loved such a sinner as I am. I am sure it will drive you to your knees if you honestly search your own lives. There is enough in the history of a single week to make you prize your Redeemer more than ever, if you fully realize the guilt of that one week, and the greatness of his grace in pardoning it. O Christian, if you would be driven nearer to your Lord, search and see, confess, repent, and seek forgiveness. Go again to the Cross because you have again felt the burden of the sin that nailed your Saviour there.

And, ungodly man, I press you also to give an account of your stewardship, because, *mayhap, the same result may come to you,* if you find that you cannot give in so good an account as you thought you could when you were wrapped up in self-righteousness. Perhaps you may be alarmed and dismayed when you see the true state of the case, and it may be that God the Holy Spirit will lead you to say, "I will go to Jesus, for I am undone without him. I will hasten to his Cross, for I need the pardon that his blood has bought. I will now go with the language of confession on my lips, and beseech him to accept me ere another year begins." I do pray at this moment that this day may be the last one you will spend in sin, and that to-morrow may be a spiritual birthday to you, the first day in which you shall rejoice in a Saviour; nay, that this very night you may be born again, and become a new creature in Christ Jesus.

And now, lastly, let us consider THE REASON WHICH THE MASTER GIVES: "Give an account of thy stewardship, *for thou mayest be no longer steward.*"

This may happen in various ways. It may be that some here may live for years, and yet be no longer stewards. A preacher may be laid aside, his voice gone, his mental faculties weakened, he is "no longer steward." One is thankful to have further opportunities of serving the Lord, and trying to bring sinners to the Saviour. Work for God while you can! It is one of the bitterest regrets a man can know, to lie on his bed, to be unable to speak, and to think to himself, "I wish I could preach that sermon over again. I did not drive that nail home with all the force I ought to have used; I have not been earnest enough in pleading with sinners, I have not wrestled even to agony over the salvation of their souls." It may be possible, my dear brother minister, that you and I may have twenty or thirty years of being laid aside from active service; then let us work while we can, ere the night cometh when no man can work. Let us seize the oar of the lifeboat, and row out over the stormy sea, seeking to snatch the drowning ones from yonder wreck, for the time may come when our strong right arm shall be palsied, and when we can do no more.

Yes, and rich professors may have to give an account of their stewardship, and be no longer stewards. There were some of that kind when the recent financial panic came; though they had much before the crash, they had nothing left afterwards, so they could be no longer stewards of the wealth that had been taken from them. It must be a cause of deep regret to men in that position if they cannot give a good account of their stewardship, because they have done but little good with their wealth while they had it; and think, you to whom God has given great possessions, how soon he may take them from you, for riches abide not for ever. Behold, they take to themselves wings, and fly away. I know of no better way of clipping their wings than by giving generously to the cause of God and using in his service all that you can. It would be a subject for continual regret to you, I am sure, if you came down to poverty, not so much that you had descended in the social scale, for that you could bear, if it came by mere misfortune through the providence of God; but if you felt, "I did not do what I should have done when I had wealth,"—that would be the arrow which would pierce you to the heart. It may be so with some of you. At any rate, I feel that there are some of you who are poor because God will not lend his money where he knows that it will be locked up, and not put out to good interest in his cause. What little you have is all hidden away, so the Lord will not trust you with more; he sees you are not fit to be one of his stewards. There are some, on the other hand, whom God has entrusted with much because he sees that they use it wisely in promoting the interests of his kingdom.

But, after all, to every man, whether he be rich, or whether he be in the office of the ministry, *there may be a close of his stewardship before he dies*. The mother has her little children swept away one after another; this is the message to her, "Thou mayest be no longer steward." The teacher has his class scattered, or he is himself unable to go to the School; the word to him also is, "Thou mayest be no longer steward." The man who went to his work, who might have spoken to his fellow-workman, is removed, perhaps to another land, or he is placed in a position where his mouth is shut; now he can be no longer steward. Use all opportunities while you have them, catch them on the wing, serve God while you can to-day! to-day! to-day! to-day! Let each golden moment have its pressing service rendered unto God, lest it should be said to thee, "Thou mayest be no longer steward."

But we shall soon be no longer stewards in another sense. *The hour must come for us to die*. Out of our large congregation we have constant reminders that those who have served us as a church, and have served God faithfully in his church, cannot abide with us for ever. One or another, whom we have loved and honoured, gives in his account, and passes to his rest. So will it be in turn with the pastor, with the deacons, and with the elders. Do not put away the thought of that day, my fellow-workers, as though you were immortal. It may come to us on a sudden; no grey hairs may cover our heads, but while we are yet in the full strength of manly vigour, you or I may be called to give in our account. What think ye? What think ye? Could you gather up your feet in the bed, and look into eternity without feeling the cold sweat of fear stand upon your brow? What think ye? Could you face the great judgment-seat, and say, "I know whom I have believed, and am persuaded that he is able to keep that which I have committed unto him against that day . . . . I have fought a good fight, I have finished my course, I have kept the faith"? (2 Tim. 1: 12; 4: 7). Oh! God be praised if we are able to say that! What monuments of mercy will you and I be if we are able to hear our Lord say, "Well done, good and faithful servant; enter thou into the joy of thy Lord."

By the fact that God is continually removing from us one and another, I ask you to remember that you also will soon depart. Therefore, be making up your account. Rest in Christ more confidently; love God more earnestly; serve your generation more intensely; live while you live; play not at living, but live in real earnest, and let it never be said of you that you trod so lightly on the sands of time that you left no impress there. Make your mark upon your age, and fill your appointed place as God shall help you, that when you are gathered to your fathers, you may not be forgotten, but the church may remember you because in her midst there are children born to God through your means.

As for the unconverted here, need I tell them that they must soon depart, and be no longer stewards? You must go from your business, O trader; you must go from your merchandise, O merchant; you must go from your bench, O artizan; you must go from your machine, O engineer; you must each depart, and go to that bourne from which no traveller returns. Be ye ready! Be ye ready! I will ring the alarm bell for some of you; perhaps my text is a prophecy meant for some man here, "Give an account of thy stewardship; for thou mayest be no longer steward." Thou hast had children about thee, and thou hast taught them blasphemy and drunkenness; or thou hast had workmen in thine employ, and thou hast laughed at their religion, or aided and abetted them in sin; thou hast had talent,

but thou hast used that talent in the service of the evil one;
thou hast had gold, but thou hast lavished it upon wantonness;
now give an account of it all! Ah! you may not heed what I say;
but you will have to heed what will be said to you at another
time. You will see this matter in another light when the death-
angel shall put his cold, freezing hand upon your shoulder, and
shall say to you, "Give an account! Give an account! Give an
account of your stewardship!" O Saviour, Son of God, put thy
pierced hand on these blind souls, and give them light, that they
may be able to render up their account with joy, and not with
grief! Give them grace to believe in thy name, and trust in
thine atoning sacrifice, for this is the way of salvation. O poor
sinners, trust in Christ Jesus and him crucified! You cannot be
saved by your stewardship, any of you; but unfaithful stewardship will ruin you. Christ crucified is your only hope of salvation. Look unto him, and live. Oh, look unto him now!

XVIII

THE RIGHT OBSERVANCE OF THE LORD'S SUPPER

"For I have received of the Lord that which also I delivered unto you, That the Lord Jesus the same night in which he was betrayed took bread: and when he had given thanks, he brake it, and said, Take, eat: this is my body, which is broken for you: this do in remembrance of me. After the same manner also he took the cup, when he had supped, saying, This cup is the new testament in my blood: this do ye, as oft as ye drink it, in remembrance of me. For as often as ye eat this bread, and drink this cup, ye do shew the Lord's death till he come." 1 Cor. 11: 23–26.

WE have no respect whatever for the ordinances of men in religion. Anything that is only invented by churches, or councils, is nothing whatever to us. We know of two ordinances instituted by the Lord Jesus Christ, the baptism of believers and the Lord's supper; and we utterly abhor and reject all pretended sacraments of every kind. And because we observe these two ordinances, and these two only, we are the more concerned that they should be properly used, and duly understood, and that they should minister to the edification of those who participate in them. We would have those who are baptized understand what is meant by that expressive rite, that they, being dead with Christ, should also be buried with him, and rise with him into newness of life. And when we observe the Lord's supper, we feel a deep and earnest desire that none should come to the table in ignorance of the signification of the observance,—or that, at least, ignorance may not be an occasion of eating unworthily; but that we may comprehend what we are doing, and understand the spiritual meaning of this pictorial instruction by which the Lord Jesus Christ would, even until the end of the age, remind his Church of his great sacrifice upon the Cross.

So, first, I will speak briefly concerning THE FORM OF THE LORD'S SUPPER.

We do not think that it is at all material where that supper is held. It is just as valid and helpful in your own private apartments, in your bedroom, or in your parlour, as it is in any place where Christians usually congregate. We do not attach so much importance as some people do to the time when it is observed; but we are astonished that High Churchmen should be opposed to evening communion, for, if any definite time for partaking of it can be quoted from Scripture, it certainly is the evening. I should like to ask the Ritualists whether they can find any instance, either in holy or profane things, of a supper being eaten before breakfast, until they invented that absurd practice. There is no time that is more like the first occasion when the Master celebrated the ordinance with his disciples than is the evening of the day. Then it was that he gathered the twelve apostles together, and instituted this blessed memorial feast. At Emmaus, too, it was at the close of the day that he was made known to his two disciples in the breaking of bread. It must be sheer superstition, utterly unwarranted by Holy Scripture, which tells us that the Lord's *supper* can only be properly received *in the morning*, and that we ought not to eat anything before we partake of the sacred emblems! We reject all such nonsense, for we find no authority for it in the only standard which we recognize, that is, the inspired Word of God. Let us see what it teaches us concerning this ordinance.

We learn, first, that *the Lord's supper should begin with thanksgiving*. So the Master himself evidently commenced it: "He took bread and gave thanks." All through the supper, the emotion of gratitude should be in active exercise. It is intended that we should give thanks for the bread, at the same time giving still more emphatic thanks for the sacred body which it represents. Then we should also give thanks for the cup, and for that most precious blood which is therein represented to us. We cannot rightly observe the Lord's supper unless we come to the table, blessing, praising, magnifying, and adoring our Saviour, praising him even for instituting such a festival of remembrance, such a memorial ordinance to help our frail memories; and praising him yet more for giving us so blessed a thing to remember as his own great sacrifice for our sin.

After the thanksgiving, it is very clear that our Divine Lord *broke the bread*. We scarcely know what kind of bread was used on that occasion; it was probably the thin passover cake of the Jews; but there is nothing said in Scripture about the use of leavened or unleavened bread, and therefore it matters not which we use. Where there is no ordinance, there is no obligation; and we are, therefore, left free to use the bread which it is our custom to eat. When the Master had broken the bread, *he gave it to his disciples*, and said, "Take, eat;" and they all participated in eating it. And this, mark you, is essential to the right observance of the Lord's supper; so that, when the priest, in celebrating mass, takes the wafer, which is not bread, and which he does not break, but which he himself eats whole, there is no Lord's supper there. Whatever it may be called, it is not the Lord's supper. In the eating of the bread, there must be the participation of such a number of faithful, godly disciples of Christ as may be present, or else it is not the ordinance which the Lord instituted.

That being done, the next thing was that, "*After the same manner also he took the cup;*" that is to say, after the same manner of thanksgiving, blessing God for the fruit of the vine, which was henceforth to be the emblem of his poured-out blood. Even so should we do. It is no vain thing to praise the Lord, though we do it twice, thrice; ay, and ten thousand times. Well did the Psalmist say, "Praise ye the Lord: for it is good to sing praises unto our God; for it is pleasant; and praise is comely" (Ps. 147: 1). Specially comely is it for us to praise our God when we are calling to remembrance the unspeakable gift of his only-begotten and well-beloved Son.

Then came the partaking of the cup,—the fruit of the vine,—of which the Master expressly said, "Drink ye all of it." Hence, when the Church of Rome takes away the cup from the people, and denies it to them, there is no observance of the Lord's supper, for another essential part of the ordinance is left out. It may be the mass, or it may be anything else; but it is not the supper of the Lord. There must be a participation by all the faithful in the cup, as well as in the bread.

Further, in order that this may be the Lord's supper in very truth, *it must be observed in remembrance of Christ*, who said to his disciples, "This do in remembrance of me." From which we learn that only those who know him much come to his table, for how shall we remember what we never knew? And how shall we remember him with whom we have never spoken, and in whom we have never believed? You are not to come to the Lord's supper to get faith; you must have faith first, or else you have no right to draw nigh to this sacred spot. What do ye here? If you suppose that this is a saving ordinance, I must say to you what Christ said to the Sadducees, "Ye do err, not knowing the scriptures" (Matt. 22: 29). Salvation comes to us through faith in our Lord Jesus Christ, and it is the result of the effectual working of the Spirit of God within us. This supper is a most instructive ordinance for those who are saved; but those who are not born again, and are not, by grace, members of the Lord's family, have no right here. They who ate the passover were such as were born in the priest's house, or bought with the priest's money; and if you have been born in Christ's house, or bought with Christ's blood, if you know, by blessed experience, the meaning of regeneration and redemption, then may you come to the communion table. But, if not, as the passover was only intended for Israel, so is this supper a family feast for those who belong to Jesus Christ, and no others may come to it; if they do come, it will be at the peril of eating and drinking unworthily, since they are unable to discern the Lord's body.

I have thus given you a very brief account of the form of observing the Lord's supper, as we find it in the New Testament. You notice that I have not said anything about a chalice, or a paten, or about consecrating the elements, or uplifting the host, and all that Romish rubbish of which some people think so much. The reason for my silence is that there is nothing about these things in the Bible. "To the law, and to the testimony: if they speak not according to this word, it is because there is no light in them." Clear away all the additions of superstition, they are but the dust and the rust which have accumulated during the ages, and they spoil and mar the purity of Christ's own ordinance.

Now, secondly, from our text, I gather THE IMPORTANCE OF THE LORD'S SUPPER.

First, *because it was revealed by the Lord himself.* Paul wrote to the Corinthians, "I have received of the Lord that which also I delivered unto you." Matthew, Mark, Luke, and John were all accessible to Paul; and, though they had not then written their Gospels, yet he could have learnt from them how the Saviour instituted the supper. But, as if Christ would not let it be second-hand, he was pleased to declare to Paul personally—to Paul himself, directly and distinctly—how the supper should be celebrated. The apostle says, "I have received of the Lord," not "*we*", not "I and the rest of the apostles and disciples," but "*I* have received of the Lord," indicating a definite personal revelation from Christ as to this matter. After the Lord Jesus had gone up into his glory, his revelations were but few; yet this was one of them. He would have his disciples, therefore, pay due attention to this important matter which he thus specially revealed to Paul.

I have already referred to the next point, but it is so important that I remind you again that *this supper was commanded by the Lord.* He said, "This do in remembrance of me;" and again, "This do ye, as oft as ye drink it, in remembrance of me." If I love Christ, I am bound to keep his commandments; and among the rest of his commandments, this one in which he here says, "This do." I might have thought, from the conduct of some professing Christians, that Jesus must have said, "This *do not*"; but as he said, "This do ye," where shall I find an apology for those who either never have done it at all, or, being his people, do it so seldom that he could not say to them, "This do ye, as *oft* as ye drink it," but he might rather say, "This do ye as *seldom* as ye drink it," since the idea of frequency does not enter into their observance of it? But what Christ revealed and commanded, it is incumbent upon his own beloved ones to obey.

Notice, again, that *this supper was instituted by Christ himself, and he himself first set the example for its observance.* As to baptism, you remember how he said, "Thus it becometh us to fulfil all righteousness," and so he set us the example in that matter; and, in the supper, it was he who first blessed and brake the bread, it was he who first passed the cup, and said, "This cup is the new covenant in my blood." If he had given the command, and the apostles had been the first to attend to it, it would have been binding upon us; but, inasmuch as, in addition to giving the command concerning it, he himself set the example of observing it, sitting at the centre of the table, with the twelve all around him, I think he has put a special halo about this ordinance, and we must by no means forget, or neglect, or despise it.

Remember, too, that *he established it on a very special occasion.* To my mind, it is very touching to read, "The Lord Jesus the same night in which he was betrayed took bread." I cannot help noticing that the apostle is very particular to say here, "The Lord Jesus." Very often, he uses the name "Christ" in speaking of the Saviour; but here it is, "the Lord Jesus," to show the awe and reverence which the apostle felt as, by faith, he saw the Master at the first communion table. Paul could not forget that, though Jesus was then Lord of all, he was that same night betrayed. He that ate bread with him, lifted up his heel against him, and sold him for thirty pieces of silver; yet, even while the anticipation of that betrayal, and all which it involved, was tearing his heart asunder, he remembered us, and established this ordinance that, by refreshing our memories concerning his blessed self, we might not be left to play the traitor, too, but might be kept steadfast in every time of trial. It seems to me that we must be specially careful to observe such an ordinance as this, instituted when our Saviour's heart was breaking with anguish on our behalf!

And do remember, too, the importance of the ordinance, because of *the peculiar personal motive with which it was instituted:* "This do in remembrance" of what? Of Christianity, and its doctrines and practices? No, but, "in remembrance of Me." You know how tenderly a thing comes home to you if a dying husband says, "This do, my beloved one, in remembrance of me, when I am dead and gone." You never fail to do that, I am sure, if it is in your power. You know how it is with a friend, who has gone from you, and who has left you some forget-me-not. You treasure it with the utmost care; the memento is very precious for your friend's sake; and our dear Lord and Master has put about this supper all the loveliness of his personality, all the graciousness of his affection for us, and all the tenderness that ought to be in our love to him. If there is anything that he bids you do, you ought to do it; but, when it is something to be done in remembrance of him, you must do it; your love impels you to do it. Are you not ashamed if you are not doing it in the most loving, humble, grateful, and earnest manner possible, as becomes the memory of him who loved you, and gave himself for you? I should not like to urge any Christian to come to the communion table; I feel as if I would do nothing to spoil the perfect spontaneity of it. If you do not love him, do not come to his table; but if you do love him, come because you love him; come because you remember him, and because you wish to be helped to remember him yet more.

There is one more thing which adds to the importance of this supper; and that is, *it is to be observed "till he come."* It is not an ordinance, then, for the first Christian centuries alone, to be, as it were, the bridge between the ceremonialism of the Old Testament and the spirituality of the New Testament. No; it is intended to be celebrated "till he come." We must keep on gathering at his table, giving thanks, breaking bread, and proclaiming his death, till the trump of the archangel shall startle us, and then we shall feel it to be truly blessed to be found obediently remembering him when he puts in his appearance at the last. As he comes to us, we shall say, "Blessed Master, we have done as thou didst bid us; we have kept alive thy memory in the world, to ourselves, and to those who looked on as we broke the bread, and drank of the cup, in thy name, and now we rejoice to see thee in thy glory." I do not know that the meeting between Christ and his people could happen at a better time than if he were to come when they were gathered at his table, obeying his command, and showing his death "till he come."

But now, thirdly, let us enquire, IN WHAT SPIRIT OUGHT WE TO COME TO THIS TABLE?

I should say, first, that we are bound to come in the spirit of *deep humility*. To my mind, it is a very humbling thing that we should need anything to help us to remember Christ. I see no better evidence of the fact that we are not yet perfectly sanctified, for, if we were, we should need nothing to help us to remember him. There is, alas, still an imperfection in our memory; and that, strangest and saddest thing of all, in respect to Jesus himself. It is extraordinary that we should ever require anything to help us to remember him. Can he, to whom we owe so much, be ever forgotten by us? The fact that this ordinance is to be observed, in remembrance of him "till he come," is a humbling proof that, till that glorious event, his people's memories will be faulty, and they will need this double forget-me-not to remind them of him who is their All-in-all.

What do I see on that table? I see bread there. Then I gather this humbling lesson, that I cannot even keep myself in spiritual food. I am such a pauper, such an utter beggar, that my own table cannot furnish me with what I want, and I must come to the Lord's table, and I must receive, through him, the spiritual nutriment which my soul requires. What do I see in the cup? I see the wine which is the token of his shed blood; what does that say to me but that I still need cleansing? Oh, how I rejoice in that blessed text in John's first Epistle: "If we walk in the light, as he is in the light, we have fellowship one with another"! And then what follows? That we do not need to make any more confession of sin, because we are quite cleansed from it? Nothing of the sort; "and the blood of Jesus Christ his Son cleanseth us from all sin." We still need the cleansing fountain even when we are walking in the light, as God is in the light; and we need to come to it every day. And what a mercy it is that the emblem sets forth the constant provision of purifying blood whereby we may be continually cleansed!

But, next, we must come *very thankfully*. Some pull a long face when they think about coming to the communion table; like Mrs. Toogood, who is described in Rowland Hill's *Village Dialogues*. She made a mistake about the week that the ordinance was to be observed, so she did not play cards during that week, and kept herself wonderfully pure, poor old soul; and then, when she found, on the Sunday, that she had made a blunder as to the time, she said she had wasted the whole week in getting ready! I hope we do not know anything of that method of keeping the sacred feast; we are to come in a very different frame of mind from that, for we are not coming to a funeral supper, but to the luxuries and dainties that become a marriage feast. Let us come, therefore, with thankfulness, as we say to one another concerning our Lord, "He is not here, for he is risen, glory be to his holy name!" These tokens of remembrance tell us that he has gone where it was expedient for him to go, that the Holy Spirit might descend upon us. Therefore, rejoice even because of the absence of your Lord, for it is well that he should be gone up into the glory. And, as we come to the table, each one feeling what a sinner he is, how unworthy he is to come, how unfit he is to sit with saints, should not each heart say, "Bless the Lord, O my soul: and all that is within me, bless his holy name"?

But, certainly, we should come to the table *with great thoughtfulness*. There are some, we are told, who do not discern the Lord's body; let us think and pray, lest we should be numbered with them. If there be no right thinking, there will be no true spiritual feeling, and there will be no Lord's supper so far as you are concerned. Think of what your Saviour suffered for you, what he has done for you, and what he has gone to prepare for you. Let us remember that the bread sets forth the suffering of his body, that the wine typifies the blood of the atonement whereby we are cleansed, that the two apart, the body separated from the blood, form a most suggestive symbol of the matchless death whereby we are made to live. Think much at the table, but think of nothing but Christ.

But come, also, *with great receptiveness*. It is a meal, you know; we receive the bread and the wine. So, come to the table begging the Lord to give you the grace to feed upon himself spiritually, that you may, by faith, receive him into your inward parts; that, in your inmost soul, you may have the virtue of his life and of his death. Come empty, therefore; for so you will be the better qualified to feed upon him. Come hungering and thirsting; thus you will have the greater appetite for Christ.

Now I finish my discourse by dwelling, for a minute or two, UPON THE GREAT LESSONS WHICH THIS SUPPER INCIDENTALLY TEACHES.

The first lesson is, that *Jesus is for us*. There has been a great dispute over this verse, "This is **my** body, which is broken for you." The word "broken" appears in some of the ancient manuscripts; but it is, undoubtedly, an interpolation. It is absent from several of those manuscripts upon which we are obliged to rely for the correct text of the New Testament; and, hence, very properly, the Revised Version reads, "This is my body, which is for you." And, to my mind, that rendering gives a new thought which is well worth having. "This is my body, which is for you." That is to say, Christ is for you; does not the supper itself say that? The bread represents his body for you; the wine represents his blood for you. We know that it is for you, because you are going to eat it. There is nothing that is more certainly a man's than what he eats or drinks; and, in like manner, when we have really received Christ by faith, there is no possibility of robbing us of him. "This is my body, which is for you." Oh, what a blessed doctrine! Lay hold of this great truth, all that there is in Christ is for you. All the fulness of the Godhead is in him, "and of his fulness have all we received, and grace for grace" (John 1: 16).

The next lesson is, that *his blood has sealed the covenant.* "This cup is the new covenant in my blood." There was a covenant that cursed us, the covenant of works. There is another covenant that has blessed the elect of God, and shall bless them to all eternity, the covenant of grace; and this covenant is signed, and sealed, and ratified, in all things ordered well; and for its seal it has the blood of God's own Son. Therefore it shall stand fast for ever and ever. So, as you partake of that cup, drink with joy, because it reminds you that God hath made with you "an everlasting covenant ordered in all things and sure."

The third great doctrine that is taught by this supper is that *believers feed on Christ himself.* Sometimes they forget this, and they try to feed on doctrines. They will make as great a mistake as if the Jew, when he went up to the tabernacle, had tried to feed on the curtains, or the altar, or the golden tongs. What did he have for food? Why, the peace-offering! When he drew near to his God, he fed on the sacrifice; and the true food of a believer is Christ Jesus himself. We can do it, and we must do it, spiritually, by having our hearts and our minds resting upon what Christ is, and what he has done, and so feeding upon our Lord Jesus Christ.

I have finished when I have mentioned one more lesson which is to be learned from this ordinance. It is clear, from this supper, that *the way to remember Christ is to feed on him again and again.* Is it not a strange thing that, if I have had a great mercy, the way to recollect that mercy is to come to God, and get another mercy? If Christ was ever sweet to my taste, the way to perpetuate that sweetness is to come and taste him again. Do not try to live upon your old experiences. Even the best kind of bread will not keep very long; it soon gets musty if you lay it by. You need to have bread constantly coming fresh from the oven. Even the manna, which came down from heaven, could not be kept, lest it should breed worms; and it is so with the food for your souls.